# THE LAST PERSON TO MARRY A DUCK LIVED 300 YEARS AGO

Pointed Essays by

## HARLAN ELLISON®

Edited by
JASON DAVIS

AN    OFFERING
EDGEWORKS
ABBEY

THE LAST PERSON TO MARRY A DUCK LIVED 300 YEARS AGO
is an Edgeworks Abbey® offering in association with Jason Davis.
Published by arrangement with the Author and The Kilimanjaro Corporation.

THE LAST PERSON TO MARRY A DUCK LIVED 300 YEARS AGO
pointed essays by Harlan Ellison®

**Harlan Ellison website: www.HarlanEllison.com**
**To order books: www.HarlanEllisonBooks.com**

Editor:   Jason Davis

Assistant Editor:   Cynthia Davis

Cover Layout:   Bo Nash

ISBN: 978-0-9895257-8-7

**FIRST EDITION**

The editor would like to thank Paul Michael Anderson,
Steven Barber, Sharon Buck, Barney Dannelke, Eric Regalado, Tim Richmond,
Rod Searcey & Dorman T. Shindler for their assistance in the preparation of this volume.

Copyright acknowledgments appear on pages 249–250,
which constitutes an extension of this copyright page.

12062016

# TABLE OF CONTENTS

"A bird does not sing because it has an answer.
It sings because it has a song."
CHINESE PROVERB

## Infamy, Infamy,
## They've All Got It in fa Me!

As an internationally noted and much-beloved author, social commentator, raconteur, film/tv scenarist, lecturer, and all-around spiffy guy, it has been my pleasure for more than fifty years to associate with, and to report on, the great, the near-great, and the schlubs. While on this long and rewarding hegira, I have amassed many wise words from my equally terrific peers, though not so many from the schlubs.

One of my favorites is this gardyloo from Herman Melville: "No great and enduring volume can ever be written on the flea, though many there be who have tried it."

Bearing the above cold dead forefront in my mind, I must admit that writing about the current state of "infamy" as it relates to what passes for contemporary American culture, is a lot like writing about how much sweat is produced by a sybaritic flea's armpit. One either tells the truth, or lies in the manner of magazines like *People* or *Entertainment Weekly*; that is, pretend all this transitory crap means something. I have chosen not to lie to you. (Though—leaping to quote another of my golden compatriots— as the Welsh novelist, Oxonian scholar, and playwright Gwyn Thomas has noted, "All writers are liars. How else can we caress the truth?")

No lies. I'm down with the Word. Open covenants, openly entered into. These are an omnipresent, usually loathsome—if not outright despicable—bunch of minimally talented, mean-spirited, selfish and obnoxious, bad-mannered, whiney and nose-picking cadre of louts, bullies, bitches, assholes, and self-aggrandizing semiliterate ego-drenched manifestations of a nutjob society that ought to be ashamed of itself for elevating to the heights of publicity and a pasha's fortune, the sort of person who ought to be condemned

1

to shoveling yak-dung in the deepest crevasses of the Himalayas.

Their ascendancy signals a kind of hideous metamorphosis in which casual and dismissable celebrity has mutated into a melding with "infamy" until they are now inseparable...a kind of shambling, slime-dripping Lovecraftian monster that has swallowed our society.

There is no longer such a thing as "infamy."

Gone, as arcane and as beyond our reanimation as the fabled T'ang dynasty blue glaze. There is nothing so low, so odious, so stomach-wrenching or sensibility-insulting that a "celebrity" can do, that will offend anyone but a Bible Belt fundamentalist (and since *every*thing gets *their* knickers in a twist, ah what the hell).

Infamy, these days, is what passes for notoriety. Notoriety, these days, is what passes for celebrity. Celebrity, these days, is what passes for impolite behavior. And impolite behavior, these days, is what would've gotten you a boot up your ass in saner times.

The truth is anathema to their ears, but here it is: these are fleas we're dealing with here.

Fleas. They stay in the news by making you itch; and all too soon the only congress we wish to have with their nasty, overwhelming presence is to scratch them or slap them bloodsucking flat.


In the same week in 2002 in which the most cataclysmic accounting scandals and bankruptcies in American history broke—WorldCom, Arthur Andersen LLP, Enron— Julia Roberts was the sacred cover icon that appeared on *thirteen* major national magazines. Infamous!

Clinton consentually got his participle parsed by Jewish American Princess Monica Lewinsky, and the Far Right jackalpack gulled the electorate into running him down and savaging him out of power; Schwarzenegger manhandled a double-six-pak of women in gyms, streets, elevators, miniature golf courses, logging camps, bidet manufacturing plants, and gunseller conventions, and the looneytoon constituency of California elected him by default as Governor.


Jack the Ripper had to put in a full day's work butchering at least five hapless women in Spitalfields in 1888 to become infamous; John Wayne Bobbitt merely needed his old lady to lop off his whangdoodle. Josef Stalin had to purge maybe as many as twenty million people (and we still haven't figured out how he did it, absent any Dachaus or

Auschwitzes) to become infamous; Michael Jackson just had to act like a carny freak and dangle a baby out of a hotel window. Stephen Jay Gould and Madame Chiang Kai-shek and Allen Lomax and Chuck Jones (Who? ask the scions of B.H. 90210) died relatively unnoticed, but the national tear-duct spigot was turned on full lock-to-lock at the demise of 30-year-old bad girl, Lisa "Left Eye" Lopes, of the rhythm&blues trio TLC. Record companies shamelessly hype bad doggerel masquerading as "street poetry" (while Langston Hughes and Jimmy Baldwin spin like gyroscopes in their graves) using the oxymoron "rap music" (giant shrimp, really unique, military intelligence), deifying musically bereft thugs who gesticulate spastically with their fingers and flail their arms like squid afflicted with St. Vitus's Dance, trumpeting their ghetto roots while moving their asses into fortress mansions among the honks in Bel Air...and the sales and audiences for classical music, jazz, blues, all go down the commercial drain. R. Kelly makes headlines for running afoul of the law over child pornography and sexual assault, and his sixth solo album debuts on the sales charts at #1.

(According to mtv.com, 14 July: "Over protests from prosecutors, a Chicago judge has granted R. Kelly permission to leave Illinois for a five-city tour in August. ... The R&B singer—free on bond after being indicted on child pornography charges last June *and apparently suffering little if any damage from the accusations*—" Italics mine.

(I've got a friend in Medieval Georgia, Gwinnett County, who hasn't even been indicted on a similar charge, and he's either been in jail or under house arrest for going on three years, he has to pay the rental fees for the in-house cameras that watch him 24/7, his 83-year-old mother hasn't been allowed to visit him, and he isn't even permitted to open his own front door.) Ah, Kelly, the perks of infamy!

As we all know, Life is not a comparison of Chamber of Horrors; nonetheless, to become infamous in times past, one had to be, say, Copernicus, Jesus Christ, Martin Luther, John Peter Zenger, Alfred Dreyfus, Joan of Arc, James Joyce, Mary Shelley. Today, you only have to be jerkazoids like Dennis Rodman, Howard Stern, or Jerry Falwell.

Let us pause, for just one pellucid moment, as we bail out some of the vitriol that threatens to swamp our li'l kayak here, and consider the term upon which we're dwelling so obsessively. Infamy. What means it, exactly, huh? Well, here's what the RANDOM HOUSE DICTIONARY OF THE ENGLISH LANGUAGE, 2nd Edition, unabridged, has to say about it:

**in-fa-my** (in′fə-mē), *n., pl.* **-mies.** 1. extremely bad reputation, public reproach, or strong condemnation as the result of a shameful, criminal or outrageous act: a time that will live in infamy. 2. infamous character or conduct. 3. an infamous act or circumstance. 4. Law. Loss of rights, incurred by conviction of an infamous offense. (1425–75; late ME infamye < L infamia, equiv. To infam (is) ill-famed

    **—Syn.** 1. disrepute, obloquy, odium, opprobrium, shame. See disgrace. **—Ant.** 1. credit, honor.

    I could've used the OXFORD ENGLISH DICTIONARY, but I sprained my back trimming some hedges last Sunday, and it was simply too heavy to schlep for use here. So go with me on this.

    Public reproach; strong condemnation; ostracism; hearty vilification, bad rep: those are the traditional, the historical concomitants of infamy. Not today. *Today*, impressionable, plastic minds of gullible young folks (what the hell else can one call an age group from 12-to-35?) are given the phrases "in your face," "pushing the envelope," "edgy," as template codes for cool behavior. Study, learn something, *know* something, have an informed opinion not fed to you by Gap ads or VH1? The words for *that* m.o. are "nerd," "geek," "wuss," "freak."

    So Pink, who was named #10 on *Access Hollywood*'s "Top 10 Bad Girls," whose video record of giving the finger to the camera is—if my exhaustive research is correct—but maybe it's insufficient, I can't be *everywhere*, fer chrissakes—somewhere above forty, gets to use up somebody *else's* 15 minutes of fame; and she has the gall, the temerity, the nerve, the *chutzpah*, to tell a recent interviewer, "Uh, like I, uh, I kinda see myself as like a, y'know, roe-ell model, y'know?"

    Terrific, just what I'd want my kid, if I had a kid, which I don't, to look up to as a roe-ell model. An attention-seeking freak within whose head exists an empty veldt whereat one cannot perceive the passage of a cogent thought. An 11-times bodily-pierced twink sans ethic, sans philosophy, sans reason for us to give a daisyfart about her comings and goings. Her Aristotelian response to most everything is flipping you the bird. Talk to me about the penalties of infamy.

Jennifer Lopez routinely travels with a 90-minion entourage of blackamoors, mamelukes, esnes, serfs, toadies, and lickspittles. There's a specialist who does nothing but Ms. Lopez's eyebrows. (How's that for a Life's Work?) According to *Radar* magazine, she has issued strict orders that she is never to be "looked at or spoken to directly." Geeeeezus lawdy! And this one'll roll your socks up and down: to stave off tantrums, stylists will routinely replace size 6 tags on clothes she buys, with "size 2." In 1999, when the cops detained her after then-boyfriend P. Doody, or P. Diddly, or whatever the hell *nom-de-chanteur* he's using this week, when *Mister* Combs was busted in a shooting in Manhattan, she is reported to have been deprived of her jongleurs and handmaidens, so she sent a cop out to get her a jar of cuticle cream. Of all the canards leveled against her it is the preceding she denies denies denies. Crucify me, I deny it! Yes I served with the Taliban and drink the blood of babies, but I did not send that friggin' cop out to get my cuticle cream, and the creep brought me some Buy-Rite crap anyhow!

Yeah, infamous behavior is *really* crippling to the rep and soul, these days.

Record mogul "Suge" Knight (that's pronounced "thug") forced a rival record industry guy to drink a champagne glass full of Knight's urine when the guy wouldn't give up Sean Dibbity's home address. A stone righteous gangsta with ties to the Mob Piru Bloods, this gleefully sociopathic bully has threatened, assaulted, intimidated, and otherwise terrorized the charnel house venue of music production nearly as long as Dillinger or Capone dominated theirs.

Model Naomi Campbell pleaded guilty in year 2000 to misdemeanor assault charges after grabbing assistant Georgina Galanis by the throat, punching her, and clonking her on the noggin with a cell phone. In a 2002 national poll, she was the runaway favorite as the Most Hated Person in Britain. Ah, infamy, doncha smell sweet!

(I have to pass on an anecdote, though it's only peripherally about Ms. Campbell. But it's a good one, so stay with me. One evening a couple of years ago, my wife and I were channel-surfing and we happened to pause for no good reason at that odious "game show," *The Weakest Link*, a hideous electronic rigadoon that rewarded the least moronic of a sextet of ignoramuses with enough money for him or her to get a lobotomy, and there stands an extremely pretty, well-turned-out young woman in an expensive suit. The harridan emceeing the show asked her the following question:

("What 'S' who starred in the film *Lawrence of Arabia* writes an award-winning bridge column?"

(The young woman thought a moment, and answered with some conviction, "Naomi Campbell."

(Now, even if one *doesn't* know the answer, which was Omar Sharif—a terrific guy, a sweet man, who *does indeed* play and write about bridge at an international competition level, though he is a consummate fish when it comes to pool, at which Peter Falk and I regularly used to beat his ass—that answer is WRONG IN SO **MANY** WAYS that it illuminates our perception of the role infamous behavior plays among *hoi-polloi*.

(There isn't even an "S" in Naomi Campbell. *Lawrence of Arabia* was released in 1962 [but was filmed several years earlier] and Naomi Campbell wasn't born until 1970. Naomi Campbell isn't an actress. Anyone who's ever seen her perform will attest to this. And she may or may not *play* bridge, but the chances of her remotely being capable of writing a coherent, well-parsed sentence about the game are roughly as salutary as the luck of a snail in a bucket of salt. Anyone unfortunate enough to have tried to read her "novel," SWAN, will attest to *this*.

(So my wife and I were both stunned and impressed by this level of ignorance, so handsomely proffered on national tv, and we decided, then and there, that *Naomi Campbell* was the appropriate answer for almost *any* question.

(What was the name of the ship that struck an iceberg and sank in 1912 in the North Atlantic? The *Naomi Campbell*.

(Who discovered radium? Naomi Campbell.

(What was John Adams's wife's name? Naomi Campbell.

(Around our house, this answer works wonders when you are tabula rasa, haven't a scintilla of a clue, don't know wha's happ'nin or otherwise have powdered parrot kibble for brains. Susan and I offer this splendid kitchen tool for your amusement.)


I could go on for decades. The complete shrike crazy pit-bull motormouth Ann Coulter, who never met a lie she didn't want to screw. Pamela Anderson, whose breasts are considered by every balsawood-brained frat boy in America worthy of being carved into Mt. Rushmore, and I suspect only keeps remarrying rocker Tommy Lee because she cannot locate an imbecile who has pierced or tattooed his body at greater measure. Whitney Houston, a live grenade from whom somebody pulled the pin decades ago. Lisa Marie Presley, who defies logic but clearly "has her price," which clearly ain't money because she has ore-cars full of it, otherwise give me one salient reason for that creepy sham marriage to you-know-who. Beyonce Knowles, Madonna, Christina Aguilera, Mariah Carey, Li'l Kim, and Britney Spears: the Slut Squad. I don't know about you, but I'm well past the horizon vanishing point of giving a flying foop about watching post-adolescent nymphs showing me their quivering butts. An ass is an egress for the transmogrified spaghetti and meatballs you had for dinner last night. Why must so much of the time of the public airwaves be given over to the masturbatory fantasies of the acne-festooned demographic, he asks, married to one of the most beautiful women in the world, who seldom finds it necessary to shake her booty in public?

Which leads me to the penultimate proof of my theme, that there *is no* infamy today, no vileness or obnoxiousness that a constituency acceptable of Anna Nicole Smith will not tolerate, if not venerate and emulate. Here it is:

Earlier this month (October 2003), the wife of the governor of Maryland addressed an audience at Hood College in Frederick, MD. It was a domestic violence prevention conference, and Kendel Ehrlich, the wife of Republican Robert Ehrlich, was trying to make the point that it is hard raising a son in these times of shaken booty everywhich-way one looks. What we call in law an "attractive nuisance." She lamented the tilt toward slutdom, and said, "If I had an opportunity to shoot Britney Spears, I think I would."

Now, I being a cruel and mordantly witty guy, think that's pretty funny. I don't for an instant seriously believe Kendel would do it, not even if she had a Glock up to Britney's temple. It was a *bon mot* voiced out of what seems to me deep-felt sadness at the low standards of public behavior in our times.

So what happened? Did the media examine this passionate misspeak by an other-wise squeaky-clean first lady? Did they initiate a six-part series on "The BootyButt: Temple of Worship?" No, the only repercussion apart from Mrs. Ehrlich having to abase herself with an apology—heaven forfend she should upset the vast lynch-mob of Spears poppets and hairy-palmed boy-terrorists who would be unhinged by her comment—was the wide dissemination of an e-mailed statement from Jive Records, the New York-based label representing Spears. "Since this unfortunate comment was made at a domestic violence prevention conference, it seems Mrs. Ehrlich has shot her own self [sic] in the foot by promoting violence."

Grand. Simply imperial! Blame the messenger, not the message. To the stocks with you, Kendel! Dunk the bitch!

If it were not for *Extra* and *People* and *Celebrity Justice* and *Access Hollywood* and *Entertainment Tonight* and *True Hollywood Story* and all the rest of the E! Channel persiflage; if it were not for *Star Dates* and *The High Price of Fame* and *Cribs* and MTV and VH1 and *101 Juiciest Hollywood Hookuss* and *It's Good to Be...*; if it were not for the thousand imitation magazines that live off studio and network handouts, and the 16 million news breaks and pseudo-journalism attentions paid to these pompous, drunken, self-absorbed, boring dummies, we might be able to clear the publicity fog from our heads long enough to realize that a society feeding off bread and circuses is doomed to pollute its commonweal so totally that we might even, weird and improbable as it might seem, elect *another* actor as our Governor, or even—ha ha I know this is silly—say, a showbiz wrestler! And they wouldn't be as smart as Ron Reagan was. Or a head of lettuce.

Ozzy Osbourne, Robert Evans, Tammy Faye Bakker, every snippy chanteuse with a piping nasal voice who calls herself "diva," which used to be reserved for Ella Fitzgerald or Marian Anderson or Edith Piaf; Jayson Blair, the dirty journalist who flummoxed the *New York Times*; Winona Ryder and Robert Downey, Jr. (whom it pains me to add to this list of miscreants, because I'm only nuts about them); hopeless drug-addicted obscenely overweight brain-damaged Rush Limbaugh; Shannen Doherty, who—besides me and Barney the Purple Dinosaur—is the only entity ever to have had an actual, membership-card *Enemies Of*—organization created just to hate her; Tara Reid, who encapsulates the arrogance and amorality of these "infamous" clowns with her response to an interviewer's cavil that she was, perhaps maybe kinda, acting like a twerp: I don't care...the only person who needs to be happy is me." Russell Crowe, Colin Farrell, even Natalie Mains of the Dixie Chicks (who was damned right correct in exercising her right to express an opinion); Angelina Jolie, Steven Seagal, Lara Flynn Boyle; holy gadzoley betty spaghetti, I could go on for decades. But why, unless you, gentle reader, are a very slow pony indeed, and need to be crowned between the eyes with a ball peen hammer!

Infamy, like everything else that isn't nailed down in our culture, has been misappropriated by the *apparat* that believes *The business of America...is business.* Whatever need be done to keep the green flowing, it's okay. And if you wait a few years you'll be working with a generation for whom Bach and Satchmo and Gershwin are white noise, for whom courtesy and not always being on your muscle and filled with purposeless angst are unknown concepts, for whom no vomitous behavior is less than cool, for whom "trainwreck television" like *The Anna Nicole Show* is Must-See Tee-Vee, and *Ebert & the Chimp at the Movies* is high kultchuh.

Just wait long enough, not very long in fact, and there will be no flea so adroit at infamous behavior that you won't greet its Fall series with huzzahs and adoration.

# ASK UNCLE HARLAN
## We answers 'em as we sees 'em

Editor's Note: Four installments of this column appeared in *Short Form* between August 1989 and September 1990. After that publication's demise, the first three installments were re-printed with new introductions in *Pulphouse*. The fourth column was never reprinted, and thus does not have a latter-day introduction. A fifth column, though alluded to, was never written.

Within very short order of your reading this, *Short Form* will be no more. I am constantly startled at how few readers of sf/fantasy have ever even heard of *Short Form*. It was a small but elegant journal of criticism of short fiction in the genre that was created and for a long while edited by Orson Scott Card. When Scott's workload became too heavy to continue the day-to-day editing, he turned the magazine over to an excellent writer and critic, Mark Van Name of Durham, North Carolina. Mark began publishing *Short Form* (though Scott continued funding the publication out of his pocket) in 1989. Now Mark's family and career(s) make it impossible for him to continue, and with one last forthcoming issue, *Short Form* will be a chapter of honorable literary endeavor one can locate only in the book of memory where *Unearth*, *Rhodomagnetic Digest*, and *Inside* claim chapters. For its relatively brief run, though, it was an eclectic, no-holds-barred publication that those in the know awaited with high expectations.

In the late summer of 1989, I began writing a "service column" for *Short Form*. The column was called *Ask Uncle Harlan*. Mark Van Name solicited it from me almost as a lark, but even before I'd completed writing the first installment it was clear to me, as it was to Mark and the readers who were in on the creation at the Sycamore Hill Writers' Conference, that we were onto something more substantive than merely a chatter column of advice to burgeoning—as well as already-publishing—writers.

*Ask Uncle Harlan* began with one dangerous ground-rule:

Absolute candor and honesty would be the response to any and all letters submitted. A word about those words: candor is easy; I am at a place in my life and career where I need cowtow to no one, where I need not fear saying those things we usually keep unsaid for fear of losing a job or alienating an editor; honesty is another matter; we frequently lie without meaning to do so. We can report only what we *think* is the truth. But more often we lie by obfuscation or avoidance of the task. It was my intention to answer every question asked of me, fully and without reserve, as truthfully as I knew how.

And so I began.

In one installment's time I felt I was setting down meatier responses to queries than ever I had done it in my essays, or lectures, or convention panels. Basically, it was a column about writing, about the marketplace, about the forces that bend and reshape writers. But I also found that few people asked what they wanted to ask straight out. The questions were couched in circumlocution. I opted for answering the questions *totally*, that is, not just what was in the communicant's letter, but what s/he was *actually* asking. That made for dangerous comment. Snide queries that seemed to be inquiring about one thing, in truth, were trying to elbow some greater answer to another out of me.

Next to my film columns for *F&SF*, these were the hardest, most carefully-written essays of my life. I wrote four installments, each one quite long. The fifth has yet to appear in the final issue of *Short Form*.

Now the ongoing chore moves to *Pulphouse*. We will begin with the first four, five installments. Each is dated as to when it was written, unaltered from its initial publication. You can play catch-up. The column will appear in alternate issues of this magazine.

I ask that you *not* begin sending in questions till you've read at least four of these previously-published sections. You can comment on them with impunity in the letters column, however, as the second rule I set for myself was never to respond to what was said about me or what I'd written in *Ask Uncle Harlan* if the comments appeared outside the confines of the essays themselves. But to any letter sent to the column...well, remember the old Chinese adage, "Be careful what you wish for, you might get it."

That second rule got me in trouble in installment number four. But that will have to wait till you see that fourth entry. And by then number five will have met the "trouble" and responded to it. Thereafter, if you feel moved to write to this column, you will find specific rules *you* must follow. Those rules grew as the column progressed, and the shape of what trouble absolute candor and honesty could bring manifested itself.

I have no idea why I am fascinated and compelled to write these pieces. They can only bring me further opprobrium than I have already managed to engender. But like some exotic narcotic, *Ask Uncle Harlan* has become a tight-wire walk that I cannot resist.

Read along for the next four installments. You'll see what I mean. And with entry number five...well, if you follow the rules for submission, we can walk that line over the abyss together. Here, then, is the first column I wrote, exactly as it appeared in *Short Form* volume 2, issue 2, published in August of 1989.

# 1: 5 August 1989

Nice looking magazine, I said to the editor, Mr. Van Name. I'd like to write for you sometime, when I get the time. How about next issue, the editor, Mr. Van Name, said. Well, I replied, we can talk about it in your Toyota van on the way to Bullock's Barbecue tonight. And so we did. In the van were three other writers in attendance at the fifth (and last) Sycamore Hill Writers' Conference. It was Friday evening, August the 4th, 1989.

What I'd like, said the editor, Mr. Van Name, is a regular column like the one you did many years ago for *Unearth*, in which you discuss little-discussed aspects of writing: how to title stories interestingly, how to create characterization in one plangent line, how to avoid said-bookisms and make big bucks. How does that strike you, said the editor, Mr. Van Name.

About as interestingly as watching kudzu absorb a fried chicken franchise, I replied. But how about a sort of *Dear Abby* question-and-answer column, in which I would respond to the often pithy and salient queries of writers and readers, seeking wisdom in an otherwise murky universe?

And so it came to pass.

This is the first installment. This column will seek to answer difficult questions on a wide range of subjects allied to the craft of writing. I will sink my hands deep into the rich loam of wisdom that covers the floor of that enormous echoing cavern I call my mind. I do that. I call it my mind.

I will attempt to be as candid as the libel laws allow, and will do my best to answer all but the most imbecile of questions. Those that fall into the category of imbecile I will merely use as an opportunity to ridicule the correspondent.

Because deadline was near, and because one must seek out lead-time material until the faithful readers of *Short Form* discover we're here, waiting for their hungering souls to find us, I solicited writers at the 1989 Sycamore Hill Conference.

These are all actual, genuine letters (Xeroxes of originals on file with the editor, Mr. Van Name). No letter will be used unless signed and dated by the correspondent.

So let us plunge into this literary adventure with the first letter to hand, the first received.

**From MR. BRUCE STERLING of Austin, Texas:**

"What do you think is the absolute worst thing about *The New York Review of SF*? Is it those godawful Kathryn Cramer things where she jaws on and on and on about differential equations and spheroid cows and other shit no sane human being will ever understand? Or is it Delany's Azathothian babblings from the all-devouring black hole of deconstructionism? Or is it those incessant, unfunny, and inevitably meanspirited attacks on Bertelsmann/Bantam that come, with amazing gall, from people who are mostly minions of The Hearst Corporation? What's the deal, anyhow?"

Mr. Sterling, author of SCHISMATRIX, ISLANDS IN THE NET, and other excellent books is, as most of you know, the aging elf of cyberpunkdom. I had hoped (a vainglorious conceit) to open this column with a craft question that might, at least for a moment, establish these outings as oases of applicable information, if not rigorous logic. I can see that is not to be the case.

We have here an example of answering the questions implicitly in the way they are posed. It would be safe to say Mr. Sterling finds the periodical in question, edited by David Hartwell and Kathryn Cramer, a less than salutary arrival in his mailbox.

Since it is clear Mr. Sterling doesn't really want to know what is the "absolute worst thing" in the journal—it will be the policy of this column to deal forthrightly and not play the duplicitous game of pretending that irony and disingenuous phrasing are intended seriously—nor does he think there is very much "right" with *The New York Review of SF*, I will attempt to answer the question posed as "What's the deal, anyhow?" Ambiguous as it may be.

It is very hard to take *The New York Review* seriously, as the magazine is so busy doing the job itself. With all the uptight posturing of a village selectman, *The New York Review* swaddles itself in a grayness of appearance and obdurate impenetrability of prose that I gather the editors think will insure its being "taken seriously." If I am to judge by the number of people who have said, in one way or another, "Oh, thank goodness you couldn't get through that spherical cow thing, either...I thought I was the only one too dumb to figure out what she was going on about!" then I am far from alone in seeing this magazine as yet another journalistic martinet intended to "legitimatize" science fiction.

In trying to answer "What's the deal, anyhow" directly, I think "the deal" is this: *The New York Review* is merely the latest tentacle of Mr. Hartwell's ongoing octopoidal attempt to rule the sf/fantasy universe.

The obvious dangers to anyone saying such a thing cannot be minimized. Mr. Hartwell, a very fine editor when he's working at peak efficiency, has a way of punishing those who cross him. I would be less than honest if I did not state at this juncture that I am one of those whom Mr. Hartwell has punished. Unfortunately—though Kafka would surely know the nature of unspecified crimes—he has never represented to me exactly why I'm being punished. That secret agenda notwithstanding, I confess to limited familiarity with the recent contents of his magazine.

Early on, I was circularized (along with most of the adult population capable of making its own bed) to write for *The New York Review*. A sample copy was included. I read the issue, found it for the most part redundant and loghorreic to the point of parody. A pedant's sugar-rush of pseudo-academic bombast.

I recall calling either Ms. Cramer or Mr. Hartwell to ascertain what sort of material they were seeking, and what rates they would be paying, but if the information I received was seminal, I've forgotten it.

Subsequently, I received a form inquiry asking me to spend many hours answering a great many dopey questions about an aspect of the writing life that I thought trivial. Yet I would have cooperated. "Good Works" should be encouraged.

However, in the same issue that had been enclosed to win my approbation, so I would expend my time and efforts in their behalf, the editors of *The New York Review* had published a review of some book or other, in which Ms. Cramer gratuitously ridiculed me for not having yet completed THE LAST DANGEROUS VISIONS. She was entitled to do so—as I am entitled to write my opinions here—but I did rather think it an olympian demonstration of *chutzpah* to ask me to enter into her service while trying to stanch the flow of blood.

I returned her questionnaire with some rude words inscribed in red, and resolved to have nothing further to do with her or the magazine.

So when you ask me "What's the deal, anyhow?" I can only say that *as I perceive it,* this handmaiden of concretized thinking—including the occasional pieces you write for them, Mr. Sterling—is merely one more strutting pouter pigeon intended to gull the academy. It will annex one more genre Sudetenland to Mr. Hartwell—who will no doubt reward these remarks with even less anthologizations than in the past—and will one day vanish, to be remembered vaguely, like the fiction of Ed Earl Repp.

What's the worst thing in the magazine, Mr. Sterling? The anal retentive dedication with which those who aspire to membership in the Eastern Literary daisy-chain try to "legitimatize" fantastic literature out of existence.

**From MR. JACK MASSA of Tucker, Georgia:**

"Two of the more accomplished writers at this conference have said they did twelve or 16 drafts, respectively, on the unfinished manuscripts they brought here. I have heard it claimed that you never revise anything. Is this true?"

Only two queries into this activity, and I'm beginning to perceive that people may not ask the real question to which they want an answer. There is something far deeper and more important in Mr. Massa's letter than explicating Ellison's work habits. Let me try an approach on this:

Yes, on sum, it is absolutely true that I write one draft. Of the, maybe, eleven or twelve hundred pieces I've written, I've gone back and done substantial work on possibly (as best I can recall over thirty-five years) eight or ten. "The Deathbird" underwent an entire rewrite, beginning to end. But "Jeffty Is Five" and "I Have No Mouth, and I Must Scream" read today in the BEST OF THE NEBULAS volume almost exactly the way they came out of the typewriter. No more than a few words or commas altered.

On the other hand, one of the four or five writers I most admire and respect, in all the world, Stanley Ellin (who was, for my money, the American Chekhov, and a writer every other writer seriously concerned about his/her work should commit to memory), well, Stan wrote short stories word by word. He would write a first line, then study it. Then he would revise it. Sometimes word by word. Then when he was satisfied with it, he'd repeat the procedure on the second line, the third, and on throughout the story... often returning to smooth or trim or refit a word, a line, a thought. His short stories are perfection by any criterion you care to apply. (He wrote novels quite differently, but that's another matter, for another time.) I would go insane trying to write like that; and I'd never write *anything*.

But as I say, the imperative I perceive in the subtext of what Mr. Massa has asked me, has nothing to do with one of the conference stellars having written twelve drafts, or another having done it sixteen times, and least of all not Ellison having done it once.

The nubbin of this, as I see it, is the freight of guilt constantly being dumped on writers because of the way they write. Unspoken, free-floating guilt based on *process*.

In a recent issue of *The New York Times Book Review* (which, sadly, dammit, I don't have at hand) I read a strange and disturbing piece about prolificity. It tried to equate—while self-sensing that it was a mug's game—amount of work done with quality of work produced. The usual suspects were rounded up: Joyce Carol Oates, Stephen King, Max Brand, Georges Simenon, Dumas *père*, Lester Dent. And since I had to rush to catch a plane, I never hacked my way through to the end to discover if the writer reached a conclusion. But if s/he did, I would bet it was an ambiguous one.

The operative problem here, as I view it, is that none of us work in a vacuum. We try to exclude all considerations of, for instance, the state of the market when we work, in hopes that the art will be pure and unbent for artificial reasons. But we do not exist in a vacuum, and thoughts always impinge. (I'll touch on that in a letter later on here.)

Part of the cultural pollution that depletes our creative ionosphere is the long-standing myth that "an artist starves for his/her art," that "you have to sell out to be successful," that "it can't be good if it's written fast."

Well, sometimes each of those is true. Most times they are untrue. Occasionally it's both. But *individually*, none of those snippets of jingoism is any truer than that all black people have natural rhythm, love watermelon, and make terrific basketball players...all Jews are good with money...all Irish are drunkards...all women are imbued with the Earth Mother wisdom...all men are rutting beasts.

But by the time a writer begins selling, s/he has had to swallow (if not absorb through the pores from the air itself) all that okeydoke about how much nobler it is to gasp away one's days in a garret, producing a single thin volume of translucent prose while shunning the corrupting influences of decent and regular meals, the love and companionship of family and friends, and a bed free of visiting vermin. We are inculcated to believe that art is produced in velvet-lined closets, and that hacks like Melville and Twain and Dickens were mere hacks because they wrote a lot, they wrote for common consumption, and that they seemed to enjoy what they wrote.

What Mr. Massa is asking, I think, is: should I feel like a fraud because I didn't agonize over what I wrote, and are you going to reassure me that if you can do it properly the first time out, that there's something less valuable about my fastwork than inherently abides in Carol Emshwiller's endless revisions?

My answer is this: every writer finds a way to work. No one way is any better than the others. Talent will out, and what you have in the storehouse is what is valuable, not how you load the bales for market.

Relax, Mr. Massa.

And by the way: what you have just read was first draft.

**From MS. PAT MURPHY of San Francisco, California:**

"As someone who lives and writes on the somewhat arbitrary and ill-defined boundary that divides fantasy and science fiction from the rest of literature, I've got a problem. The fantastic elements that appear in my stories are often not the central motivating element that traditional science fiction and fantasy demands. I've been selling these stories to sf and fantasy markets, and people don't seem to mind; but I feel as if I'm getting away with something. What do you think? Should I feel guilty?"

Ms. Murphy, first of all, and at core last and only, is that you are a remarkable writer. No one who could write THE FALLING WOMAN need ever feel guilty about *any*thing. You can commit great crimes against humanity and still sleep like a babydoll.

Do *I* think you should feel guilty?

That's dumb. First of all, what the hell does it matter whether I ascribe guilt-producing motivations to what you do? In these matters I think it presumptuous of us to decide what is worthy of guilt for others. That you *ask* me if you should feel guilty is another matter. And it ties into Mr. Massa's query.

Even as the mainstream and society in general have cobbled up these mythic bugaboos for us to deal with, so too has the sf/fantasy genre erected warning signs. One of them is that *this* is sf and *that* is fantasy and this over here, well, it doesn't seem to be either, so it can't strictly speaking be either, and therefore must be somehow less valuable, or bogus, or "getting away with something." That's horseshit.

Once upon a time, one of the best of us, Ted Sturgeon, grew so demented (with absolutely proper cause) at the life of poverty and dichotomous adoration/rejection through which he was suffering as a "science fiction writer," that he decided to do some mainstream stories, and sell them in markets where he could achieve some general community attention. Two of these stories we all know.

He wrote a story titled "Loneliness" and another called "Hurricane Trio" and he sent them everywhere; and they were roundly rejected. The mainstream didn't want no fuckin' upstart fantasy guy smudging their pages. After all, they'd let Bradbury out of the ghetto, and one of *those* people was enough.

And so, finally, in dejection and frustration, Ted offered them to Gold (or Pohl, who was working with Gold) at *Galaxy*, and Horace (or Fred) knew he needed the money, so they said, just stick in a sci-fi device, and we'll buy them. So Ted did. He added a flying saucer to the former (which was retitled "Saucer of Loneliness," an enamel-scraping awkwardism that bugged Ted till he died), and ESP or psionics or somedamnthing to the latter, and they became "science fiction stories." And they sold.

Were they frauds, had Ted gotten away with something, did it matter?

Well, they weren't frauds, they were just two good mainstream stories with dopey sci-fi gadgetry Crazy Glued to them. Did Ted pull a fast one and should he have felt Murphyesque guilt over it? I say no, because he gave the reader full value. They were Sturgeon writing well, and that's all *any* reader has a right to demand of us, that we write well. Did it matter? Yes, it mattered, because Ted had to fudge those stories to get them into print, and that did some small mayhem to the honest presentation of his art. But it was a choice he made.

Just as *you* make the choice when you decide to add that talking frog or cybernetic dinosaur or Other who might be an alien in an otherwise mimetic story. If it's sales you want, or simply the end-result of seeing that over which you've slaved appear in print, rather than taking up residence in a filing cabinet, it is a compromise you have to make for yourself.

As one who maintains he is *not* a science fiction writer, but simply a *writer* who has written some sf, among the many forms employed to tell stories, I have no such qualms; ergo, no guilt.

"All the Lies That Are My Life," without even a scintilla of sf/fantasy in it, unrewritten for the market, was rejected throughout the mainstream, and wound up eventually in *F&SF*. It also got on the Hugo ballot. I didn't change it, they ran it, they voted for it, and though it lost the Hugo, it was exactly the story I chose to tell, unwarped for marketplace.

I think you should feel guilty only if you've fucked up your story for artificial market demands. If the readers seem to enjoy it, and the editor has paid you good money for it, figure they're adults and know how the world runs. If you *keep* feeling you ought to feel guilty, well, then perhaps you'd better look more deeply into what you're writing, what you call it, and if you're in the right genre. It is possible, you know, to ignore the labels entirely. They mean nothing; they are marketing tools for those who would keep all things neat and tidy: Vonnegut is literature...over there; Murphy is science fiction...over here. I've spoken and written endlessly at the invidious nature of that categorization.

But inevitably, because you're good, and because you care about your work, you will have to consider if you care for *yourself*. And at that moment you will know if you want to undergo the pains and setbacks that will be your lot if you decide you're bigger and better than a stupid label.

On the other hand, you could ignore this answer and just keep doing what you're doing. And feel guilty about it.

In general, my feeling is that any Pat Murphy story is a valuable icon, and filling that piece of the universe with Murphy, which keeps that piece of the universe from being possibly filled by Judith Krantz or a great many sf writers I could name, is a Good Thing. An intelligent reader, whether of *Asimov's* or *The Atlantic*, should treasure the gift and eschew the labels. If the tunnel-visioned need the label more than the art, I say fuck'm.

I had two more questions. Good ones, from John Kessel and the editor, Mr. Van Name. But I'm tired of writing right now, so I'll save them till next time—adding to them a few of the questions we trust will be generated by the general readership.

The procedure on this will be simple: keep your question to one side of a postcard clearly addressed to *Ask Uncle Harlan* in care of the editor and this publication; your query must be signed and dated, anonymous or undated postcards will be ignored; your submission of a question waives right of privacy, and all queries become the sole property of the columnist, who may some day use them in a collection of *Ask Uncle Harlan* columns. When the editor, you know who, has a batch at hand, he'll forward them to me. Do *not* write me directly; everything must go through the publication office. I'll try to answer at, well, shorter form, from now on.

This time, I thought we should get acquainted. And remember: if your question is snotty, you'll get that kind of an answer. If it's seriously posed, I'll answer in kind. This first column should show you what I mean by that. And finally, address all unpleasantries to the editor, Mr. Van Name.

Don't bother laying them on me. I don't give a hoot.

It was only a month between the writing of the premiere installment of this service column, and readying of a longer second outing, the piece you are about to read. You were introduced to *Ask Uncle Harlan* in *Pulphouse* #6 (25 Oct 91), with publication of that first column, originally published in the limited-circulation journal *Short Form* in August of 1989. Excluding the new introduction I wrote for that first reprint installment, it ran a length of 4000 words. By the time I got to penning this second column, a month later in September 1989, the wordage had grown to 5500.

(Installment 3 was almost exactly the same length, but by the time I hit installment 4 in June of 90, the length had extended to 11,500.)

I was learning something extremely troubling, and it was this: it is far easier to ask the question than it is to give the answer. And a damn sight more succinct.

Take for instance the opening salvo of installment 2, beginning below. The excellent writer John Kessel (GOOD NEWS FROM OUTER SPACE) used only thirty-two words to ask his question, but it took me more than 3000 words—ten and a half double-spaced manuscript pages—to answer the question as completely as I was able.

In bogus courtroom dramas on shows like *Matlock, Civil Wars,* and, yes, even *L.A. Law*, people are constantly being commanded to "simply answer yes or no, Ms. Smith, just yes or no!" And if you are as naive as those who believe the oft-repeated clichés of television (like: it's sitcom-simple to marry an American just to get to stay in the country; or: those smarmy remarks made by men and women on *Studs* and *Love Connection* were actually made by them, and not cobbled-up by the production staff; or: the hero cop or p.i. can get hit in the shoulder by a .45 slug, and just keep coming, as if there were no such thing as inertia, systemic shock, or blinding pain) you will believe that's how it is in an actual court of law. In fact, and despite the growing senile behavior of Judge Wopner, one is never required to douse one's answer with an idiotic yes or no. Unless one is so intimidated by the questioning attorney or the judge or the venue that one becomes the sort of petrified yotz who *deserves* to be so improperly badgered. In fact, one is almost never cut off as summarily as are the actors facing Ben Matlock or Victor Sifuentes.

And so it is with these columns. Like Kessel's query, almost every problem has a yes *and* no answer. To deal with the questions superficially, to answer briefly but incompletely, would be to deny the basic criterion for these pieces, which is: we answers 'em as we sees 'em. Fully, annoyingly honestly (as best I can perceive the truth), and in response to not only the question *as presented*, but to the underlying, between-the-lines larger questions being asked. (For instance, somebody writes in: "How does one break into writing?" and s/he is *truly* asking, "How can *I* break into writing?" Answering the question as stated wastes time for all of us. Duplicity is not necessarily the operative problem—though that is sometimes the intent—but getting to the substantive core of the question *is*.)

And so I leave myself open to "How he does go on!"

But since the most annoying kind of people are Those Who Never Get the Word, those who come into a press conference or symposium or letter column or *life* just a little late, and who ask questions others have asked and had answered a hundred thousand times before, I would rather respond completely to a query and then, should the same or similar question present itself at a later date, I can just refer the tardy interrogator to a previous column.

So in the long run it serves the commonweal to "go on" at length and wring from the question everything I know on that topic. I do, however, try not to be boring about it.

One more thing.

I made it *extremely* clear last time that we were starting these columns with four or five that had already seen publication in the now-nearly-gone *Short Form* in 1989–90, and that we did *not* want questions submitted just yet. I asked that interested parties hold their new queries until the four, five older installments had been published, at which time a complete set of ground-rules for writing to *Ask Uncle Harlan* would be put forth...and then you could inundate me.

There are Those Who Never Get the Word, or in this instance, those who simply Cannot Read. We got a couple of submissions. I sent them back with rude remarks. I suspect the people who got their questions returned with rude remarks were deeply offended.

I have no problem with that.

# 2: 27 September 1989

**F**rom MR. JOHN KESSEL **of Raleigh, North Carolina:**
"Can a writer get control over the cover art on his/her book? If so, how does s/he do it; and is it a good idea to do it if s/he can?"

Ticklish question, even though the answer is an unqualified *yes, absolutely.* Ticklish, because there are risks attendant on the effort; greater risks if you succeed; cautions that must be entered; and a lot of subtextual ancillary psychology, self-evaluation, pragmatism and commonsense necessary to informing that unqualified *yes.* You wouldn't think the water would run so fast and so deep at just thirty-two words of query, would you? Well, they do; and it's a long answer, if it's to be a complete and correct answer; and I suggest anyone who, with Mr. Kessel, cares about this matter, pay very close attention.

It is my presumption that Mr. Kessel asks this question of me, rather than of, say, Isaac Asimov or Ursula Le Guin, because he is aware of how closely I have aligned myself with that *yes* almost since the beginning of my career. Consequently, there will have to be more than a smidge of personal history passim my answer. Self-serving is not the measure in such reminiscence: it is my hope that anecdote will serve to illustrate the points of tactics and risk. By way of credential to be *offering* such medium- to high-risk suggestions.

I sold my first novel in March of 1957. To the late Walter Fultz, a smashingly adroit editor, when he was working for Lion Books. It was a juvenile delinquency novel based on my stint with the Brooklyn gangs, and it was called WEB OF THE CITY. Though Lion was not noted for its artistically enriching covers, Walter and I had a working agreement that he'd show me sketches before a final selection of artist was made. *That is the first thing you must obtain, by contract preferably, if you want a say in how your book will finally look when you see it on the airport racks.*

Merely asking your editor, in that chicken-peep way you have of speaking to Him or Her, will not suffice if you want to "get control" as Mr. Kessel phrases it. (In fact, you don't want to "get control." You want to be accorded a voice of equal impact in cover decisions with those of the marketing people, the art department, the editor, and the designer. If what you want is clearly and intelligently conveyed, if your desires are taken into consideration, and if you get to see all the work as it progresses, then control can remain with the publishing house. If you operate off the basic concept that the publisher and you are *partners* in this project, then one need not strut around like an *Oberst-gruppenführer*. The hardest part of this scheme is getting all responsible parties to understand that you are deeply concerned, and that unilateral decisions will result in extra work, extra expense, and dust-ups that will only slow the process. *Control* is not the desired end-result: a terrific cover *is*. Work toward that goal.)

So make sure the publisher doesn't spend money paying for false starts. If—preferably guaranteed in your contract or in a binding sidebar letter—you get some say in which artists are considered for the job, which one is selected, and what those first sketches look like, you'll be cut into the loop right from the start. To *become* part of that loop, look around at local bookstores and newsstands for artists whose work you think reflects what you want the book's cover to say, whose style and design sense are sufficiently unconventional to make a statement that forces their titles to stand out from the mass of books demanding the potential buyers' attention. In the case of hardcovers, the name of the designer is almost always present, as well. Note it. (And if you don't know which part of that fine dust jacket was the conception of the designer, and what part was artwork done to direction by another hand, then forget "getting control" because you don't know anima from animus, and the job is better left to professionals. But, assuming you do...)

If they're paperbacks, invest the money to buy those two or three that feature one or more artists you'd like to have considered for *your* book. If they're hardcovers, you can buy them if you think it's worth it, or just jot down the title and publisher, as well as the artist and/or designer names, and send them to your editor. Or go through your own library for recently-published hardcovers that say what you want your book to say visually. Xerox the dust jackets. Send them. Xerox the pb covers. Send them. Do it three or four times when you're in the earliest stages of pre-production, the same week they sign the contract or they've accepted the manuscript. Get them used to the idea that you are *interested*, that you are *concerned*, that you have some thoughts on the appearance of the book, that you want to be in the loop.

And that means from selection of designer and artist to the point of first sketches. Fax becomes a good idea at this point, and I'll get back to it in a moment.

But, back to personal history. Lion bought WEB OF THE CITY. But Lion went under in a complicated distributor realignment, sometime around late '57, and my manuscript was part of the assets sold off to other companies. Walter went on to work for Knox Burger at Gold Medal, and I lost track of WEB OF THE CITY.

It was not until I was serving in the U.S. Army, at Fort Knox, Kentucky, in 1958, that I learned the fate of my first novel.

I had managed to finesse myself into a job writing for the post newspaper, *Inside the Turret*, and had further managed to convince the Public Information Officer in charge of the paper that what was desperately needed to better the souls of the damned at that installation was a column reviewing the latest paperbacks. Thus, as a matter of course, boxes of pb's arrived for me every mail call. And one bright day, I received a packet from Pyramid Books.

Standing in the dayroom of the company HQ, I tore open that box and shuffled the half dozen titles, to see if there was anything that caught my fancy. Halfway through the pickings, I encountered a book with one of the most off-putting cover illustrations I'd ever seen. It was clearly a j.d. novel, luridly and badly illustrated by an artist who had, surely, been engaged as part of a hire-the-handicapped program. The title of the book was RUMBLE. I was *so* put off by the cover and the tawdry treatment of the contents as indicated *by* the art, that I put the book aside.

It was not till later that night, when filing the books for later attention, that I noticed RUMBLE had been written by someone with a name exactly like mine. I had to look twice, because the fine novelist Hal Ellson was still very prominently being published during that period; and I was prepared to commiserate with him for having been maledicted with such an abominable cover design. Not to mention that awful title. RUMBLE. Oughhh. But no, the name of the author of RUMBLE was the same as mine, poor sod.

If I seem to be recounting an incidence of unparalleled denseness, take it as reaction-in-kind to what *you* felt when you saw, for the first time, what they'd done to *your* book. Denial is the overwhelming passion. No, this can't be happening to me! This is a nightmare! I slaved a year or more over this novel, and it is now unquestionably consigned to the toilet! Deny, deny.

At that moment, as I realized Lion had sold WEB OF THE CITY to Pyramid (like a bond slave intended for the most demeaning labor on the plantation, cleaning the grease trap, draining the swamp), as I understood that for the rest of my literary life I would be the author of something called RUMBLE, I was overcome with a Scarlett O'Hara-like determination that "as god is my witness, I will never be hungry again!" That is to say, I would never again abrogate my responsibility to work I'd spent a piece of my life producing, never again sit humbly and trustingly and patiently—like a bond slave—as unseen forces did what they wanted to do with *my* book! Sit and wait to see if I'd come up lucky and the job had been done skillfully, appropriately, in a manner that would not demean me or my work, even as the work was offered in a manner that would make it commercially tasty; or come up impoverished with an inept, ugly, degrading trashpackage, turned out with a shrug and a cavalier "Well, win some, lose some" dismissal by nameless, faceless men and women in sales and art departments. Those whose salaries and reputations were predicated on the totality of what they did, not like mine and yours, rest on that one maladroitly proffered package.

(And I was to understand very soon that those nameless, faceless men and women *never* get blamed for the puny sales of the book. *You* get blamed. You're a hack, a bum, a minor talent; and we feel just *sick* about it, Mr. Kessel, but your last book didn't do as well as we'd hoped, so we'll have to decrease the advance on this new one. We're just *sick* about it, but the p&l is boss, you know; business is strictly business.)

At that moment I began to establish the credential that permits me to answer Mr. Kessel's question fully and authoritatively. As Scarlett lay vomiting up that radish in the scorched fields beyond Tara, swearing she'd never again be the pawn of unseen forces, I vowed to sit in the face of any publisher who undertook to become partner with me in the presentation of my work.

*Which is the second thing you must possess, if you want to retain some control over your career, your literary destiny: a sureness of self, a trust in your own worth, a certainty that They may or may not know what They're doing, but that you must be in on the decisions from the start.*

You are a cottage industry, a one-man or one-woman shop. You cannot immaturely put yourself in the hands of people who have *many* irons in the fire, people to whom your life and work are important only in degree to the enthusiasm you can generate in them; people who have a million odds and ends demanding their time; people who may mean well, but who may sacrifice you to considerations urgent to them but utterly beside the point to you...and bitch if it goes sour.

If you place yourselves, thus, in their hands, like trusting children, then you have no right to piss and moan about what the book looks like. If it's awful, it's *your* fault. Every time.

So I began finding artists whose work I admired, whose style seemed to be out of the ordinary, whose vision reflected what I was putting between the covers.

Leo and Diane Dillon, Jim Steranko, Barclay Shaw, Jill Bauman, Ilene Meyer, James Gurney, Michael Whelan, David Reneric, Dario Campanile, Charles Bragg, Don Punchatz, Mike Presley, Richard Corben, Jane MacKenzie, Ken Steacy, Vaughn Bodé, Ed Emshwiller, Kent Bash. And others: either as illustrators of the stories in magazines, or on the books. The Dillons on thirty covers, Barclay on sixteen.

And along the way, because I was permitted to work with such special people, I developed a design eye. And began coming up with the concepts.

I have no artistic ability whatever. I cannot draw, I cannot sketch, my "art direction" with the talents with whom I've been privileged to work is almost entirely verbal, because my "sketching" is stick figures and at best pathetic. But I can *see* what that book looks like in my head. And I can convey that.

*Which is the third thing you must possess: an understanding of design.*

Now here's an important caution. All of us *think* we can do better than the publisher. We *think* that. It comes with the arrogance of being a writer. But many writers don't have that additional skill. We know we hate what they did, but we haven't any better way to suggest to them. At this stage in my career I *know* (not think, but *know*) I can design a book that will catch the eye of the bookstore buyer. I offer as credential those Barclay Shaw editions from Ace and Bluejay, last year's Houghton Mifflin collection ANGRY CANDY, and the recently-published HARLAN ELLISON'S WATCHING from Underwood-Miller. If you happen to have the chance to examine them, I think you'll find that they buttress what I'm saying here, rather than my just blowing smoke.

But don't get into this cover control thing unless you have some solid, demonstrable evidence that you know how to put together a cover concept that will work. And remember that what works for a hardcover doesn't necessarily work on a paperback, or vice versa. They are radically different venues.

Be pragmatic with yourself. The size of your name may mean much to you ego-wise, but unless you have a following, an audience that will remember your last book with affection, your name need not dominate. Similarly, you may need the ego-boost of embossing, die-cuts, foldover covers, wraparound art, curlicue writing in silver...but those may not serve your purposes for *that* book.

There's already too much of that wasteful expenditure being practiced in the New York houses, and all it does is raise the per-unit cost on the title. Better to have a strong, single image that arrests attention, with the title (if it's a good one) and a catchy blurb line featured. Reign in your need for strokes, and relentlessly concentrate on creating a cover that will jump out at a casual buyer. Research has shown that the average paperback buyer stands back about five feet from the racks, and does an eye-scan. So tiny portraits, complex scenes, unreadable type, or copy printed in colors that blend into the background tone defeat your purpose.

Metallic inks or foil printing may make you think you're a hotshot, but of all the momentary fads that have enchanted those who try to outguess the competition for buyer attention, the lure of metallic printing overlays is the dumbest. They catch light in a peculiar way; and rather than reflecting in the buyer's eye like sunlight off a sniper's rifle, they merely serve to make the words illegible. And that, combined with a demented penchant for script with curlicues and tails and flourishes, effectively renders the message as gibberish. Avoid it, I beseech thee.

Work through your editor, at the start. Demonstrate to him or her with the evidence of those Xerox copies of covers that work for you, that you do understand design, marketing, the problems and realities of bookstore stocking, airport newsstand passenger flow, the psychological value of color and type integration. (Some familiarity with THE LÜSCHER COLOR TEST—Random House, 1969—cannot hurt. A primer of basic understanding about what colors people respond to, and in what ways they respond.)

Speaking knowledgeably to your editor will convince him or her that it will be okay to pass you along to the art director or whoever is assigned the job of designing your package. And it keeps you in the loop.

Do *not* let weeks and months go by without asking "what's happening with the cover?" Don't pester, but don't let any one conversation with the publisher—about *anything*—pass without your inquiring. Keep them aware that you wish to be consulted!

But if you have managed to get the editor and/or publisher to agree to clearing the sketches with you—and with fax capability this no longer presents a deadline problem for anyone—and as much a Luddite as I seem to be because I still use a manual typewriter and won't go to pc, I urge any writer who wants to run his/her one-person shop efficaciously, to get a fax at once, but make *sure* it has "halftone-plus" for receipt of artwork—and if you have convinced the editor that you do, in fact, know what you're doing, then stay with the cover process all the way to the end, making sure you see a color Xerox of the finished art, overlays of type to be used and the *colors* of those lines of type, and the copy itself.

A word about cover quotations.

I don't think they count for shit.

If you can manage to get George Bush or Tom Clancy or Mother Teresa to say the book is the best thing since the Bible, maybe it can pick up a sale or two for you. But not even Stephen King or E.L. Doctorow means much these days. Blurbs come and go, and I'm convinced no one pays much attention. A good *New York Times* review means something, but short of that, you're just feeding your ego again, and playing into the traditional thinking at the publishing houses. Just as I would sacrifice *all* advertising in *The New York* or *Los Angeles Times*, *Locus*, *Publishers Weekly*, or *NY Review of Books* for a good, big full-page ad in *TV Guide*, so I would happily pass on all words of praise from other writers for an inspired blurb line on the cover that chills the reader and captivates his/her attention. The object is to get the book into a buyer's hands! Never forget that.

I've gone on too long. I know that. Sorry. But I'm trying to cram everything into one *précis*. If I've overlooked anything, just Ask Uncle Harlan for specifics and I'll return to this matter in another column.

But here's the final caution. And take it to heart.

You will generate some animosity trying to get into the loop. Publishing houses have art and design departments that are run like feudal duchies. No army co-op messhall is run by a ruthless NCO more imperatively-territorial than a paperback art department. They resent "outsiders" sticking their noses into their affairs. They will resist. You must stay on top of what is being done, and speak *directly* to the art director in charge of your book. Your editor has his/her own ass to protect, and this makes additional work for them, so handle it yourself. With humility but professional strength make friends of the art director, the layout person, the copywriter, the designer... all of them. Talk to them directly, but climb the chain of command through your editor.

But know that they will call you a pain in the ass when you hang up. They'll do that until they get the slicks of the cover in their hands. Then, when they see what a nifty piece of work it is, they'll take all the credit and be ready to listen to you on the next book.

Go cautiously. Step by step, without forcing your opinions or suggestions on them. Use the old dodge of letting them believe *they* understood that the most easily-read type is yellow against black. Let *them* believe they were daring and original in departing from the traditional design to produce this elegant package. Politic is the word. I know that sounds odd coming from me, but I've learned to do it, and as a result, I can live with the books I've had a hand in fashioning; and those books have *always* sold better than those I let go through the maze untended.

I hope that answers your question, Mr. Kessel. Perhaps more than you cared to know.

But now I must press on.

**From MR. F. BRETT COX of Durham, North Carolina:**

"At the 1989 International Conference on the Fantastic in the Arts, Robert Silverberg gave an extremely gloomy speech in which he said that the literary aspirations of the 'New Wave' had been trampled by *Star Trek/Star Wars* fans and teenagers who refuse to read anything that doesn't extend over three volumes. The only bright spot he cited was 'a minor renaissance' (I believe those were his words) in sf short fiction, primarily centered around *Asimov's*. Do you agree with this? What is your assessment of contemporary sf?"

One comment before I answer. It seems as if every question at hand is from someone living in North Carolina. I didn't set it up this way, friends. The Kessel question, and one from the editor, Mr. Van Name, were given to me personally as I was writing my first installment; and they've carried over. It may not be necessary to answer Mr. Van Name's poser, for reasons that need not concern you. But apparently all these others got to Mr. Van Name first, because the correspondents were in his neighborhood and they got their copies of the last issue early. Let us hope for a greater geographical diversity henceforth. Nonetheless, as the subhead says, we answers 'em as we sees 'em. If we don't sees 'em, I can't...well, you get the idea. But...to work:

Do I agree with Mr. Silverberg's assessment of the current state of the genre? Agree, hell, I said it first! I said it, for the record, in 1966 when *Star Trek* was taken to the bosom of sf fandom. Though the series was not immediately successful as far as NBC was concerned, through word-of-mouth efforts in which I had a hand (he said humbly, but historically-correctly), or a mouth (he said with some chagrin), it became the Thing Incapable of Being Killed with which we live today.

I said then, almost a quarter-century ago, that *Star Trek*—and later, *Star Wars*—provided a cheap jack way for publishers to add sf to the easily-exploited genre presentations of mysteries, romances, westerns, spy novels. I was laughed at. Roundly.

One of the biggest laughers was Lester del Rey. It is more than slightly ironic that Lester, and his late wife, Judy-Lynn, are one unit of the three I most blame for the current wretched state of what passes for commercially-published sf. Don't ask me to name the other two. This will already stretch my friendship with Lester, to have placed him in the camp of the despoilers.

But at that time Lester, and many *many* others, called me a Gloomy Gus, the specter at the banquet. *Star Trek* and *Star Wars* would, they rebuffed me, open the market for Our Thing. No it wouldn't, I howled. It would open the market for *Star Trek* and *Star Wars* spinoffs, and we would plunge willingly into the trap of writing idiot space opera, because it's the lowest common denominator of sf for the masses.

I took as the basis for my prediction the success, at that time, of the dreadful Perry Rhodan novels that Don Wollheim was reprinting from Germany, and the several series imitations they had spawned. An audience that has trouble reading Barry Malzberg and Tom Disch and Kate Wilhelm already, I said, will find its pablum in formulaic novels using these tv cliché characters. And because of the broader base of readers for this simplified drivel, the money will be tantalizing to writers. It will turn good writers away from "difficult" work as they (rationally and quite properly) look to their own survival. They will see big bucks being made by hacks, they will rationalize that since they like *Star Trek* anyway there isn't anything much wrong with getting a taste themselves, and what the hell, ain't I entitled to live decently for a change, haven't I spent ten years writing high-falutin' sf that gets great reviews from fanzines but doesn't make a dime beyond the advance?

Saul Bellow wrote, "Writers are not necessarily corrupted by money. They are distracted—diverted to other avenues."

One may feel that writers like Vonda McIntyre or Piers Anthony, who have done brilliant work in their time, have expended valuable, unrecoverable years on projects "unworthy" of their talents, but I suggest that anyone who dares to make that judgment is being presumptuous beyond the limits of fair comment. Laboring in the vineyard for a tiny coterie of aficionados, for the momentary approbation one gets at a convention or in the book reviews in *Locus*, as one's contemporaries collect enormous royalties, placement on the *Times* bestseller lists, ego-enrichment by publishers formerly acting with olympian disregard, and a chance to break loose from the ghetto, may seem small, bitter, and cheap reward after a while. Before any of us revile our friends for acting in their best interests, we'd best be damned sure we wouldn't do exactly the same if presented with the opportunity.

Money is what they throw at us to divert us, and even if the money isn't a consideration—some of us really don't care much about it—that money brings with it the attention and feeling of worthiness we usually are denied. And if you'll permit just one more quotation, that latter lure is often more enticing than dollars because, as Quentin Crisp observed, "Artists in any medium are nothing more than a bunch of hooligans who cannot live within their income of admiration." I'm the worst offender in this regard, so

I feel empowered to point it out to the rest of you.

Thus, in my view, the sorry state of the genre is mutually attributable to editors who have become purchasing agents for bottom-line books demanded by their employers' p&l statements, and by good writers looking out for the main chance. That includes all the writers who have been pushed into writing windy trilogies by their editors playing on authors' hubris. ("This is a significant fantasy idea, far too bold and sweeping to be done merely as a novelette. It requires three *books*, possibly six, maybe nine!") It also includes all the writers of lesser or greater ability involved in these abysmal shared-world trivialities. And the writers doing spinoff titles based on "ideas created by" big-name authors; and the writers doing novels set in the worlds of famous short stories; and the writers doing interactive multiple-choice "novels" for dweebs with videogame mentalities; and the writers of adaptations of banal movie scripts.

Understand: I respond to the question pragmatically, and in so doing I am compelled not merely to say yes, I agree with Bob Silverberg's judgment of the condition of the form, but to state *why*. That means pointing the finger. But I do *not* pillory any of the writers or editors on whom the shoe above fits. Who am I to tell Bob Silverberg that he betrays some idiotic Noble Cause by writing his "Heroes in Hell" stories? By what right do I tell dear Ann Crispin that she should forgo her *Star Trek* novel annuity because it Betrays the Art. Only a knothead would waggle a finger at Owen Lock or Jim Baen and tell them they are bad guys for publishing greater and greater numbers of Tolkien imitations or paranoiac military sf, when they are making money at the task, *which is what they're in business to do*, because it offends the tender sensibilities of Those Who See Greatness in SF.

Yes, I see the state of the field as being more wretched than ever I can remember its being previously; as minimally-talented amateurs are raised instantly to the heights of pr-puffery; as older writers rewrite their previous successes again and again; as experimental writers opt for "family" by aligning themselves with one fad school or another; as good writers who've grown weary of relative poverty and relative obscurity succumb to the cheapjack blandishments of big-money houses, skimming not creating.

It is, in my view, the worst time for new writers. They do not get the gradual training they need to insure a career that will last, and that will mean something when it's ended. What they get is promotion and virtually no editorial direction that can better their craft. The short story markets that were the training ground in years past, are now only supplementary to the trilogy markets. And if there is "a minor renaissance" in the short story, it is because every writer has some special work in him/her. It *will* get written.

They understand that new-wave thinking (in the classic sense of that phrase, not the jingoism of sf historians) will not be looked on with much favor by the publishers, so they write the ideas as short stories. And so, we get the occasional killer piece—like Connie Willis's "At the Rialto" in the current *Omni*, excerpted from MICROVERSE— that reminds us just how enthralling can be this art-form, when the artist is eccentric and goes full tilt dammit. If there's a "minor renaissance" in the short story, perhaps that explains it: there are still good ideas out there, and intellectually-hungry writers needful of setting them down. The ideas cannot be bludgeoned and put on the rack to fill a fat novel, or a trilogy, but they *must* be attended to...and so, we see the fresh writing being done in the shorter form.

There is also the possibility that the new attention being accorded impressive short story writers in the mainstream—Ethan Canin, Tomas Rivera, Amy Hempel, Tobias Wolff, Marianne Wiggins—signals one of those periodic attacks of ennui with the overblown novel that the Eastern Literary Establishment suffers. It may be that the "minor renaissance" Silverberg perceives in the genre's short product production, is a resonance with the larger literary world's turning Chekhovwards yet again.

So in summation: yes, I agree that the genre is in dire straits, and no, I haven't tumbled to the "minor renaissance" Silverberg notes, but that doesn't mean it ain't there. I think, as a rule of thumb, that the best, most innovative work in *any* genre is always done in the short form, like pathfinders searching out new passages through the concrete mountains, and that may be what Bob is seeing. I hope he's correct in his analysis.

### From MR. CHARLIE MARTIN of Durham, North Carolina:

"What do you do when you have a story that you like and you believe in and you've written as well as you know how, and you've sent it out to everybody and no one else likes it?"

Thank heaven, at last, a question I can answer briefly. When you say "no one else likes it" I hope you also mean to say that they gave you *reasons* for their reactions. If they did, then run a correlation. See if the reactions dovetail at one or more places. If five people told you they didn't believe the ending, then that's the place to start examining the piece. If no one gave you specifics, then you're in the dark, of course; and simply hearing "I didn't like it" won't serve your needs.

In that case, I commend to your attention this pragmatic method:

1.  The story may be *exactly* right the way it is, in terms of what you wanted to do

with it. In that case, fuck'm. You wrote it, you did what you wanted it to do, and that's that.

2.  But if you also want to sell it, then the core fact you learn from the rejections is that it didn't work. At least not in the way you wanted it to work. And that might mean...

3.  You weren't good enough, or smart enough, to carry it off. I've found that to be the case with stories I wrote in the past. I had this great idea, but I simply wasn't educated enough in some special area to provide the backup information that gave it verisimilitude. Or I wasn't old enough, and hadn't had sufficient life-experience in that specific of the human condition to make the characters believable. So...

4.  Put it in the drawer. And don't think about it, or look at it, for two years. Live your life, write other things; and in two years come back to it and read it as if someone else had written it. I'd make book that you'll find it's not as perfect as you'd originally thought. And the weaknesses will leap at you. *Then* rewrite it, and send it out again.

That's it. I'm pooped. This is, after all, a journal called *Short Form*—as my wife just pointed out—and I never intended to go on at such length. But as you can see, the simplest questions in terms of being stated, require a lot of back'n'forthing to answer. I'll try to do better, that is, shorter, in future installments. There has to be a way of accomplishing this short of Dear Abby slickness.

I just haven't found it yet.

One last comment. Last time, I made some remarks about David Hartwell and *The New York Review of Science Fiction*. They were, in part, the sort of things that no one could enjoy having said about them or their publication. I would be less than evenhanded if I did not mention that when Mr. Hartwell was apprised of my comments, and he read them, he dropped me a note saying "I will do my best not to be extremely annoyed by them."

One can hope for no more decent response. This comes under the heading of *mensch*, a Yiddish word that indicates a person of considerable class and composure, which is what Mr. Hartwell is, in my book. I thought you ought to know this.

**I**f you've been following the renascent progression of this column, a *service* column intended to make your life as a writer easier and more productive and more self-assured and more creative and, yes, even more financially remunerative, you'll know that we now come to the third installment, originally written for *Short Form* (edited by Mark Van Name, financed without editorial control by Orson Scott Card) in December of 1989. For those coming late to these columns, the synopsis is simple: I began writing these pieces at the request of the editor of *Short Form*, and the one absolute unbreakable rule was (and is) that I would answer every question asked of me with total honesty (notwithstanding the universal truth that, like you, I am wrong in my perceptions as often as you, but that I would not *consciously* stray from what I *perceived* to be the Genuine Right Stuff). That means the *whole* truth, even the parts that make you uncomfortable. Further, to implement honesty, I would undertake to answer the *real* question, the core that lay within sometimes-obfuscated query.

We've all read fantasies in which the protagonist wishes for everyone to "tell the truth" and what horrors ensue as characters in the story are denied the acceptable white lies or kindly euphemisms that permit us to live our lives with civility. If someone who looks like hell asks, "How do you like my new do, I just came from the stylist?" and you reply, "What you look like is something that Dr. Moreau might've designed if he crossed a peccary pig with a bowl of oatmeal," you may be telling the truth *as you perceive it*, but you would be needlessly cruel and for what purpose? There are untruths or dissemblings that we all use just to get through the day.

But I'm denied even those. If you Ask Uncle Harlan a question, you'll get the un-adorned response. If you don't want to hear it that way, just don't ask.

As Edna St. Vincent Millay put it: "It's not true that life is one damn thing after another...it's one damn thing over and over."

Be that as it may. Truth unadorned; and exhaustive answer, conveying everything I know to that question; and no responses to complaints about me or the column in the letters section, only replies in the venue of this or that installment, where the query appears. You can pillory me with impunity in the letters dept.

I wrote four columns for *Short Form* between August of 1989 and June of 1990.

We're working our way through those already-published four columns at the moment. There will be a fifth column done for the swan-song issue of *Short Form* any day now, and then that one will reprint here, and then...we start fresh with new essays prompted by the readers of *Pulphouse*.

Do not, repeat DO NOT send any questions now. They'll be shredded. Let me catch up. Let *Pulphouse* catch up. Next time we do #4, and quickly thereafter #5, and *then* we'll open the window for your angel-winged missives. Right now, here's 5300 excellent words from December of 1989.

# 3: 19 December 1989

**From MR. GREGORY KUSNICK of Sonora, California:**

"What are the pros and cons of writing books on spec? Are editors receptive to completed works, or would they rather buy something they can steer? Does having a boxed up manuscript in hand cut any ice at the bargaining table? Is the work itself well served by being finished first and sold second?"

I'm absolutely in love with this question.

And like all honestly-phrased questions, its simplicity bears within its presentation a commonsense answer. (As opposed to *another* sort of question, examples of which have appeared here in the past, and which species will manifest itself once again next time, where the very phrasing of the question is disingenuous, duplicitous, and insulting.)

The answer, of course, is that the writer is *always* better served, artistically and market-wise, if the book is completed before it's sent to be pawed over by the sausage packagers.

The *only* benefit, as far as I can perceive, of selling a book on the basis of a concept, or an outline, or a 10,000 word chunk and an outline, is that the writer will be subsidized while doing the writing. Now that may seem swell, on the face of it, but one is never really subsidized to the degree that provides genuine creative freedom, but only to the degree that a new, artificial and arbitrary, parameter has been added to the equation. In addition to the built-in problems of working with the story materials—as *they* work with *you*—of evaluating pace and vigor and proportion as you pummel your way through, often so close to the work that you can't know whether you're on top of it or sinking beneath it, as you cope with the warping of your daily life and the stresses put on all your

37

relationships because your primary devotion is to the work...and human situations are being shunted aside or patched-over till sanity returns, you have taken on a foreign master.

No matter how understanding, or kindly, or attuned to your needs the buyer of wares may be, s/he is a foreign master, and you must consider his/her vested interest, consciously or unconsciously, every day of the writing. If the buyer of wares (hereinafter codified as the BOW-WOW!) is patient, understanding, relaxed in his/her schedule... even then, it's an assumed jot of sidebar consideration that diverts the stream's direction of flow. Perhaps imperceptibly. Perhaps obviously. Never inconsequentially.

But if we're to deal with reality here, rather than some never-never land fairytale simulacrum of the real world, we must look at the totality of all auctorial experience from that of the first freelance Australopithecine hired by a precursorial yuppie *h. erectus*, say, an early model Java Man, to redecorate the upwardly-mobile cave...to the bushy-eyed, bright-tailed communications B.A. grad who last week sold a high-concept story-arc to HBO Films. And in such examination, seek though we may, we find not one incidence of an artist being anything but beset, lumbered, troubled, chivvied, unsettled, or otherwise distracted by the presence in the creative situation of an outside intelligence, a straphanger reading the newspaper over one's shoulder, a *presence* (no matter how benevolent) whose needs, demands, and feelings must be taken into consideration.

That's what they *do*. They're the Pope. It's their *job*!

The instant someone gives you financial support, they think they have the right to know what's being done with it. "As long as you live under *my* roof, young (man) (woman) (choose one), you'll abide by *my* rules!" There is nothing of philanthropic dispassion when a publisher contracts for a book. Lou Aronica is not one of the Este patriarchy, endowing a painter of frescoes simply because it's his nature. He's logging on a new "product" and though he may allow you to work at your own pace, in your own way, for a while—shorter or longer—at some stage of the game he'll start asking questions, wanting to "see some progress," suggesting things that seem to him rather more interesting in the already-submitted pages than other things about which you're enamoured. Bending, controlling, venturing opinions, as you phrase it—steering. That means your little caravelle rides not on the natural tide, but tacks to the effort of a guiding intelligence, not in full your own.

Mr. Kusnick opens his question with the phrase "writing books on spec." Know this:

Until the moment the writer speaks to the BOW-WOW! the book is subject to but one master. The book is yours. It is not, therefore, "spec." (It just dawned on me, there might be some rank amateur, simultaneously suffering from mental retardation, who doesn't know that "spec" is short for *speculative writing*, i.e., writing done for an editor or publisher, without a firm commitment from the editor or publisher that such work will be purchased once produced. It is work done on the if-come. It is work done with, at best, a dangled carrot of, "If I like it, I'll buy it. If I don't like it, you're shit outta luck, Johnny." The term "spec writing" was unheard in my days as a magazine and paperback original writer. One either did the whole book or story, or in the case of paperbacks did ten thousand words and a good outline, and sold it up front. There was no such thing as "spec." As far as *I* know; though there were no doubt examples of that procedure between some parties; I just don't happen to know of any. The term comes from the television industry, which is run in a very different manner from the world of publishing. "Spec writing" is *verboten* in Hollywood, entirely through the good offices and stern strike history of the Writers Guild of America, west. In days of yore—even as recently as 1962, when I got here—there were a hundred smarmy ways for a producer or studio to get you to do work on the cuff. Through the past three decades, the WGAw has strengthened its Mimimum Basic Agreement—available to you if you write to the WGAw in Los Angeles—so that it is a punishable offense to con a writer into doing work on the if-come. That's why I find some of the newer, younger horror writers, who think they're buying their way into the game by doing spec scripts, so pathetic. They will be used, rewritten, paid chump change, get no screen credit, be denied membership in the Guild, and will eventually be shat out the other end, having been used by unscrupulous film "entities" for the naïfs they are. So there *are* foolish amateurs, all puffed up with their sophomoric sense of invulnerability, who still practice spec foolishness; but it's universally held to be an odious and stupid practice.) So the term "spec" really doesn't apply when you're writing without assignment or contract from a publisher. The book is yours. Until you bring a BOW-WOW! into the equation, at which point, even by having a conversation and hearing that commercially driven "input," the book becomes, in some way large or small, *theirs*, as well.

It's the Heisenberg Uncertainy Principle.

By the very fact of other eyes watching, you and the work are affected.

Of course, there are hacks, doing hackwork, who don't care. What they do is a performance, anyhow. And it cannot be any more corrupted by having been steered by an editor or publisher or purest market considerations, than it has been by the impure motives for having entered into the project in the first place.

But none of you is one of those, so we need not be concerned with that aspect of the question here.

Which brings us back to that "pro and con" thing, where we left it a moment ago. The only positive aspect, as I've suggested, is being endowed to do the work. Literary food stamps. Auctorial grant of aid. Subsidy.

And as I said earlier, even that is hokeypokey, because one is never paid what one needs to do the job at one's chosen pace. It's like television: if it takes you $273,000 per episode to do the series, the most they'll give you is $195 to $240. You *always* have to go to deficit financing. If you figure it'll take you a year to write the novel, how much is it going to cost you to live, without taking on work that will put food on the table but divert you from the major effort? Ten thousand, twenty thousand, fifty? Have you a spouse? Have you children? Have you debts, prior commitments, health problems, extenuating circumstances such as an invalid relative you must support, or living with you? Exactly how *much* do you need to have laid back, to take you through the full extent of creating this work?

I promise you, if it's ten grand, they'll offer you three. If it's twenty-five, they'll offer you fifteen. And beyond that level, forget it. The more they give you, the closer they want to watch you. After all, they have "publishing committees" and bookkeepers who know only the bottom line, who do not get the same erotic rush as your editor, from thinking of themselves as part of the Literary Community. The ones who control the purse strings are businessfolk, and they are substantially less tolerant of writers who don't produce what they were paid to produce than are the editors who serve as double-agents, climbing the corporate ladder while attempting to keep the approbation of the creators.

But what of the value of a sounding board for the work in progress? Isn't that a big plus? To have a professional right there at beck and call, paying *you* for the privilege of giving you his or her honed opinion about how you're doing! Isn't that a big item on the pro side?

You keep wanting to set up housekeeping in dream castles in never-never land. You really must get a grip.

Do not delude yourself that an editor over your shoulder, someone whose personal career rests in part on how well you do, whose existence can be in some way, large or small, threatened by how well s/he guessed at your potential, can keep you on track. They don't have the time. That was years ago, chum. Today they are "purchasing editors" or "acquisitions editors" or galley slaves recently graduated from some eastern college and working for peanuts. Senior editors, who should have the smarts of Maxwell Perkins or Victoria Chen Heider, are, in my opinion, for the most part callow and as badly suited to their positions as a drayhorse is to a run in the Kentucky Derby. They haven't the equipment, even if they had the inclination and the time, to do the work of depth that is needed to "steer" a writer. Bad enough if you're a newcomer; impossible if you have a reputation. An editor that good just doesn't exist in the genre today. That'll win me no looks of love from my friends Ginjer and Beth and Sue and all the rest, but as far as I'm concerned the only editor at the moment who has the right stuff is Mike Seidman over at Zebra, which is why I've placed twenty-two books in his hands. But that's a side-bar for another time.*

You are *always* better off doing the work solo, unaided, not showing it around, not seeking justification or "input," and definitely not seeking financial backing from a publisher. You are much better off as a negotiator (or as a product for your agent to negotiate) if you have completed the book. If you have written it the way *you* want to write it.

Because they'll offer you more money for a finished item.

Because you'll have a vested interest that will keep you from bending to whimsical demands that you alter the book for this or that bogus reason.

Because you'll have the strength to walk away from a lousy deal.

Writing is, and should be, a solitary endeavor. It isn't like writing tv scripts, where you perform as you create. It is one of the few processes left to us by which we can commune with our higher natures, understand our place in the chain, speak to our times and those who will come after, and in short, grasp hold of our destiny and control it. To offer any of that, *a priori*, to an outside intellect, for *any* amount of upfront jack, is to piss in the chicken soup.

**From MR. DANNY REID of Chapel Hill, North Carolina:**

"Last issue you mentioned Stanley Ellin as 'one of the four or five writers I most admire and respect...' Who are the others, and why?"

Hoist by my own hyperbole. There are, of course, more than four or five writers whose work I admire and respect; and suddenly being asked if Ellin is one of the top five, who are the other four...well, of course, that's a trap of my own making; and

---

* This has nothing much to do with the issue at hand, but having written the answer to Mr. Kusnick's question, I realized I might be making some trouble for Mike Seidman at Zebra, and so I called him to ask if what I'd written seemed accurate. He agreed, but asked that I mention that the 22 books he has bought of mine are *not* being marketed as science fiction, that Zebra does not *publish* science fiction, and that sf writers should not be misled by my deal with Zebra into thinking it's a market for sf.

had I known someone was going to take the remark literally...as I suppose I intended it to be taken in the specific case of Stan Ellin...I would have circumlocuted in a more evasive fashion.

But having been pinned by my own infelicity of speech, I'll try to be as brief and as forthcoming as I can.

Stan Ellin absolutely *is* in the top half dozen of any Most Admired list I might draw up. And there is not one of you out there, no matter how arrogant, how excellent in your craft, who cannot learn from simply reading him. Not one of you.

As for the rest of the list, it reads like this:

Frederic Prokosch

Kate Wilhelm

Jorge Luis Borges

Franz Kafka

W.S. Merwin

Gerald Kersh

Donald Westlake

And that makes eight, not four or five. So sue me.

As to *why* each of these writers is on my Most Admired list, the reasons are multi-farious, not just through the group of eight, but from writer to writer, with several qualities in each writer's work commending that talent to me. Trying to run it down slickly—Kafka's surrealistic intensity; Merwin's mythic references, concision, ability to compress a novel into three lines; Kersh's inexplicable way of delineating an entire complex character with one salient flourish; the vast weight of intellect Wilhelm brings to usually ordinary story materials—is a trick, not an analysis, and it would take me thirty thousand words to explain in complete rationale why these eight top my list. So I serve you best, in answering your question, Danny (and the rest of you reading over his shoulder), by simply saying, if you want to find out what makes them better than you or me...go read them. Stop trying for the bullshit crit-lit analysis, and go find their books, and *read* them. Not as you read this week's trash Tor output, or Ace abominations, but *read* them as supplicants, as students coming to sit at the feet of the masters.

And just because I put them at the very top, steals nothing from, say, the next two down—Zoé Oldenbourg and Bernard Wolfe—nor from the next three down—Mark Twain, Thomas Hardy, and Shirley Jackson—or the next four—Fritz Leiber, Wyllis Cooper, Konrad Lorenz, and John O'Hara—and not even a jot is stolen from the fiftieth on the list, who may be Luisa Valenzuela or Tom Disch, both of whom have taught me important lessons.

In short, this is a mug's game, unworthy of any of us, particularly when some idiot fan journal demands we "name our top ten of all time" or somesuch flummery. It's a Miss America contest, and beneath any writer to participate.

Nonetheless, I was asked the question, I've answered it honestly, but I think it's fucking foolish; and I wish I'd never expressed myself in a manner of such sequential superlatives. I feel like a damn fool, and I hope you're satisfied, Danny.

**From MR. STEVEN J. VAUGHAN-NICHOLS of Lanham, Maryland:**

(1st Question) "Once upon a time, would-be writers had drilled into them the laws of manuscript preparation; how much the paper should weigh, double-space not single-space; and how wide the margins should be. Those lessons still need to be taught with a few updates, like *thou shalt not print on a dot matrix printer with a bad ribbon*. My question is: some publications, mostly computer magazines, but a few others, will now accept manuscripts either on disk or by electronic mail. It seems reasonable to expect other magazines to get on this bandwagon. Do you have any suggestions for proper manuscript formats for the '90s?"

(2nd Question) "I'm an up-and-coming writer of non-fiction, but like so many people in that situation, I'd like to publish fiction as well. Is it worth mentioning my non-fiction experiences in query or submission letters to fiction editors?"

Like everyone else, I enjoy playing the know-it-all. I suspect that out there among you breathes not a single soul who does not puff up like a blowfish and bask in the warmth of having been the one who twisted the stuck ketchup cap off the bottle. But, like most of you, there are times when I have to confess that I am the wrong person to be asking for a certain piece of information...or even a particularly good gut-guess or extrapolation. Such is the case with Mr. Vaughan-Nichols's first question. (I'll be replying to these two separately.)

I use a manual typewriter.

I have never worked (save for *very* rare instances, on deadline or away from my office, when pressing circumstance required and I had no alternative) on an electric typewriter. I have *never* written anything on a pc or "word processor."

Let's not make a big thing of this.

I understand the need for proselytizing on the part of those of you who are simply in love with these idiot machines; but it is a messianic imposition on my good nature that I long ago ceased to countenance. It's like having endless *Watchtower* flacks banging on my door, or veering too near the maw of a Scientology Center. I do not plump for a return to the manual typewriter, nor even a taking-up once more of the goose quill. I figger everyone is entitled to earn his/her keep with the mechanism best suited to his/her needs. Such a sanguine and humanistic attitude, however, does not seem to be the course of those who speak of "accessing data" or suchlike.

It is strictly a personal matter, between me and my conscience, like my attitudes toward politics and religion. My theory of the preferability of writing on a manual machine as opposed to "word processor" is that one should not be a Luddite (I have a fax machine and a Xerox in my office), that one should avail oneself of modern technology, but *only* to the degree that the technology is useful for getting the job done by one's own rigor...and beyond that all one is doing is keeping up with the Joneses, playing with clever toys, or making hackwork easier. For me, the level of technology that best serves my purposes is an Olympia office standard (I have four of them) or, when on the road, an Olympia portable (I have four of these as well).

But it does mean that I'm hardly the guy to ask about "proper manuscript formats for the '90s."

Bearing that in mind, here are the only thoughts in reply that I think may be useful:

What worked on a typewriter, ought to serve equally as well for a manuscript prepared on pc. Double-space, 24 or 25 lines to a page, margins at about 12/72, with an inch margin left and right sides, and an inch to an inch-and-a-quarter top and bottom...on an 8½x11 sheet of white bond, of course. As for format, I have found that the most universally accepted laying-out of a manuscript is the one to be found in Scott Meredith's book WRITING TO SELL, originally published by Harper & Row in 1950 and revised in 1960 and 1974. This is the very best one-volume source, of all the books on "how to be a professional" I've seen and read, available to the writer who perceives that being an author is a business, as well as a vocation. Everything you need to know about manuscript page-headings, cover sheets, query letters, space breaks...all of it...is there, simply and sensibly proffered. There may well be a more recent revised edition than the 1974, which I own. And it will very likely deal with pc formats and suchlike, if it exists. This is the book Budrys gave me when I was just starting out, and I recommend it without reservation.

(This testimonial for the book, however, should not in any way be construed as a testimonial for Mr. Meredith as a literary agent. That is another matter entirely.)

One thing I *do* know for sure about manuscripts produced on a screen and then printed off a disk: justifying the right-hand margin is punctilious, amateur horseshit. And using a bookface type that makes the manuscript appear to have been set in type for publication, as columns, with script, with all the appurtenances of a finished magazine or book publication, is very close behind in the horse puckey sweepstakes. When you send in a raw manuscript, it ought to *look* as if it came from human hands, not Xeroxed from some magazine.

It seems to me, *en passant*, that concern about "format" is a concern with the chrome and digital dashboard readouts on a vehicle that continues to give you nine miles per gallon.

Not meaning to sound too lofty about this, but it's *what* you have to say, Mr. Vaughan-Nichols, and how *well* you say it, that matters most. Within the fairly flexible parameters of the format equation for an editor's understanding that s/he is looking at the work of a professional, rather than an amateur who sends in the story in pencil on lined paper, you can stop worrying about "new formats." The tried and true look of a manuscript is probably your best template.

Beyond that, you may be trying to say with fancy footwork what you cannot with style and content.

As for question number two, yes, of course you should mention (in brief) any publications of consequence you've had, even if they're non-fiction and you're submitting to an editor of fiction. Whatever can convince him/her that you know what you're doing, that you're not a dub, is to your advantage. I cannot conceive of an editor not being impressed that you have had three long essays in *The New Yorker* or *Harper's*. But by the same token, I cannot conceive of an editor thinking that your running column on gardening in the *East Weewaw Suburban Greensheet* has much to do with your ability to write galaxy-spanning adventures that will make boys and girls of all ages gasp in wonderment. Commonsense should rule your name-dropping.

Don't try to impress anyone, you'll never be able to snow them. Simply try to reassure.

**From MR. MARK VAN NAME of Durham, North Carolina:**

"Your career has been characterized by struggles. Struggles against the evil acts and evil men and women you perceive in the world, struggles that you attack Zorro-like, sword-pen in hand. Sometimes your attacks have been *ad hominem*, in whole or in part. Sometimes that is certainly deserved, but how does one know when? Also, the level of vehemence in your voice often seems to change the plane of the discussion, away from the issues and into a spitting contest.

"Case in point: some paragraphs of your earlier response to Bruce's letter. I don't know Hartwell, so I can neither refute nor support your assertions about him. More important, do they, and the overall tone of that answer, advance the cause of critical discussion, or are you merely showing off?

"Just where does one draw that line, anyway?"

I'll make this short, because this is precisely the kind of question I *don't* want to deal with in this column.

Mr. Van Name is referring, of course, to my reply to Bruce Sterling's letter in the first installment of this series (Vol. 2 No. 2 August 1989). The question was about *The New York Review of Science Fiction* and it was asked in Mr. Sterling's usual arch fashion. And was answered in the same vein. In my second installment I made note of Mr. Hartwell's gracious reaction to what I'd said, and stated that he was a Class Act. That's the background of Mr. Van Name's question.

The answer is this: how the hell do *I* know where the line should be drawn? Maybe I *am* just showing off. Hell, I don't *think* that's what I'm doing, but who's to know? Certainly *I* don't know.

But I suggest it's not something I care to get into. The purple prose of Mr. Van Name's opening, all that hyperbole about sword-pens and Zorro and evil men and women and great struggles...that's Mr. Van Name's characterization and, if I may suggest it, his attempt at peering into my psyche. It's *his* interpretation, and I assure the readers of these words that I do not perceive of myself (at least as Uncle Harlan) in the role of Simón Bolivar. I'm here to answer questions about writing, not about me and my personal life. The earlier query from Mr. Vaughan-Nichols prompted a little of that— about manual typewriters—but I'm uneasy spilling my personal life *in this venue*. Heaven knows I do it freely enough everywhere else. I'd very much like to keep this column as purely free of personal trivia as I can. I may not always be smart enough to accomplish that end, but believe me when I say I'm *trying*.

Let me, for a moment, address one element of Mr. Van Name's analysis of my forensic debating technique. He suggests that because of "the vehemence in my voice" I may be lowering the intellectual tone of the discussion at hand. He may be correct. On the other hand, I like to think of it not as vehemence, but as *passion*. My response to many songs that reach my ears is a visceral one. If a thing is worth debating, it should be worth debating full-out, without regard to How Good One Looks. And there is a rule of thumb I use when committing myself to the discussion, and it is this:

Don't let the other guy set the tone.

Very often, proponents of a position will undertake to set the ground rules for what *kind* of discussion you have, by the tone they employ at the first horn blast. For instance, if you go back and re-read the Sterling *question* that Mr. Van Name cites as case in point, you will see that I addressed the *way* in which Mr. Sterling couched his query, as much as I did the actual content. To have answered it with a pretense that Mr. Sterling was asking what he asked all wide-eyed and innocent, would have been to play his game. I chose to treat his secret agenda as well as his open request.

If someone adopts that nose-in-the-air, Boston brahmin, Late George Apley attitude in a letter that nonetheless boils down to personal attack, to attempt answering it in that tone of voice is to deny my feelings and to operate on the playing-field another has chosen, usually from a position of highest ground and unassailable strength. No, I prefer to recast the battlefield; and if that occasionally means I don't dance the pavane as stately as the attacked wished, well, one should never expect a greater nobility of one's adversary than one possesses oneself.

I'm not sure that impassioned response to duplicitous query "advances the cause of critical discussion," but then, was it critical discussion to begin with, or just another attempt to slip one past and do some sneaky damage...I don't know, kiddo.

The line is drawn where it happens to be drawn, each time out. And if we go overboard, well, it seemed like the right thing to do at the time. Better than that, and with the assurance that Uncle Harlan is *trying* to be fair and evenhanded, I cannot reassure you.

I still have at hand a long-held letter from Orson Scott Card, and a new one from Richard Kadrey. I'll try to include them next time.

It's been a shitty end-of-year, my right leg is in a cast up to my knee, I had three hours under the knife at Cedars-Sinai a week before Christmas, and I'm feeling as ebullient as a carbuncle right about now; so I'll go quickly, and wish you all a better decade a-coming.

# 4: 28 June 1990

There is a powerful scene in the Dalton Trumbo screenplay for the Kubrick-directed *Spartacus* (a scene not found in Howard Fast's exemplary novel) in which, after the defeat of the slave army, the Roman cohorts assemble the battered remnants of that vanquished rabble in an attempt to discover which man among them, if still alive, is the instigator, Spartacus. It is the obsession of Marcus Licinius Crassus (as portrayed by Laurence Olivier) to crucify this seditious and charismatic rebel in such a public and brutal manner that it will snuff the flame of freedom these self-proclaimed "unchained souls" follow. But the face of Spartacus is unknown.

So an announcement is made to the survivors huddled in chains on the hillside. You will be spared. Slaves you were, and slaves you shall remain, but your lives will be spared. One condition only: the slave Spartacus, alive or his body, must be identified. Let him give himself up, or be given up by others, and you will be spared the awful death of crucifixion.

There is a momentary beat of expectation as the camera holds on Spartacus (Kirk Douglas), chained between the poet Antoninus (Tony Curtis) and the Jewish gladiator David (Harold J. Stone). Spartacus rises, to give himself up; but as if all three were on the same spring, Antoninus and David rise with him. And before Spartacus can speak, the Greek poet says, "I am Spartacus!" and an instant later David says, "*I* am Spartacus!" and then, one after another, each of the bloody ex-slaves stands and declares, "I am Spartacus!" "*I* am Spartacus!" "*I am Spartacus!*"

In the case of the tardiness of the appearance of this issue of *Short Form*, I cannot in conscience permit the editor, Mr. Van Name, to take the blame for that which is my responsibility.

I cannot permit his crucifixion for my dilatory behavior. The simple truth is that poor health and other pressing deadline demands compelled me to shunt this (admittedly pleasant but financially non-remunerative) literary indulgence onto a side track till it was convenient to expend the time on something of less than a survival nature. I take writing this column as seriously as anything else I do, but it is a luxury, a hobby...an indulgence. And sometimes, well, the real world demands in a louder voice than does the editor, Mr. Van Name; or the readers of *Short Form*.

So do not accept any bogus apologies by the editor, Mr. Van Name, in any other section of this publication. He is only rising in the fetters to declare himself Spartacus out of a misplaced sense of loyalty to his volunteer columnists. The buck stops here.

Oh, and one other small preliminary note. Because I answer the questions you send, I am in the enviable position of being able to respond to any personal attacks with virtual impunity—like a stand-up comedian eviscerating a heckler in the audience who is too stupid to understand that the guy with the microphone *always* gets the last thrust in. Because of the unfair power this gives me—I have a soapbox much higher than the other guy—I've chosen not to respond to any of the comments made about me or this column that appear in the *Letters* section. Were I not trying to be absolutely even-handed about answering the queries you send in, I would likely have jumped into the *Letters* section myself, to respond to those *most* peculiar remarks of Ms. Janice Bridge in issue number 7; or to point out to Mr. Charles Platt (issue number 8), author of PLANET OF THE VOLES and GARBAGE WORLD, that he is possibly being presumptuous when he tells the author of "I Have No Mouth, and I Must Scream" and "'Repent, Harlequin!' Said the Ticktockman" and "The Deathbird" and a few other items, that his manner of producing such works of fiction is flawed.

But I have this column as a forum, and so the *Letters* section of *Short Form* will never see a communiqué from me, nor a response to any criticism of me or this series of outings. You have total and complete latitude to express yourself, assured of an impenetrable barrier between me and thee. Knock yourself out.

Ah, *but*...

If you make the mistake of sending a letter directly to this column by way of the editor, Mr. Van Name, and it is a letter of insult or capricious mischievousness, be prepared for as honest and direct an answer as I'd give if it were a request for information on a matter of writing...which is what this column is supposed to deal with.

And now...to work:

**From MR. PETER WONG of San Francisco, California:**

"What difference is there, if any, between writing sharecropping novels and writing tv series scripts or writing a novel for a pulp series?"

On reflection I'd say there isn't much difference. All three are creatively thrombotic. If we accept the widely-held belief that "good Art is never created by committee"—and I think we all *do* believe that, by way of no less demonstrably valid evidence than our own experience—then simple logic dictates the answer.

Now, if I read Mr. Wong's question as being precisely what is on the postcard, with no subtext, then the answer I've given is direct and sufficient. If, on the other hand, I address a possible interpretation that restates the question like this—

"If you're so dead set against shared-universe, 'sharecropper' books, suggesting that they are demeaning to the work, to Art, and to the abilities of individual writers who do this sort of thing for money, aren't you being hypocritical putting others down when you do the same sort of thing as a scenarist for a series on tv, which is no less a 'shared world' situation?"

—then the answer becomes somewhat more needful of backup; though the answer remains *yes*.

(I don't want to put words into Mr. Wong's postcard. He may have been asking exactly what the question-as-phrased asks. If this woolgathering is of my own supposing, I apologize. But on the off-chance that this is yet again an example of someone phrasing a question in the subtextual "Have you stopped beating your mate" manner, I'll proceed with the exegesis.)

I confess never having considered this. Yes, I suppose it *is* hypocritical to decry writers wasting themselves, in my view, while performing the same sort of peonage in another medium. I'm not going to spend more than a beat or two by way of self-defense as this is a new thought for me, and I need time to work it out in my head. With a little luck I won't spend that time trying to justify the dichotomy. However (he said, putting up his dukes), I suspect in some unconscious part of my brain I came to the same conclusion Mr. Wong may or may not have cleverly suggested in his seemingly innocent query. I say that because, after ten years of writing for many different tv series, I found I could not with any degree of comfort or self-satisfaction write anything dramatic or unexpected in the series format. If I wrote *The Man from U.N.C.L.E.* and a segment of *Star Trek* early in my film/tv career, it was because that was what there was around to be written, and I did it because I enjoyed writing for television in those dear dim days.

But if Mr. Wong, or anyone else sufficiently bored with the important things in life that they would waste their time on it, cares to examine my film/tv credits, they will find that scripts I've written for anthology shows far outnumber those I did for series with established characters. We're talking here *The Outer Limits, Twilight Zone, Alfred Hitchcock Presents, Circle of Fear, Darkroom*, and other shows that were self-contained stories.

In fact, I ceased writing for series television in November of 1970 (on record, in my second collection of tv essays, THE OTHER GLASS TEAT), at which time I swore I'd never write for another series if I could avoid it in any way, and would thereafter concentrate on writing only pilots and tv movies. I kept that promise until November 6, 1984 when I joined the staff of the new *Twilight Zone* and went back to writing teleplays. (That was fourteen years. Not too bad. And when I went back to working in that medium it was not on a series with continuing characters, it was, again, an anthology.)

Hmmm. The more I examine this, the more convinced I am that my pronouncements about the strangulating conditions extant in "series" writing, whether shared-universe books or series tv, are deeply-held beliefs. Apparently, without realizing it, I was decrying the concept of writing endless sequels—doing coattail writing with other people's plots and characters, warping stories to fit existing guidelines—in my own career, as well as in my public statements. Hmmm. I may have just dodged the hypocrisy bullet.

And so, having ruminated this out before your very eyes—and if I haven't, I'm sure the *Letters* section will be rife with indictments—let me complete that *yes* answer by reiterating that *any* auctorial medium that crimps a writer's full range of story and characterization choices is operating on a lower level of excellence than I think we should demand for ourselves. It is one thing to write a story for an anthology, even one predicated on a single-note theme (and I've personally received solicitations in the past couple of months to write stories for anthologies about "evil cities," "fantasies in which water is a prominent element," "dark fantasies about merry-go-rounds," "serial killers," and "talking animals"), no matter how bizarre or apparently dopey, because one retains full control of what is written; and it is quite another thing to have to shoehorn a personal vision into the narrower and narrower box provided. The more effluent the restrictions—*Star Trek* books, *Wild Cards* universe, *Heroes in Hell* scenarios, sequels and prequels to famous stories from years past, *Robot City* and *Thieves' World* and *Liavek* and *Witch World* patchworks—the fewer choices are left to the writer with a need to create new and individual situations. Shackles.

Which is not to say there hasn't been some terrific writing done, even in these formats. I've read a lot of it and enjoyed a lot of it. But it does sadden me to see as original a writer as, say, Sheckley, doing sharecropper work in the universe of Harry's *Bill, the Galactic Hero*. And I know that when I say "shackles," there are writers who will counter: "Challenges!" Well, all right, I'm not going to get into a battle of the saxophones over that; I think it's ego and (in Mr. Platt's perception) hubris. Like the fan activity of trying to write a story in which the word *the* never appears. Challenge, maybe, but as I clock it, it's like the whistling pig: interesting trick, but what else can it do?

To summarize, Mr. Wong: the fewer masters a writer serves when s/he is fine dreaming, the better. If your work is going to succeed or fail, let it be on your own terms, and not on those of factors over which you had no control.

**From MS. GINA DeSIMONE of Baltimore, Maryland:**
"I hear you'll only write with manual typewriters—no computers. What's the big deal?"

Answered this one in detail last time. Not again. What bemuses me, though, is why this question should ever be asked by *any*one, much less by three different correspondents in three successive issues. Isn't it the quality of what one produces that counts—whether on manual typewriter, electric typewriter, pc, or quill pen—and not the manner in which it was physically transcribed? Aristophenes worked with papyrus and stylus, never had to change a ribbon, never even heard the words byte or modem, and turned out some pretty fair copy.

The resonance I get from this peculiar business is the many times at parties when those who were drinking took offense that I wasn't. "C'mon," they'd say, nudging me with an elbow because their hands were occupied with glasses and bottles, "don't be a party-pooper. Take a little drink. Be sociable."

No, thank you.

Now, can we *please* go on to matters of greater import?

**From MS. TONYA R. CARTER of Chapel Hill, North Carolina:**
"I have published three fantasy novels (all in collaboration) and am concentrating more now on my solo work. Recently I was discussing my work with an agent and he told me that doing a multiple-book series is the way to find success in the writing business. When I replied that I deplored the trend in fantasy toward trilogies, etc., he said that it wasn't really a trend but a 'requirement'—that single books just don't find as much favor with publishers these days. What do you think of this? Can it be true? Say it ain't so."

Sure, I can say it ain't so. It ain't so. Now I've said it, kiddo, but what I said ain't so. Because it am so.

Whoever that agent was, he was giving you a kind of very good, very sensible, very pro-survival, very pragmatic, very market-savvy advice. That it is (in my opinion) horrific and ultimately destructive advice is quite another matter.

Look: I can give you all manner of high-flown, Art-for-Art's-sake bullshit, but I'd be doing you a disservice. The major publishers are no longer the bailiwicks of ladies and gentlemen, engaged in a lofty calling. The Pantheon brouhaha is only the latest miasma of ethical pollution to blanket the industry. And if you're unaware of what's been going on at Dutton and Lippincott and Doubleday and McGraw-Hill and Random House— and the Pantheon matter—then you're not serving yourself in the Author As Cottage Industry sense, because you're permitting your remove from the center of publishing, which is New York, to keep you uninformed. Living in Chapel Hill does not mean you must be ignorant of what forces are at work in your chosen field. You can subscribe to *Publishers Weekly*, or read it each week at your main branch library or at the University, and you'll be as knowledgeable as the CEO of Time-Warner. But if you are operating off antiquated or woolly-headed mythic ideas about what the book publishing industry is like, and how it works, then you're a blind woman trying to milk an elephant; a paraplegic signed up for a dance marathon; a poor sap trying to beat the house odds.

Pasteur said: "Chance favors the prepared mind."

If you even have to *ask* the question, it means you're heading toward the rapids in a cardboard kayak using a noodle for a paddle.

Now, I'm assuming a lot about you. I'm inferring from the (perhaps intentional, perhaps mock-serious, perhaps satiric) naïve way you presented the question, and the question itself ("Say it ain't so, Joe!"), that you really *don't* know what's going on in the upper reaches of Manhattan, where editors are told by their superior editors, and the superior editors are told by the publishers and marketing mavens and trend analysts and bookkeepers, to buy books in tonnage lots. What was hellishly conceived and then brought to a fine system by Judy-Lynn del Rey has become Accepted Wisdom in every major hardcover and paperback house: if one book can sell well, have 'em do it again, then have 'em do it three or four more times...get them to do a series of space-war epics, get 'em to return to the world of Xanth till we wanna nuke the fuckin' place, get 'em to wear our patience so thin that we ignore anything else the writer ever produces, thus wasting someone's career by short-shrifting the long haul and making the quickbucks now. I'm *assuming* you don't know how important the bottom-line became for the accountants and foreign masters who, decades or so ago, began to dominate the NY book publishing arena.

If I'm reading into the letter what isn't there, well, you can just chalk it up to getting a slightly longer answer than you wanted.

But if I'm correct, and you don't read *PW* weekly, and you haven't made it your business to learn the business, then this will be good background material for you. For instance, one of the most atrocious phenomenon in publishing today is the callous abandonment of books when an editor moves to another house or is fired. They call such books orphans. The two most recent examples to come to my attention (involving authors who've asked me not to use their names) are these:

An author who had a moderately successful first horror novel with a hardcover house that recently fired its entire staff, had his second novel scheduled for mid-June release. He had laid on a major signing at a prestigious bookstore in one of the four top sales cities. A week before the signing, I called him to mooch a copy of the new book. He said he hadn't seen it yet. I said, "You're kidding!" He said no, he wasn't kidding; he just hadn't received his author's copies yet. I said, "But if pub date is this Friday, and you're signing this Saturday, you should have had copies in your hands two months ago. If not part of the standard shipment, then at least a couple of hand-bound copies." He said he hadn't seen a thing. I told him he'd damned well better call the publisher the next morning and demand that half a dozen copies be sent by overnight express. He said he'd do it.

(An example of a knowledgeable writer who didn't know that part of the business.)

He called me the next afternoon. His editor was gone. Editor's assistant was gone. Senior editor, gone. The executive editor in charge, gone. He was shunted from person to person, left on hold, reached temps who were "only here for the day, sir, so there's no need to yell at me, sir, and I don't have to listen to that kind of language, sir, and it's not *my* fault you've been put on hold and transferred around for half an hour, sir," and then she hung up on him. (But don't forget, that's NewfuckingYork and we're all supposed to accept the fact that everyone in that rotten tooth of a town is too busy bemoaning the death of the freewheeling '80s to hire people who can answer a switchboard or take a message without being so goddam rude you want to take an Uzi to them. It is, after all, the wonderful center of the oh-so-*courant* publishing industry, and we poor yotzes out here in the colonies can't be expected to appreciate what exacting lives are lived by the folks at the publishing houses who can barely make it through the day without a three-hour lunch break. But I digress. We certainly mustn't show our bad humor by suggesting that simply making a phone call to that patch of plague on the Hudson is enough to poison your soul for the rest of the day, 'cause heaven knows, good help is *so* hard to find these days.)

And finally, he reached somebody or other. Who got around to telling him they'd decided to postpone his book past the optimum summer sales period, and had rescheduled it for the dead dog days of August or September, because they'd needed the release slot for a book that one of the new staff wanted to get on the stands fast. You know how it is. It's just business.

And what about my signing this Saturday? he asked.

What signing? they asked.

The signing at which I'm going to look like an asshole because there ain't no books there, *that's* what signing! he said.

What'd they say, I asked him. He was silent a moment.

"Basically," he answered, "what they told me was, 'Tough shit, trooper,' and they pretty much shined me on and hung up in my face." What can he do about it? He can do squat about it, is what he can do about it.

The other writer, when his imprint was sold to a larger house, and he was abandoned to the "tender" mercies of a staff that hadn't contracted for the book, didn't like the book, didn't care about the book, didn't very much want to publish the book, was stuck with the book, wished they'd never heard of the book—and felt in each of those particulars in exactly the same way about the book's author—when that writer demanded to know why his book had not been interior designed and typeset in the manner he and the former editor had agreed on, was told—through a very sweet young woman who had been in the business exactly eight months—"I was told by the senior editor to tell you to go fuck yourself, sir."

Both of these are true stories.

The first author is financially pretty well off. So he's been able to absorb the penalties on plane tickets and hotel reservations that had to be cancelled when the pr jaunt he'd put together *himself* for eight cities cross-country had to be shelved. And he's been able to hire a publicity woman (at his own expense) to take up the slack, because his poor little orphan of a novel is not only not getting any promotion from the publisher, but in their flack newsletter his name was misspelled! As for the second writer, he just had to swallow it. The book is truly abandoned, and for him it's like a love affair that went very ugly, very quickly. It took him four years to do that book, and he's had to reconcile himself that no one will ever see it, that it won't earn back its advance, and—most galling of all—that the sonofabitch publisher who never wanted to do the book, who inherited the book as part of a merger deal, will continue to eat half his paperback (and possibly film) royalties till the day he dies. He is learning the business the hard way, and fast.

This is an ever more common nightmare. It was a fact of life in the movie and tv business from the git-go, this abandonment scenario: you'd work on a screenplay for a year, and just as you were handing in the final draft there would be a palace revolt at the studio or the network, and everything would get shook up by Coca-Cola or Kinney or Tri-Cities, and out on their asses would go all the sweetly supportive execs who'd cajoled you into spending a year of your creative life writing this wonderful script, and in would come a new batch of faceless M.B.A.-toting *wunderkinds*, and they would sooner suck off a diseased dalmatian than support your pissy little project, because if they do, and it's a success, it'll redound to the reputations of the schmucks who were jettisoned, and if it fails it only goes to prove that the Corporation was correct in booting out the dead wood and bringing them in to save the day like Mighty Mice. That was s.o.p. in the movie business since the earliest days, but those of us who have a foot in both camps thought we could always take a breather in books till things settled down at the studios, and maybe we'd get the script back on turnaround. We always thought publishing was above all that kind of crap. But now, with the same conglomerates owning studios and production companies that have bought their way into publishing (for "diversification"), they've brought their policies with them, and it's no different in New York than it is in Hollywood. There is no place left to run.

So if you ask me what do I think of that, and do I think it's so, and say it ain't so, what I tell you is this: you'd damned well better retool. You'd damned well better divest yourself of the charming naïveté that widened your eyes when that agent told you publishers are *requiring* trilogies. And here's the best piece of advice you'll ever get from me: read the following books. Get each of these five books, and keep them right there on the shelf, close to hand, next to your Roget and your rhyming dictionary. They're not books about the art and craft of writing, which are luxuries. They are books about the *business* of not getting screwed in the writing game. They are necessities.

THE BUSINESS OF BEING A WRITER by Stephen Goldin and Kathleen Sky (Harper & Row, 1982, $13.95).

FROM PRINTOUT TO PUBLISHED by Michael Seidman (CompuPress, Inc., Albuquerque, 1988, $9.95).

HOW TO BE YOUR OWN LITERARY AGENT by Richard Curtis (Houghton Mifflin, 1983, $10.95).

STAYING ALIVE by Norman Spinrad (Donning, Norfolk, Virginia, $5.95).

THE WRITER'S LEGAL AND BUSINESS GUIDE (Compiled and edited by Norman Beil for the Beverly Hills Bar Association Barristers Committee for the Arts, Arco Publishing, Inc., New York, $9.95).

All of the foregoing assumes you really were startled by that conversation with the agent, and that you haven't prepared for your career by studying the environment in which your work will be bought or rejected for reasons that may have nothing to do with your artistic abilities.

So when the agent tells you it is a pressure tactic, that it is almost *required* of you to sign up for a trilogy or longer series if you want to "make your name" in the genre, what he's telling you is that the "name" you will likely make for yourself is *hack*. And if all you're seeking is a living, something to keep you out of the nine-to-five grind, an occupation instead of a career, he is probably giving you good advice. He is talking solid sense commerce, state of the market...not Art.

The opinions I'm giving you here, in this overlong answer, are predicated on *my* belief that writing is a holy chore; that you write first because you have the desire, the hunger, the obsession to do it, and second because of the money. I've said it before (to the point of dreariness), but thirty-five years preparing to go to work as a writer and *staying* a writer have not altered that belief. But these advisements come with the warning that if you follow what I suggest, you probably won't get rich, you'll likely never become a "popular" writer, your road will be a good deal longer, and unquestionably stonier.

Writing, say, novels in a pulp series—going back to Mr. Wong's question—can imbed in the minds of those who critically evaluate a writer's worth, the impression that the writer is a by-the-pound drudge, a competent hired gun who can fill those low-level, non-promoted slots in the monthly release list that *must* be filled, one way or the other. If not by minimum-advance novels in some dopey western or slasher or sci-fi series, then by crossword puzzle collections or one of the million self-help books from some specialty hardback publisher who'll be delighted to get a two or three thousand dollar paperback reprint.

This is the graveyard of books. And those who toil in the earth of that cemetery are thought of with dismissal and casual disrespect. They're like a last-minute date on a Saturday night, when all the A-list people are taken. The writers are seldom considered for the "quality" jobs. Even when they attempt to break out, to write something original, or to cross categories, the unspoken stigma remains. They aren't taken seriously.

Good writers like Bob Vardeman and Dave Bischoff and Simon Hawke have had to swallow that bitter pill, through no greater sin on their part than wanting to earn a decent living.

Award-winning writers like Anne McCaffrey and Isaac Asimov and Philip José Farmer have been made financially secure, but at the cost of their auctorial vitality, having found themselves being lured back again and again to series they have drilled till the wells have come up dry dusters.

Frank Herbert, as dear and as talented a man as he was, as conscientious and committed a writer as he was, should have seen that the commercial interests inveigling him to return to Arrakis book after book, had their own exchequers at heart—and didn't much care what happened to his reputation.

Edmond Hamilton was a muscular talent, a writer of considerable originality and endless invention. But for the better part of two decades—through the Forties and Fifties—he was thought of by the *capos* as little better than a pulp hack, because he had created and written so many Captain Future novels for Standard. It took the belated publication of "What's It Like Out There?" to shock the Establishment into reevaluating him. But it had been twenty years in which he had languished in a kind of critical and creative Coventry.

Yes, there have been writers who've made their careers with the series—Evan Hunter as Ed McBain, Faulkner with the Snopes novels, Proust and Ian Fleming and Chester Himes and Lawrence Durrell, to cover most variations—and I'm not suggesting it *can't* be done. But for every rare instance you can cite of a Lone Ranger making Fran Striker a wealthy man, for every Edgar Rice Burroughs becoming a millionaire with a Tarzan or Barsoom repetition...there are a hundred writers who have mired themselves in the tiny bog of one idea that lies at the corner of their full acreage of ability.

As Trevanian wrote in SHIBUMI (and forgive me for citing this endlessly): "Do not fall into the error of the artisan who boasts of twenty years experience in his craft while in fact he has had only one year of experience—twenty times."

The publisher will not look out for you; the agent will try if s/he thinks of you as friend or special talent, but s/he can only do so much; other writers are too self-involved to give you the bad news that you're getting stale, and the worse news that you're thought of in the industry as second-string; critics are too busy savaging you to care that your heart is breaking and your talent is eroding.

And that leaves just one, with a primacy of interest in what you're doing, how you're holding up, how far you can go, how contentedly you'll die. And that one is just you.

We are, none of us, free of the pressures and considerations of the marketplace. We doubt our ability to exist at the highest level of Art, we are distracted by simply surviving; we must live, we must tend to our responsibilities, and we must sometimes make accommodations. Out of lack of ego, out of fear, out of bad advice, out of our minds to pay the mortgage and to buy a kid a toy. We sell ourselves out. But when it comes to giving a deep damn about the final judgment of our work, it is only each of us who can decide the point beyond which we bruise our talent and our reputation and our ability to bounce back one more time; without hope of recovery.

If you are told that publishers are *requiring* that you stretch a good one-book idea to an attenuated three or more, you can be told by a million people that it ain't so, but the truth is—it *is* so. Publishers have a bottom-line to think about, and editors have to fill those slots one way or the other; and they just don't have the time or the insight or the heart to give a shit where *you* will be, ten years from now—or even five.

I have given you an answer. But it is just *one* answer; and it doesn't count for much. The answer you need is the one you will arrive at when the crunch-point comes. When they offer to buy your soul, I hope this answer will recur in memory and will advise you to read carefully the unwritten small print too many good writers have already overlooked in the glare of green.


**From MR. RICHARD KADREY of San Francisco, California:**

"For the last couple of years I've read a lot about the powerful influence of the big bookstore chains on the publishing industry. Even more disturbing, I've recently heard about publishers deleting some books before publication because the big chains either didn't order enough, or because they were made nervous by the book's subject matter. If all this is true, are we at the mercy of some hideous conspiracy or simply suffering over the deeds of some pale little shitbirds?"


Steps back in utter amazement! Looks at Mr. Kadrey and blurts, "Where the hell have *you* been for the last twenty years?" Realizes he is being impertinent and likely embarrassing a guy who asked a perfectly polite and rational question, and gets all flustered. Didn't mean to offend. Quickly buries the thought, *There are always Those Who Don't Get The Word*, and tries to offer a weak apology for his stupefaction that anyone even remotely concerned about publishing doesn't know that this has been the *status quo* for at least two decades; and wonders how the hell he's going to bring Mr. Kadrey up to speed without boring everyone else with a horror story they know all too well.

Tries this:

Everything you've read or heard about the power of the chains is dead correct, no matter how bizarre the anecdote. It is even worse than you may think. Though there has been a strong resurgence of the independent bookstore—as reported steadily in *Publishers Weekly*—and my recommendation to Ms. Carter to get and read *PW* regularly goes double for you—and a concomitant downturn on the expansion curve for chains, that have had serious financial reverses these last three or four years, these are (relatively speaking) only blips on the chain power 'scope.

Because I was so taken aback that this question had been asked, and knowing that answering it would only restate what most people already know, I checked in with a half dozen top-level executives and editors at publishing houses in New York (none of whom are sf/fantasy people), to ascertain if there's anything new I could report. They told me it's business as usual. Things remain as they have been for years and years, as regards the symbiotic relationship between major houses and the biggest chains. Or is that a *parasitic* liaison? To hear the editors tell it, they are mere pawns in the ongoing sales/distribution game.

Is it a conspiracy? Well, in some ways, it is. As you would surely agree if you'd been following the reports in *PW* of lawsuits brought by associations of independent bookstores against various publishers these last few years. Lawsuits that proved there were hard and soft houses that were giving larger discounts to the chains than they were to the little individual bookstores. I'd have to go back through three or four years of issues of *PW* to give you specifics, but I *think* I'm accurate in stating that every one of those litigations was adjudicated in favor of the small stores, on the basis of unfair competition, restraint of trade, and a plethora of other multisyllabic charges.

But it hasn't diminished the power wielded by the major chains.

Here are the principal players:

WALDENBOOKS, INC.: a 100% owned division of K mart, with 1500 outlets nationwide. The President and CEO is Harry T. Hoffman.

B. DALTON BOOKSELLER: a 100% owned subsidiary of Barnes and Noble Bookstores, Inc., with 774 outlets. Leonard Riggio is the President and CEO with Stephen Riggio as COO and Executive-VP.

CROWN BOOKS CORPORATION: an affiliate (34% ownership) of the Dart Group Corp., with approximately 260 outlets. Co-Chairman of the Board of Crown (and Co-Chair of Dart) is Herbert H. Haft; and the guy you see in the tv ads is Robert M. Haft, who is the President and CEO of Crown.

BOOKSTOP, INC.: based in Austin, Texas with outlets mostly in the South, but moving fast in California (they've opened in San Diego and other venues), they are smaller by far than the three previously-noted behemoths, but they're hungry and they're coming on at a dead run, with 24 outlets at last count. At least three of these stores are called BOOKSTAR, as in the New Orleans shop where I did a writing-in-the-window gig just last March-April. The CEO and Chairman of the Board is Gary E. Hoover; the President is Steve Mathews.•

On the other side of the net we find the assorted publishers who have chosen to play ball with the chains, seemingly to the point of total disregard for the welfare of the independent bookstore; an endangered species, not only reeling from the increase in price of books that they must sell at non-discounted prices, and the rise in illiteracy that has cut away their base of customers (an illiteracy compounded of not only inept education and its fostering of fear about reading, but of forty years of television viewing), but reeling from the actively malevolent practice of opening a Crown or a Waldenbooks in the same block with an old, established, full-service shop that simply cannot compete with the tv-hyped, discount-festooned, audiobook and videocassette inventoried yuppie-heavens

---

• Subsequent to writing this section, I came across a news item in the June 1st, 1990 *Publishers Weekly* (invaluable magazine!) that not only updates but keynotes exactly how carefully the deck has been stacked. Here is that news item:

### CROWN SELLS INTEREST IN BOOKSTOP TO BDB FOR $8.3 MILLION

Crown Books Corp. has sold its minority interest in Bookstop to BDB Corp.—which consists of Barnes & Noble, B. Dalton Bookseller and Bookstop—and dropped its lawsuit against BDB. Crown stated that BDB paid Crown about $8.3 million for its share in Bookstop and other considerations.

The battle between Crown and BDB was set in place in September last year, when Crown acquired 40% of Bookstop's outstanding common stock, representing some 20% of all Bookstop stock, for $5.8 million. Crown president Robert Haft called the purchase "an extension of our existing business."

A month later, Barnes & Noble/B. Dalton announced that it had acquired 62.5% of Bookstop's outstanding stock, and thus a controlling interest in the company.

In January of this year, Crown sued BDB, charging that Barnes & Noble was forcing it to sell its interest in Bookstop and relinquish its two seats on the board of directors.

Founded in 1982, Bookstop had expanded to 21 stores—primarily in Texas and Florida—by July 1989, when the board asked founder Gary Hoover to step down as chief executive officer. He was replaced by Thomas Christopher, former executive vice-president of operations at Pier 1 Imports. It was widely rumored at the time that Bookstop was losing money and therefore causing concern among investors.

Bookstop expanded recently into California from its base in Texas and Florida. It specializes in 10,000 square foot stores with broad selection and discount prices.

—JOHN MUTTER

where Sidney Sheldon and Judith Krantz and Garfield are the pantheon of literary gods.

What can we say of these publishers? Well, here's an extract from the May, 1990 *Village Voice Literary Supplement* symposium on publishing in America. The writer is Lew Rosenbaum, Manager, Guild Books, Chicago:

> Increasingly the conglomerates have entered publishing, because their profits require a new market to penetrate. And as in all other industry, they squeeze out independent producers, independent retailers. They flood the market with "product" and then destroy it when it doesn't sell. They declare a price war, and once they win a greater market share, prices resume their inflationary spiral.
>
> And what is the result of this concentration of wealth? Columbia University recently surveyed visual, literary, and performing artists. They found that 77 per cent work other jobs to support themselves; that 75 per cent earn less than $12,000 from their art; and that more than 50 per cent earn less than $3000 from their art. This wasteland looks a lot like *Roger and Me*, but with different names and faces. For Roger Smith read Si Newhouse. For unemployed auto workers read authors one royalty check away from out-on-the-street.

And it is in this matter of "product" that the effect and impact of the chains' back-stage presence most grievously makes its feral primitivism felt.

It is not merely that the majority of New York houses shamefully and sycophantically curry favor with the chains by sending their salespeople to see the executives, to find out what trends or specific authors are currently being smiled on with favor—which would be loathsome enough were it the worst—but in selected genres there are *caporegimes* whose attentions are sought. (The *capo de tutti capos* only deal with top of the line stuff.)

For instance, a few years back, when B. Dalton was the bitch after which the hounds sniffed, if one wanted to get good display for non-fiction, a rep from your publisher would try to get a lunch date with Brian Baxter; if Del Rey or Ace wanted to get an inside track with the science fiction buyer, it was David Thorson to whom they'd send their rep, leaking charisma and toadying in such a way that the Dalton "specialist" would offer his "input"—usually by indicating which upcoming authors carried promotable cachet à la the TV-Q ratings the networks use—and the publisher's emissary to the Court of Kublai Crown or suchlike would dutifully take notes; if general fiction or essays, it was Mike Hejny. (I have no idea if these guys are still the stiles one must turn at Dalton to get to the fast track. There are no doubt all new names and faces.) But remember: these buyers were not around the corner on Lexington Avenue, so a lunch date was merely the work of picking up a phone and saying, "I'll meet you at noon at La Petite Ferme." B. Dalton's headquarters are a long business-class flight away in Minneapolis.

And though the editors and executives you might buttonhole on this matter will deny it, deny deny, deny it...even if you threaten them with nailing their puppydogpet's head to a coffee table...at least three editors to whom I spoke in preparing this answer admitted that "well, we show them the slicks of covers we have upcoming, and if they say it doesn't move them, well, then we send it back to the art department for a revamp." The houses continue to declare publicly that editorially they are strictly autonomous, no pressures. But the pragmatic reality is that if—as happened at Pocket Books a while ago—a rep takes the stack of forthcoming covers in to one of the chains, and the purchasing entity says, "Why are you doing a BEST OF WILSON TUCKER? His name doesn't mean anything any more. We can't move this one," then are we to consider it mere coincidence that the most recent (at that time) Pocket Books collection of "Best of—" titles, a Wilson Tucker collection, gets dropped from the announced schedule for several years?

But the influence of the chains goes beyond such fiddling. (Even such fiddling as impedes or even scuttles a writer's career, when one considers that the NY publishing *apparat* is a hive of gossip and rumor and free-floating opinions that take on the force of reality if circulated widely and often enough. It is also the explanation for our bewildered queries, *Who decided Stephen Coonts is hot? Who decided Amy Tan is bestseller material? Why does Viking suddenly promote John Mortimer as he's never been pushed before, with 50,000 first printing and $50,000 ad/promo budget? Who's been watching the Great Clock of Fad closely enough to declare that Jay McInerney and Tama Janowitz have outworn their welcome but Tobias Wolff and Ethan Canin are "in" this season? Where did Gary Devon come from so quickly? How come Ray Feist was sizzling hot for one book, then became hardcover poison?*)

Some undated time ago, publishers decided if a few good words of advice out of Minneapolis or Austin were money in the bank, then why not try for the strongbox full of bearer's bonds; and they began showing raw manuscripts to the secret arbiters at the chains. I'm not talking about sending bound galleys or page proofs or even Xerox copies of books already purchased; I'm talking about your agent sends in a crossover suspense thriller to your publisher, and your editor's selection committee isn't dead certain it's your time to get out of the ghetto, so your editor, on the q. t., sends a copy of your *unpurchased* manuscript to the hardcover fiction guy or gal at Waldenbooks, and coyly asks, "Whaddaya think of this? Think it has, er, uh, *breakout* potential?" And the word comes back from this isolated opinion-maker, this stock&inventory intellect, this keen literary mover and shaker—and you sell or get rejected, in large part, because the conglomerate has been reassured or contrariwise has been told you ain't got the right stuff.

Hell, you could nail the editor's aged and decrepit granny's head to the coffee table next to Fido's, and they wouldn't cop to *that* one. But it's true.

Yes, luck and skill play a large part in your future, but as large a part is played by a warm or lukewarm or tepid or corpse-cold reaction by someone out there whose name and involvement you'll never know about. Yes, books are dropped from schedules because the chains aren't interested. Yes, writers get lower advances on their next book if the chains report they didn't do well with your current one. Yes, the chains have enormous power.

Are they the Villains of this piece? Hell, no. They're flattered when their opinion is sought. They all think they're experts, and they can't wait to demonstrate their acumen. (And if you've ever been in a Crown Books emporium, and you've dealt with the average clerk—who is still in school, is being paid coolie wages, and who thinks Shirley Jackson is maybe Michael's brother, and refers you to the sex education section when you ask for a copy of Gide's THE IMMORALIST—you can extrapolate just how deeply grounded in literary history may be the judgment visited on your poor submission.) They didn't demand the power, it was Uriah Heepishly proffered by conglomerate-owned, committee-run, arrogantly but culturally illiterately-edited publishers.

Now do you see why I was thunderstruck that you asked such a naïve question? Answering those few lines you sent in is a task that cannot but grow discursive, infuriating, frightening, and dismaying. Perhaps we should go back to why I use a manual typewriter.

**From MR. TARAS WOLANSKY of Jersey City, New Jersey:**

"...when I heard you speak [at SUNY, Stony Brook, 1988] about censorship and the First Amendment, I wondered if it didn't sound like special pleading: 'The government should regulate all industries and occupations,' says the liberal writer, 'EXCEPT MINE!' To what extent is writers' love of the First Amendment nothing more than self-interest? Just how important is the kind of First Amendment absolutism we have been enjoying for the last couple of decades? Great Britain and Canada, to name two, seem to get along very well without it."

There are so many assumptions stated as fact in this letter, that to answer it with any degree of thoroughness would lead me into an essay easily as long as this edition of *Short Form.*

There are half a dozen *ways* of answering it.

For instance:

You say that my lecture sounded like special pleading. That I seemed to be saying writers alone should be permitted to the full measure of Free Speech, but everyone else should be muzzled, partially or totally. Okay. That's what I was saying.

You have a problem with that?

Or, for instance:

You use the adjective *liberal* with more than a whisper of denigration. Why? "Liberal" is defined in the RANDOM HOUSE DICTIONARY OF THE ENGLISH LANGUAGE as "favorable to progress or reform," "favorable to or in accord with concepts of maximum individual freedom possible, esp. as guaranteed by law and secured by governmental protection of civil liberties," "favoring or permitting freedom of action, esp, with respect to matters of personal belief or expression," "free from prejudice or bigotry; tolerant," "open-minded or tolerant, esp. free of or not bound by traditional or conventional ideas, values, etc.," "characterized by generosity." Antonyms are given as "reactionary, intolerant, niggardly."

*Liberal*, before the unholy corruption of the label by the likes of Nixon, Reagan, and Bush; Hoover, Meese, and Agnew; Haig, Quayle, and James Watt, was synonymous with *progressive*. Until Bush despicably referred to Dukakis as a "card-carrying member of the ACLU" in the same tone of voice as generations of paranoid Cold Warriors had used the phrase "card-carrying member of the Communist Party," for no nobler purpose than to get himself elected, standing up for Free Speech and the First Amendment as a member of the American Civil Liberties Union was considered a mark of good character and fairness. But to the debased electorate who shrieked in terror at Bush's revelation, "liberal" became the sort of word that corrupters of the language employ to besmirch the intentions of, say, writers.

Or, for instance:

You make it abundantly clear that you believe we have been enjoying "First Amendment absolutism…for the last couple of decades" which sounds suspiciously like the language and belief of those whose political and religious and social attitudes are most commonly considered leaning toward the right. If you truly believe there has been anything like "First Amendment absolutism" in this country, at any time since Hoover was in office, much less the last couple of decades, then you simply have not been listening to the voices of the disenfranchised and lobbied-against. Exactly why do you think Nixon had his thugs covering up the Watergate break-in with such frenzy that he chose to risk ruin and impeachment rather than let it be known he had tried to silence Daniel Ellsberg? Absolute freedom of speech…you actually believe we've had it in this country for at least two decades? I'll take up a collection to buy you a good radio that can only be tuned to the news stations; and I'll use the extra funds to buy you some magazine subscriptions to the sort of horrible "liberal" journals that endlessly chronicle the plight of school teachers who try to teach THE GRAPES OF WRATH and CATCHER IN THE RYE.

Or, for instance:

Neither Canada nor Great Britain "seem to get along very well" without freedom of speech protection. In Canada there is film and magazine and book censorship and banning of precisely the same sort we fight here in the States. Recently, whole shipments of comic books sold without comment in America (and France and Italy and elsewhere in Europe) were seized by Canadian customs officials because they, personally, thought they were "seditious *and* dirty." In Great Britain, one nationally-known police official in Manchester, whom Britons refer to as "Hang 'Em High" Anderton, decided that no one should be allowed to view a videocassette in the privacy of his/her home that Anderton considered "obscene." And so movies in Great Britain are regularly edited *here in the States* for bowdlerized versions shipped overseas—acceptable to this one man. They're getting along just fine, you think? I urge you to present that point of view to Michael Moorcock or Brian Aldiss or Neil Gaiman or Alan Moore, and then stand back.

But I finally decided to answer your question like this:

There is no middle-ground for free speech. You are either 100% foursquare for the First Amendment, or you're not. When those who wish to make exceptions to the First (and they abound—every individual or group you might imagine wears the attitude of the Ayatollah toward Rushdie at some time or other) start in with their Joe McCarthy-Cotton Mather-Phyllis Schlafly diatribes against this remark or that painting or some other "offensive" novel or non-fiction work, they instantly offer as their cachet for shutting someone up, the drag-line scent of child pornography. They immediately rush to the farthest extreme and kill everything in between, just to achieve their sanctimonious ends.

Writers of any kind, not just writers of fiction, serve the philosophy imbedded in Thoreau's dictum: "He serves the state best who opposes the state most." Torquemada is always with us, whether named Jerry Falwell or David Duke or Jesse Helms. Do I make a special plea for the absolute right to voice *informed* opinions, and to write whatever it comes into my head to write? You bet your ass I do, Mr. Wolansky. And if you think anything less is acceptable, I suggest you do some brushing up on your history. There are already a sufficiency of boosters who will wave the flag and promulgate the delusion that everything is Just Peachykeen in This Greatest of All Nations. These are the same people who would rather snarl at the Japanese for their trouncing of us in the marketplace than admit that we've been strutting around like King Shit since World War II, playing Jack Armstrong and trying to convince everyone that we are John Wayne perfect. They are the folks who don't really want any stirring of the porridge. Calm is what they seek. And writers only keep that pot boiling. As Arthur Miller put it: "Society and man are mutually dependent enemies and the writer's job is to go on forever defining and defending the paradox—lest, God forbid, it be resolved."

Now. Let me pause. A question-and-answer exercise is fruitless in this context. If you truly believe what you wrote, then I must tell you with all candor that I perceive you to be One of Those Who Didn't Get the Word. And so that you will *get* the word, I will attempt to narrow down the vast topic you raise by focusing on just the most recent, most outstanding example of attempts by Those with an Agenda to curtail First Amendment freedom.

I speak of Senator Jesse Helms, and his close-to-successful attempts to strangle the National Endowment for the Arts. If you ask the questions you ask, Mr. Wolansky, then I suspect this matter that has filled the news for the past year has escaped you.

And I have the means by which you can answer these questions for yourself. In the Spring 1990 edition of *Comm/Ent*, the Hastings College of Law journal (University of California Hastings College of Law, Volume 12, Number 13), there appeared a lucid, exhaustive, and mesmerizing article by Stephen F. Rohde, a well-known attorney and student of the Constitution. It is titled "Art of the State: Congressional Censorship of the National Endowment for the Arts."

This reasoned and thorough study of the Helms restrictions is available to you. It costs a mere ten bucks, which covers the cost of printing and mailing. It is obtainable from:

The Law Offices of Stephen F. Rohde
1880 Century Park East, Suite 411
Los Angeles, California 90067

You have asked me a question to which the answers seem very clear. The answer I choose to give you is embodied in that booklet. Spend ten dollars. Send for it. If reading what just one purblind, bigoted, power-besotted and narrowminded man wants to do to tell *you* what you can see and hear and read doesn't give you all the response you'll ever need, then not only did you come to the wrong guy for clarification, but we must thereafter view each other as holding inimical views.

And, finally, here is the first answer that occurred to me when you asked if I was indulging in special pleading when I spoke against censorship and in favor of unlimited free speech:

Yessir, you perceived correctly. It *was* special pleading. But it wasn't for me. I was pleading for *you*.

I'm done answering Mr. Wolansky. But for the rest of you, here are some words from an unlikely source. "The world needs writers. We will always be necessary. There are few professions that can claim that distinction."

The man who wrote those words was Rod McKuen. See, gang, Henry David Thoreau and Oliver Wendell Holmes didn't have all the great lines.

I've gone on far longer than I'd intended. One never knows how deep the water is, no matter how many times one has taken the dive. I'd hoped to get to Scott Card's excellent query from 'way back last September, but it's another complex one, and I beg Scott's forbearance till next time; and I'll get to it first next time.

---

Editor's Note: There was no fifth installment. With the author's consent, the fourth and final installment of *Ask Uncle Harlan* has been edited to omit a missive that has—in the years since its original publication—been revealed to be a forgery.

The following essay, written 19 September 1991, appeared in the 1991 World Fantasy Convention progress report #3 and in the convention Program Book. It was also sent to 60 Arizona newspapers. It later appeared alongside the reprint of the first *Ask Uncle Harlan* installment in the 25 October 1991 issue of *Pulphouse*.

# An Accomplice
# of Liars & Forgers:
An Ethical Position Paper by One of the
Guests of Honor of 1991's 17th Annual
World Fantasy Convention in Tuscon

It now appears ultimate and inevitable: I am destined ever to be in trouble with the righteous state of Arizona, cradle of liberty, home of the brave, land of the free, bastion of moral rectitude, and otherwise nifty showplace of honorable America.

The last time was back in 1978, when I was to be the highly revered and oh-so-personable Guest of Honor at the 36th World Science Fiction Convention (aka Iguana-Con) slated for the Hyatt Regency Hotel in Phoenix, Labor Day weekend.

Well, if you recall—and many of you enjoy memory retention at a level we usually associate with things one might win as a prize at a carnival ring-toss—there was this big brouhaha going on about the Equal Rights Amendment in 1978.

(Note the ERA: twenty-five words intended as Amendment to the U.S. Constitution, as follows: "Equality of rights under the law shall not be denied or abridged by the United States or by any State on account of sex." Every poll estimated that between 65–68% of the American public was in favor of passage; yet on 24 June 1982, because of the determined refusal of fifteen states to ratify, the ERA was defeated. Along with a fistful of redneck states, Arizona was in that group.)

Having had my consciousness raised from the primordial muck where, as an average American male born in the '30s and inculcated in the ways of society during the '40s and '50s, it had wallowed happy as a pig in puke—raised howling and whining like Baby

71

Sinclair by the none-too-tender devices of women far wiser than I—I'd been involved with passage of the ERA for a number of years. To the extent that the National Organization for Women had given me this actually rather tacky medal for efforts above and beyond: an actual by-count total of more than 1100 hours spent on the lecture platform, in states so backward and depressing that not even obsessive ERA fanatics would consent to venture to those venues. Eleven hundred hours *actually talking*, which does not include the hundreds and hundreds of hours spent *getting* to and from those places, or the hundreds and hundreds of hours spent in dingy motels waiting to speak, or spent having "courtesy dinners" with the local NOW/ERA chapter officials. (You want to know from boredom? From massive heartburn? From conversations without charm? Go have dinner with the well-meaning, gracious and grateful people who bring you to their environs in service of a Holy Cause. It is to gnaw off one's own wrists.)

So by 1978, I had this sorta kinda moral dilemma where Arizona was concerned.

Because, you see, I'd accepted the Guest of Honorship of the Phoenix convention several years earlier—as is the m.o. of selecting World SF Conventions—and now I was in substantive conflict with myself. Even as I fought for ratification of the ERA, so I buttressed that position by refusing either to do business in, or visit, unratified states. I was turning down $5000-a-night speaking gigs in Illinois, Florida, Georgia, and other benighted pus-pockets of institutionalized inequality.

But if I was boycotting unratified states, what was I to do about my promise to be Guest of Honor at an Arizona convention that would be (they advised me when I tried to back out) "crippled, ruined, sued, shot down in flames?"

On the one hand, I'd given my word. And those who've gotten it know that it may take me fifty years, but I keep my promises. And that goes for THE LAST DANGEROUS VISIONS, too, despite meanspirited assholes like Greg Feeley, Christopher Priest, and other similar running sores who have nothing better to do with their time than stick their beaks into other people's business just to see if they can make the meat twitch.

On the other hand, I'd been annoyingly, publicly vocal about boycotting ERA-unratified states.

Immovable object, unstoppable force. Cute li'l fella squozed in the vise.

My then-assistant (now married to Mike Moorcock) came up with a spectacular solution to the conundrum. Linda Steele suggested we rent a Winnebago, load it full of supplies, drive to the Arizona border, fill up with gas in California, go on into Phoenix, and live out of the motor home for the duration of the convention; thereby maintaining the economic boycott, even to the extent that the Vice-Mayor of Phoenix (a woman) had the parking meters hooded, so we didn't even have to stoke *those*! All I had to do was live in the Winnebago without air conditioning, and try to sleep in 116° heat.

Well, we did just that. We didn't spend a cent in the state (though Jerry Pournelle continues to try to pin on me the rap of having slept one night in the convention suite, and of having bought a candy bar, neither of which is true, but fer pity's sake, folks, that's thirteen years ago, and it was bullshit then as it is now, talk about how some people need to get a life!) and I performed every function as a highly-visible Guest of Honor. Even won another Hugo.

But you cannot *imagine* the amount of crap that was visited on me and those who supported my behavior. You'd've thought I'd given them one-way tickets to Devil's Island! How *dare* I bring moral, ethical, and political considerations into the arena of fan frivolity!?! How *dare* I suggest others do as I had done, boycott the state by staying not in hotels but at public campgrounds or in private vehicles, denying Arizona even one penny of succor!?! It was the big flap of the convention. Just shut right down all the arguments about The New Wave and Heinlein's latest novel.

There was even a death threat, and the hotel called the cops, and they came with sniffer dogs and silent, stealthy SWAT teams, and suchlike. And the cops suggested that I really shouldn't encourage the crazies by wearing a chambray work shirt with a gigantic bullseye appliquéd on the back.

But when it was all done, and I drove that long drive back to Los Angeles, having eaten my cake and holding onto it as well, I felt genuinely spiffy. False heroism, of course; but it is a rush, folks, I gotta tell you. Now I knew how Ralph Nader feels *all* the time.

Yet time passed, even if the ERA didn't; and here comes a year or so ago, and I get the call from Bruce Farr, Chairman of World FantasyCon for 1991, and he asks me if I'd do him and his group the honor of being one of the two Special Guests, the other being this woman who, when we got married, proceeded to take the side of the bed I'd slept on for fifty years, without even asking and I'm not pissed-off about it or anything, she's a wonderful woman, and I haven't even *this* much rancor at her usurpative behavior despite the fact that I haven't had a decent night's sleep since she insinuated herself into my life six years ago and my back cries out for Doan's Pills five times a day simply because I turn and turn all night trying to find those comfortable places I wore away for years, and don't give it a moment's thought, *because I sure as hell don't*!

So. Would I, in tandem with She Who Drools on the Pillow, my most excellent wife, The Electric Baby, would I be Special Guest? Heh heh. *Would* I!?! Hell, I'd only been waiting seventeen years to be asked. Half a dozen times in previous years, FantasyCon convention committees had sought to have me as the GoH (you see, I have this sorta kinda longstanding career in fantasy, as opposed to sf), and they'd been politely but firmly advised that the Shadowy Ancient Old Ones who ruled the FantasyCon venue from behind-scenes would sooner see Charlie Manson or maybe Jeffrey Dahmer as GoH than the dreaded Ellison...

(Sidebar. Here is your latest bulletin from the Council of Politically Correct Language. You are no longer permitted to refer to people of my height—which is 5′5″—as "short." We are now to be referred to as *vertically challenged*. Just as those who formerly were tagged with the opprobria "crips" or "handicapped" now insist on the nomenclature *differently abled*, and we are no longer correct in using the words "dead people" for those who are, in fact, *differently alive*, so we must now have the good sense to refer to Jeffrey Dahmer not as a "cannibal"—sheeeesh, gnaw one paw and they give you such a bad rap—but as *dietetically challenged* or, more elegantly, *nutritionally esurient*, as Daniel M. Pinkwater said to me yesterday when we were discussing this and his radio commercials.)

...so would I accept, pretty please? Like I was really this hard to convince guy, right? So I blithered my yesyesyes, and Farr went off and won the convention bid, and I forgot all about it, and time passed, and one day I got this call from Bruce or one of the other card-carrying *nuhdjes* who haven't given me a moment's peace for the last thirteen, fifteen months or so, and I'm asked about what sort of travel arrangements I want to make, and I ask *arrangements to where?* and the voice down the line says, "Why, to Tucson, of course; for the World FantasyCon."

And I suddenly realize, with more than a smidge of horror, that Tucson is in Arizona; and I've been at odds with Arizona yet again, for a couple of years, because...

Arizona is one of only two states in the entire goddam union that doesn't have a paid Martin Luther King, Jr. holiday, and I've been boycotting Arizona again, and holy geez, gang, but it's more than a decade since my *last* horrific go-around with Arizona, and here I am in the same bloody stupid impossible ethically-twisted situation as in 1978. And I drop my head into my hands and begin to weep like a true movie buff in 1967 when George Kennedy won Best Supporting Actor for *Cool Hand Luke* when it should have been Eli Wallach for his role in *The Good, The Bad, and The Ugly*, because there I am, right in the ka-ka again!

Now let us pause for a moment, for a history lesson. Painless, I promise. But necessary in a nation where 68% of all college seniors tested were unable to name the adversaries of the United States in World War II; where only 22 of 1300 U.S. newspapers carry disclaimers with horoscopes, advising they ain't really "science" but simply horse-puckey; and where, in a recent National Geographic Society survey of more than 1600 adults, about only one-third could locate Vietnam on a map, 75% couldn't find the Persian Gulf, and 45% didn't know where Central America is located.

The Reverend Martin Luther King, Jr. was a black man who was as pivotally responsible for the successes of the Civil Rights Movement in America during the '50s and early '60s as was John Adams for the successes of the Continental Congress in 1776. To many people, he is the personification of strength and courage and decency, all that is best in the American character; and for most black people in this country he is as close to a demigod as anyone born of man and woman can get.

On November 3rd, 1983, a man who was then President of the United States—his name was Ronald Reagan, but you may remember him from *Hellcats of the Navy* (Columbia 1957) or as the host from 1962 to 1964 of tv's *Death Valley Days*—signed into law a bill establishing the third Monday in January as a paid legal holiday, Martin Luther King day. Its first nationwide observance was to be January 20th 1986.

On 6 November 1990, Prop. 302 upholding the establishment of a Martin Luther King/Civil Rights Day was voted down by the people of Arizona 533,510 to 516,274. In case your math skills are worse than your memory, that was a denial of the holiday by a one percent difference. 51% of the people of Arizona said no to that which is observed by more than 120 nations, the U.S. government, 48 states and...*21 Arizona cities*!

To this day, Arizona remains one of only two states (the other is New Hampshire) devoid of a legal, paid King holiday.

Prop. 302 *passed* in Maricopa County (Phoenix), Pima County (Tucson), Coconino (Krazy Kat) and Apache and Santa Cruz counties. It failed out there in the rural counties. Polls showed that voter age was a big consideration. Under-35 voted yes by 56%; all those Good Amuricans over 55 voted no by 57%. The minority vote was small. And the constituency that had kept King Holiday Legislation from advancing out of committees to the full Arizona legislature in 1972, 1975, 1976, and 1981–1985...the swell guys and gals who elected a loudmouthed bigot, homophobic racist, sexist demagogue named Evan Mecham as Governor...the freedom-loving and equality-espousing Arizonans who learned all about the joys of patriotism at the knees of John Wayne, J. Edgar Hoover, Richard Nixon, George Wallace, Orval Faubus, and Lester Maddox...well, they had their way.

And the rest of the country turned away from Arizona with the taste of ashes on its tongue. These are not Americans, we, said. We looked at this creep Evan Mecham, with his tawdry appeals to the basest and vilest instincts, to racial fears and illogical demons, and we could not believe that in this day and age the people of Arizona could be party to such despicable behavior.

Well, in fact, most Arizonans *couldn't* take it. In 1988 Mecham was indicted on charges of fraud and perjury, charges related to illegal campaign donations. He was convicted, he was impeached, he was tossed out of office on his ass. (And was acquitted of criminal charges in June of 1988. But at least he was wrenched away from the controls of the engine of state.)

Governor Rose Mofford took over, but the damage was already done. Mecham and his 51% of the population had become so detestable in the eyes of decent men and women that convention after convention decided to cancel plans to meet in Arizona. The NFL pulled the Super Bowl. Church groups canceled. No one with any self-respect would book into the state. It cost Arizona more than $30 million in lost revenues.

And Mecham, even out of office, continues to lobby against the holiday, as the rest of the nation watches...and boycotts Arizona.

(There is more, much more history that I could set down, dates and details, chapters and verses, names and addresses. In preparation for this statement I read hundreds of pages of information, prepared for me by Victor Dricks of Phoenix Newspapers, Inc. But you can check out all of this on your own. I'm sure the nitwits who attacked me for my ERA position have already begun to employ their vast cool intelligences to justify the moral and social positions of skinheads everywhere, in aid of slaying the message by badmouthing the messenger.)

Now, if you ask why I take all of this so seriously, I guess I have to cop to a personal tilt here. You see, for a lot of other reasons, but mostly for this one, I admired Martin Luther King enormously: I was one of thousands who flew to Alabama in 1965, just another one who marched along behind him, from Selma to Montgomery, as State Troopers and Alabama National Guardsmen pointed rifles at our heads, as elegant white women mooned us from their porches, as Alabama intellectuals threw dogshit and garbage on us as we passed under their windows. Like everyone else in that long, sweating, frightened line of men, women, and children, I was there in large measure because of the heroic image of Martin Luther King, Jr.

So there I found myself, late last year, having given my word, having committed myself to appearing as Special Guest at a convention being held in a state that believed (at least 51 percent) that "Martin Luther King may not be worthy of having a holiday established for him." Committed to attending a convention in a state where hundreds of other conventions of nobler intent had chosen to give a pass. And I tried very hard to get out of my commitment. I urged and begged and worried the question with Bruce Farr and his people for months. They were concerned, because they had advertised my name. And this time I had no Linda Steele to think things through for me, to come up with a clever and all-around satisfying coup that would serve both masters of my conscience. This time I had to do it alone.

And I anguished over it; truly descended to bloody cuticles trying to reach an equitable solution. I know that has the tinkling resonance of foolish melodrama to many of you for whom such situations pose no concern. I look at the roster of schools where students have been expelled for cheating; I listen to the comments of the Roving Reporter as he interviews men and women in the streets, who think the worst thing Charles Keating did was get caught, same for Nixon, same for that great hero Ollie North; I speak to network executives who have no sense of shame at the garbage they continue to slather on the screens of a nation's most perfect opiate. And I recognize that in many ways I'm a buffoon for my constant carping about this'n'that. Conscience is a cartoon in America today.

*What am I to do*, I thought, over and over, for weeks. If I now take the route of convenience, then having walked that other road more than a quarter of a century ago was adolescent foolishness, and nothing more. If I stand on my hind legs and bark about this, if I boycott the convention and the state, what harm do I do to the Committee and that portion of their lives invested in this event?

And then, too, I could not shake from my mind the admonition of the French philosopher Charles Peguy: "He who does not bellow the truth when he knows the truth makes himself the accomplice of liars and forgers."

And then, one day, as if a silken breeze had found its way into the impacted confusion that filled my brain, it all became sweet and simple to me. I had the answer. I knew what to do.

Screw it.

In truth, who gives a damn about one dead nigger.

It's not as if it were something urgent, something real, like going to a convention of fantasy fans and having a good time!

There are all kinds of *real* problems to worry about:

Are fantasy trilogies ruining the genre?

What's happened to the market for short fiction?

Will there be any *really* good parties to attend, or just a lot of boring get-togethers?

Why should I befuddle and bedevil people, get in their face, suggest that social considerations have any place in the world of quests for golden chalices and unicorns and the enchanted dagger of Neptuna? Why must I bother the *status quo* with crap like abortion rights and censorship and arming drug dealers if they're anti-Commie and the death or imprisonment of students and writers in a hundred different countries? What the hell has that got to do with a World Fantasy Convention?

This King character got blown away a long time ago. Worrying about some croaked jigaboo who's long since been put on the worm's menu is counter-productive, annoying, out of line, out of place, out of touch, out of my mind. Screw it!

So what if gang kids slaughter each other, and Native Americans who ought to be happy we call 'em Indians are losing their heritage, and "developers" are paving over the whole damned planet, and the ozone layer is jazzed? Hell, Pournelle and Niven and one of their proteges have even written this swell paperback about what pains in the ass these whale-loving, tree-hugging ecology freaks have become. *That's* the real world, not all this brain-busting worry about things over which we have no control.

Let's party, dudes!

So I'll be there, right there in Tucson, along with all of you who can't be bothered worrying about this senseless boring crap. We can sycophant one another, and tell each other how terrific we are, and how we have the edge on the Mundane Crowd, and piss off to what's going down in Croatia and South Africa and the inner city. We know what's important: the quest for the Jeweled Girdle of Garnorathanath!

It's fantasy, guys and gals. Fantasy is our life. It's the wave of the future. And who cares where the party is being held, as long as we can root for our ball teams and toss down a brew or two and get laid once in awhile, so what if some fag actor withers and pukes and dies in pain from getting sex in a perverted, disgusting way! I finally got the message:

We exist in dreams. Dreams we substitute for life and pain and responsibility. Dreams we write to lull others into the world of sleepwalkers. Dreams that we ennoble with aphorisms, apothegms, epigrams, and epigraphs! We are the dreamers, by jingo. Noblest of the noble. Those who exist outside the dreams may struggle and starve and sleep in the streets, but what the hell has that to do with us? We've got a costume ball to worry about, is my macho barbarian armor on straight? (Yeah, I *know* FantasyCon doesn't have one of those embarrassing, adolescent, outdated, bad publicity costume balls, but you get the general idea.)

I accept with pride and genuine humility the role of Special Guest. And don't blame anything on the Committee of the World Fantasy Convention; they had no hand in this. I held a gun to their heads. Run this statement, I said, or I duck out on you and leave you without your star buffoon!

They had to do it.

So direct your comments where they belong.

And if this statement offends you, well, geez gang I'm sorry as hell about that. But in truth, at least 51% of the Arizona audience has sure as shit offended me.

Now let's have a most superior party!

Editor's Note: The following essay originally appeared—in an extremely edited form—in *Newsweek*. This is the complete text.

## Strangers in a Strange Land

Everywhere, today, the question is being asked: what did the Heaven's Gate cultists have to do with science fiction? Try this for an answer: *nothing*.

They had *everything* to do with that hideous verbal crotchet "sci-fi," however. And they are light-years apart, so don't confuse them. At peril of your life.

Almost exactly one year ago, my heart tried to kill me. Before I could die, they cracked me open and did a quadruple bypass. But for a moment, I shook hands with death, and in that bonding I got a tough insight; and this I now know for certain: In those gasping last moments of the Rancho Santa Fe cultists, as they were descending into their death sleep, they were thinking *Please help me*; I'm going into the darkness and I need to know! Yeah, we *all* want to know...the answers that make sense of a world growing ever more complex, of lives that seem to be controlled by forces too big for our puny intellects, of a journey without sufficient noble purpose.

Traditionally, answers have been sought in philosophy or religion or mysticism of one kind or another. What's the sense of it all, in a bewildering universe that doesn't seem to know or care that we're here? But from those sources no fully integrated or fully satisfying answers have come.

And those answers may not be anywhere in the literary genre called science fiction, either, but one thing is for *damned* sure: they are not to be found in the cheapjack foolishness of "sci-fi."

The concepts that abound in fantastical literature have the magical capacity to inspire dreams that become enriching reality. Science fiction, like *The Whole Earth Catalog*, is only an implement, a tool of the mind's imagination. It employs the technique called extrapolation, allowing us to play the game of *what-if*? A game of intellect and daring, of special dreaming and determination not to buy into all those boneheaded beliefs that always tell us we're too stupid and too inadequate to prevail. That we need some kind of mythical alien or supernatural babysitter to get us over the rough spots. Science fiction says otherwise. It is an idea-rich literature that is, at core, hopeful and progressive, that always says—with a nod to the reawakening of a competent human spirit—there *will be* a tomorrow. It may be troubling, and it may require us to get a lot smarter, but there *will* be a tomorrow for us to work at.

"Sci-fi," that hunchbacked, gimlet-eyed, slobbering village idiot of a bastardized genre, says only that logic is beyond us, understanding must be crushed underfoot, that the woods are full of monsters and aliens and conspiracies and dread and childish fear of the dark. The former is a literature that can open the sky to all the possibilities of change and chance; the latter is hysterical and as overripe as rotten fruit, that can turn all rational conjecture into a nightmare from which one escapes only by phenobarb-laced apple-sauce or a slug of grape Kool-Aid straight up with cyanide. The former says responsibility for your life is the key; the latter assures you that you ain't got the chance of a hairball in a cyclotron.

And *that* is the dichotomy of science fiction, as opposed to the tabloid mentality of UFO abductions, triangular-headed ETs, reinterpreted biblical apocrypha, and just plain bone stick stone gullibility. It is obscurantism and illiteracy, raised to the level of dogma. It requires that you be as ignorant today as you were yesterday, that you be no brighter than the sap who keeps playing three-card monte on a street corner with a hustler who will *never* cut you a break.

"Sci-fi" is what the Rancho Santa Fe sleepers bought, in that flashy but adolescent shell-game called *Waitin' for the UFO*. They were philosophical suckers who turned away from the genuine wonders of the real world and all its solvable mysteries, to embrace the sophomore horse-puckey of astrology and government conspiracies and recastings of Jesus as a deep-space navigator. That has nothing to do with the problem-solving and curiosity of science fiction...it has *everything* to do with the monster fear and dread produced by the dumbness of "sci-fi."

Stop being exploited by greedy thugs who only want to sell you movie tickets and poisonous delusions that enrich them by your stupidity and fear. Because the truth is in this: neither Heaven nor Hell, and certainly not a flying saucer, can be found in the tail of a comet.

## Struggling for Interior Logic

Only two kinds of people watch *The X-Files*. This is not arbitrary; we have irrefutable statistics. You could look it up.

The first sort of viewer watches the show faithfully, is scared or edified or made querulous by the series, thanks the invisible gods of tv for at least one show that doesn't put you to sleep or turn your brains to *purée* of bat guano, and returns to a normal life beset by the realities of taxes, conglomerate takeovers, cholesterol, and lousy drivers.

The other phylum of *X-Files* viewers believes to his/her soul's deepest depths, some or all of the following:

• John F. Kennedy was assassinated by a secret cabal made up of Mafiosi, CIA renegades, Beltway insiders, high-wire psychopaths, demented Texas right-wing power brokers, and cheap thugs who were once corrupt cops or aldermen; a cadre numbering in the hundreds, if not thousands...all of whom are better able to keep a world-shaking secret than anyone else in the civilized world. Not a *yenta* among them.

• Aliens who—depending on how much backlighting and blown smoke is present— appear to be either light blue, pukey green, or battleship gray, whose sole purpose in this complex universe is to drive straight here from WHEREVER, mostly to perform rectal examinations on semiliterate soybean farmers and defrocked auto parts salesmen, despite the certain knowledge that one, or at least three, such colonoscopies oughtta tell even the most retarded third-year med student what the human plumbing system looks like.

• The woods are full of yetis, sasquatches, abominable snowpersons, Loch Ness plesiosaur, elves, gnomes, færies, sprites, dryads, unicorns, and unnamed terrors that lie in wait for anyone who identifies with the characters in a Freddy Krueger movie or wears a red jersey like those *Enterprise* extras who are always first to get an arrow through the forehead.

• James Dean ain't really dead. He's actually living out his days, hideously disfigured from the car crash, in a mental institution in rural Indiana. Elvis not only rules, but he walks. Marilyn was poisoned by the CIA and Bobby Kennedy, who was himself later snuffed to keep it quiet.

I could go on for days.

We live in a world where far too many people cannot distinguish between reality and fantasy, between shadow and image, between primetime and *The 700 Club*. As I sit down to write this, late in October of one of the last years before the millennium, I call to mind something I heard three hours ago on CBS radio. What I heard was this: A government oversight study of the state of American education concluded today that less than 12 percent of all graduating students have a grasp of simple science. We're talking here the basic laws of physics and the way the universe functions, not arcane and abstruse stuff like analyses of muons, quasars, or the proton synchrotron. Just simple stuff like inertia, gravity, and the trajectory of a bullet through some other gangbanger's brain.

There are two kinds of people who watch Chris Carter's brilliant series. The first recognizes that this is the product of a single intelligence, melding with other talented people to formalize a secret dream. They perceive that it has ever been so with television. The only good stuff is traceable to one creative impulse, whether Buck Houghton or Steve Bochco or Joe Straczynski. *Au courant*, these viewers were onto the series long before *TV Guide* lumbered into its slipstream. Forty million viewers cannot be misled for this long (though I am bewildered by the duration of *America's Bloopers & Pratfalls*, or whatever those blights are called). This first kind of viewer is intrigued by surmise, by the what-if game, by the pleasures of tolerable terror. They understand it's just a goof, it's only fiction.

The other kind of viewer believes in that crap called "sci-fi"—a very different horned creature from the respectable literary genre called science fiction, or even speculative fiction.

Sci-fi is believing giant ants can be produced by hitting them with gamma rays, because you're too ignorant ever to have heard of the inverse-cube law.

Sci-fi is a studio head or network exec or production honcho insisting there be a big bang sound whenever there's an explosion in space, despite the fact that an airless void cannot carry sound.

Sci-fi is dumbing down every good idea that speculative fiction produced in something over 70 years. It is drooling idiocy like *Independence Day*, and Roger Corman ripoffs starring Pauly Shore (a marriage made in heaven).

Sci-fi is what the Heaven's Gate cultists believed that sent them spinning into oblivion.

*The X-Files* walks a narrow ledge over a frightful abyss. On the one hand, it is in the great and grand tradition of all speculative fantasy constructs. It suggests, it hints, it asks what-if, and it plays the dicey game of forcing the viewer to suspend disbelief...at least for the time it takes to watch a segment. But on the other hand (which is green and has only three tentacles on it), the seductive, mythic subtext fosters and enforces and encourages the illogical and obscurantist urban fantasies of the mass people who actually believe a tv hero can take a bullet in the hip and not phase-out instantly with systemic shock.

Carter said in a recent interview, "Paranoia results in a hyperintense way of looking at the world. I don't think that's a bad thing."

Well, uh, er, maybe so, Chris; but even as I agree that no artist should be held responsible for the demented beliefs of an audience that looks on the Shroud of Turin as anything but a 16th century scam, that thinks what they see in tv advertizing in any way veers near accuracy, that actually voted for Bush or Clinton or the little guy with the weird ears...so I also agree that giving the yahoos a visual fix every week, that reinforces their gullibility by telling them Atlantis exists and plants can talk and flying saucers use us as frequently as a Motel 6, is a dangerous game to play as we stroke through these muddy waters toward the year 2001.

History shows us that millennial lunacy recurs. It isn't anything mystifying that *Newsweek* need pose as a conundrum on its cover. It's just the way we are. We're a weird, mostly dopey species that would rather believe that the Red Sea parted than that maybe it was low tide and the story got all bunged up over the centuries. Whether it's the dancing madness, or the tulip frenzy, or the proliferation of astrologers and spiritualists, we're ready to believe it, no matter what nutsiness it may be.

I watch *The X-Files* with regularity. Wouldn't miss it. If I'm out engaging in my life, I tape it. But I gotta confess, it's more than the unresolved plot lines, desperately struggling for interior logic, that gives me the whim-whams.

It's wondering how many of those video zombies actually believe Carter and Mulder and Scully are reporting the Real World.

Editor's Note: The following essay served as the introduction to the third volume of Pulphouse Publishing's five-book, limited edition of THE COMPLETE SHORT FICTION OF ROBERT SHECKLEY, which contained the Ellison/Sheckley collaboration—"I See a Man Sitting on a Chair, and the Chair Is Biting His Leg"— referenced in this essay, and collected in Ellison's PARTNERS IN WONDER. In 2015, Ellison contributed narration to Skyboat Media's audiobook of Sheckley's UNTOUCHED BY HUMAN HANDS.

# The Brides of Sheckenstein

Robert Sheckley is an important writer. Okay, enough of that.

Now let's talk about the interesting stuff. Did you know that Sheckley, through most of his wastrel life, has been an unregenerate slut? Did you know that, apart from the possibly *hundreds* of women whom he has infected with diseases so nameless that one must speak in tongues to designate them, that Sheckley has actually been legally (if not ethically) married at least four times?

And, yes, I am prepared to admit—if bolted down and subjected to the touch of metal objects left long in the brazier—that a) Robert Sheckley and I have been disgustingly close pals for more than thirty years, b) Robert Sheckley is among my top twelve or thirteen favorite writers, the sort whose each new book I welcome with huzzahs and smelling salts, and at which event I set aside whatever worthy tome I'm then reading, in order to indulge myself with a guilty pleasure, c) Robert Sheckley was to have been the subject of a very long, detailed, annotated, and cross-indexed academic study I intended to write a few years ago, for a pittance, but then the fever passed and everything was okay again, d) Robert Sheckley has long been a god in my eyes, but the advent of remedial laser surgery has helped just a lot, and e) if *anything* I write here is taken seriously, let it be this: Robert Sheckley, in my view, has been *the* stylist of the breakthrough Fifties' attitude in fantastic literature.

(Here is the moment of serious comment. Pass on, if genuine remarks make you nervous.

(If I were to be asked by the editors of one of those big-time "encyclopedias" of sf and fantasy: Who, among all the prominent writers from the beginning of the '50s through to the latest flavor-of-the-genre, do you think has had the greatest, *and* the most unsung, effect on literature? I would answer, without a blink, "Robert Sheckley."

(Because he wrote so well, and he wrote so fast—because he was a professional, and that's what he did for a living, *he wrote*—instead of hanging out at the coffeehouses or in the middle of a pack of adoring writing students hanging on his salted-nuts philosophies as other, *many* other, writers did—and still do, needing the sycophancy—and because he was so successful so quickly—and because, for instance, he was selling to *Playboy* for big bucks when most sf writers couldn't crack that market, and Doc Lowndes over at Columbia Publications was shorting the writers at the back of the magazine so he could pay Sheck a half-a-cent-a-word more to be at the front, and Ballantine was publishing UNTOUCHED BY HUMAN HANDS long before they did story collections by older, more established, "worthier" writers—he was the object of envy and calumny, the truly innocent victim of opprobrium and meanspirited gossip spread by a group of New York professionals who were nasty shits and battened so much on the bile they directed toward Sheck, that if one were to dig up their corpses a thousand years from now, one would find their bodies intact and uncorrupted by the warmth of death, still in full possession of hair and teeth, fingernails trimmed though caked with dirt, their execrable selves maintained in pristine awfulness by the snide and odious embalming fluid of maliciousness.

(But it was Sheckley who, after Alfred Bester, had the most profound effect on the young writers of my generation. If it had truly been Asimov and Heinlein who had formed the way of writing that created Poul Anderson and Frank Herbert, then it was for damned certain Alfy and Sheck who shone brightest for me and Zelazny and Silverberg. And while Roger and Bob might have no difficulty owning up to their debt to Alfy, I think it might take a long moment of reflection for them to perceive how important Sheckley was, as their literary world-view was coalescing.)

He wrote so simply and compactly, so cleverly and with so much diversity, it looked like a performance to the less-talented. And the worms despised him for that. He was Fred Astaire: he danced so well, it looked uncomplicated, easy to emulate. Until they tried it. And fell on their asses. Then they despised him the more. Because there was depth and complexity in the simple devices he used. While they were proffering cathode tubes, he was working with microchips.

Readers today may know none of this. As I have said elsewhere, to the smug, arrogant, culturally illiterate trolls of the MTV generation, nostalgia is breakfast. Even so, there are debts that should be acknowledged.

I'm glad I don't have to be the bore who does it, however.

Because, though I am happy to admit all of that, from a) to e), I would much rather talk about the women Sheckley has been married to. And if you ask me *why* I pass up this opportunity to laud one of my best friends, a superlative writer, and a man who seldom picks his nose in public, in lieu of which I discuss personalities unknown to the purchasers of this rather expensive volume, I will answer: because I have been trained in beastly behavior, not to mention the midrash, at the scabby knees of Sheckley; and this is no more than he deserves. Ever, we seek balance in the Universe.

I first met Sheckley in 1953. I was still in high school. I'd run off when I was thirteen, but had gone home to Ohio off and on, until my father died in 1949. Then I lived in Cleveland with my mother until I managed to graduate from high school, which took a very long time, as I recall. But I wandered around the country a lot. And I visited New York. And I worshipped Sheckley, because he was the rising star of that time, and his work was so antic that I knew we'd be friends, even though I was just a kid and he was a crepuscular Methuselah, all of twenty-five years. So I managed to cajole Sheckley's phone number and address from, I think, Ayjay, and I called him, and he erred on the side of courtesy—as he continues to do to this day—saying something noncommittal, like come to visit one afternoon, sometime, kid; and I was there within the hour.

He was living, I'm pretty sure (without actual recourse to spending money by calling him for the facts, and who needs the facts anyhow, when making it all up has so much more vigor) on West End Avenue, uptown, at 103rd Street.

That was inordinately posh turf in those days. Before the coming of the Victim Culture and "entitlement" and the invasion of the army of the homeless and all the other benefits accruing to thirty-some years of Republican largesse; but I digress...

He lived high up in the face of an expensive apartment house, and when I entered the expansive living room, that looked out on the Hudson River, the space was flooded with sunlight; and he had his typewriter set up on a long shelf arrangement in front of one of those windows, and there was a sheaf of typing paper on one side, pristine and sparkling in the sunlight...and on the other side was a slightly smaller sheaf of pages filled with *story*.

I was ushered into the apartment by Bob's first wife, Barbara. She left me alone for a few minutes till Sheckley himself would make his appearance to the fanfare of trumpets, sackbut, lyre, and dulcimer. In those few minutes, I stole over to the typing area where grandeur was born again and again on a regular basis for approximately three cents a word on demand, and I read what was in the typewriter. It was one of the "Finn O'Donnevan" stories, I think. (In those days, because there were so many magazines to fill, and because pay was so small, and because a hot young writer was fired up to write but didn't want to dilute the value of a byline, almost everybody worked with two or three pseudonyms, strictly for commercial reasons. "Finn" was Sheckley's most prominent. In that way, he could have two or even three stories in a single issue of *Galaxy*, which was the top-paying market for magazine sf fiction those days, thereby even further endearing himself to less-talented writers who were selling parts of their childrens' bodies to kind strangers on upper Broadway.)

I recall distinctly reading that page rolled onto the platen. It had something to do with Billy Batson, and maybe Captain Marvel, and something to do with Billy being in a big mailbox on a street corner.

(I have never been able to track that story down. It may have been a snippet Sheckley threw out, or lost, or never used. But I never forgot it. Years later, when I was writing what Silverberg thinks is my best story, "At the Mouse Circus," I used that image. Billy Batson carrying on a conversation while peering out of a mailbox slot. It was perfect for my purposes, and since I'd never located it in Sheckley's works —though I think I've read about ninety-five percent of what he's published that has come into my hands—I figured such a powerful memory-turned-icon should not go to waste. So don't tell *me* that Sheckley didn't have major impact on my young and fevered brain!)

Well, the point of all this hugger-mugger is that it was Barbara Sheckley who opened the door into the world of Bobbo for me. She was a pretty woman, young in 1953, well turned out, eminently at home in that (I imagined) palatial eyrie in the Manhattan sky. To a hick from Ohio she was a Grande Dame.

I remember little about her except that she offered me a cup of coffee, and that she and Sheckley had a fierce argument over something inconsequential. Because I am of Jewish descent, and so is Sheckley, and so was Barbara (*née* Scadron), it was a form of discourse with which I was all too familiar.

Among my people, it is called *geshrying*.

And what is it, *geshrying*, you ask? Stand in the middle of an echoing space. Empty, preferably. Try a mini-mall in your neighborhood. Now put your hands to your temples, clutching your hair in all the fingers, and try to rip the hair off your head while shrieking at the top of your lungs. Also, attempt to pop your eyes out of their sockets, swallow your tongue, and recite all the generations of biblical elders in some lost language, while pushing the veins of your forehead out through your scalp. This will, in some small way, approximate the *geshry*.

They had this, uh, disagreement.

I don't remember much more. I didn't see Sheckley again for years. He had met Barbara Scadron at New York University, in Irwin Shaw's writing class. They were married from circa 1951 till circa 1957, though they separated in 1955 and Bob went off to live in Lester del Rey's old apartment, a dark and depressing cell in the West Sixties, where Lincoln Center now rises. It is my gut feeling that he was unfaithful to Barbara for much of that time. I have no proof. But I certainly hope she was likewise.

Now we come to Ziva who, among all the various mates of Sheckley, I most admired and adored. First of all, the former (and presently) Ziva Kwitney was drop-dead gorgeous. Blind men on Amsterdam Avenue smiled when she passed, and went to their graves fulfilled. Flowers blossomed where she walked. The sky above her was always gingham or pastel pink. She was smart as a cookie, had very fine and slim ankles, knew how to win an argument, was old world gracious though thoroughly modern and up-to-date, and was (as Daniel Manus Pinkwater phrases it) "no beck number."

Sheck met Zee on a blind date that had been set up by Fruma Klass—who is also one of the classiest and most terrific women you'd ever want to meet, despite her malicious putz of a husband—and she set up the date in 1956 after Bob and Barbara had gone plop! Now, if you ask Sheckley how he met Ziva, he'll tell you blah blah blah on this blind date arranged by Fruma, at which time he saw Zee for the first. In his telling, Fruma is the *shadchen* (for the *goyim*: look it up) and Sheckley was this dashing young scrivener-cavalier, sweeping off her feet the luscious but naïve ingénue. On the other claw, you could have something like the truth, which is a lot more interesting, not to mention serving as a strictly terrific lesson about not trusting Sheckley's wretched memory. Hell, when *he* tells it, Fruma arranged the date in 1957, which is clearly nuts, because by 1957 he and Ziva were already married. The year of the event was 1956. Tertiary syphilis is a ghastly way to go; first the memory, then the sense of humor, then the knees, then the rack and pinion steering...

Anyhow, the way it played was like so: Sheckley had separated from Barbara. Jason had been born in 1952. He was three when they split up. Now Bob is living in this squalid airshaft Lester had deliriously conned him into believing was capable of domiciling humans when, in truth, it was like something out of the darker sections of Mervyn Peake's GORMENGHAST trilogy. Now it's roughly two years later, and Sheckley is parceling out his time among three activities: writing for penurious sums and parting with as much of the money as Barbara can track down for the support of Jason...dating a woman named Phyllis, whom I only vaguely remember...and chasing giant mutant cockroaches the size of IRT subway cars around the kitchen of what will one day become the home of the Metropolitan Opera. (Lester, of course, had fled the scene, and was living in opulence in Red Bank, New Jersey, where Evelyn spent most of her time cauterizing his wounds from the cockroach attacks.)

Cut away from the dashing young scrivener-cavalier, and let us move in for a medium close shot of young Ziva Kwitney, recently returned from Israel and now enrolled at NYU. One day early in 1956 she picks up a copy of the then-young *Village Voice*, and sees an ad in the personals that says something like:

```
              WRITERS!
     PUBLISHED, UNPUBLISHED!
      Let's get together for
     conversation, literary
    stimulation, professional
          assistance; let's
            form a group!
            CALL: SAM
```

So Zee calls this number, and it turns out there is no "Sam" (well, actually, "Sam" was alleged to be a poltergeist, but that's another psychoanalysis entirely). Now, for members of the MTV generation, the name Dave Mason will mean nothing. That is to say, it never meant much to members of *my* generation, either, but at least Mason was current at the time, so I can tell you about him, and in this one instance do not feel at all uneducated if you've never heard of him.

Dave Mason was this guy who hung around New York and East Coast fandom, eventually wrote some science fiction, got a book or two published, did this and that, and spent most of his time—if I recall correctly, and I probably don't—well, he spent a lot of time trying to get laid.

Which is what this advertisement in the *Voice* was all about. There was no writer's group, there was no "Sam," but when Zee called the number she got Dave Mason, who began to hustle her with a line that so quickly turned her off, she hung up on him. So then Ziva called her friend Fruma, and they goofed on this character who was trying to meet women with such a lame action. So then *Fruma* called Mason, and he tried to put the move on *her*. So Fruma made a date with him for the following Friday night. So then Fruma calls Ziva and tells her what went down, and they giggle for a while, and then Fruma suggests to Zee that she call Mason *again*, only this time she should put on her famous Russian accent, and pretend to be someone else. So finally Zee and Fruma get together, and Ziva makes the call to Mason, and she tells him she's "Svetlana" or somesuch name, and she does it all in this husky, sexy whisper kind of voice, and Mason goes all over himself trying to haul her in. So Fruma scribbles a note to Ziva saying, "Insist on the date being Friday night!" and Zee does so, and Mason goes er, um, and asks if she's available *any* other night, and "Svetlana" says no, impossible, and so he agrees.

Now, comes that Friday night, and Ziva has made arrangements with Dave Mason to meet him in front of the cigar store on the corner of Christopher Street and 7th Avenue, at Sheridan Square. And of course Mason has broken the date with Fruma, in high expectation of meeting the mysterious Svetlana.

Now, he stands there, and he stands there, and he stands there. Because neither one of them show up. They do, however, walk by incognito, staring at the geek scuffling his toe and waiting for the Siren of the Steppes to manifest herself.

If you'd ever met Dave Mason, this would be a really funny story for you. Since you haven't, well, take my word for it.

Anyhow, eventually, for reasons that passeth understanding, Fruma goes out with Mason. Go ask. He takes her to a science fiction party. Some semi-pro fan group. And there Fruma meets the guy she will eventually marry, whose name I would sooner choke on a chicken bone than mention here. And in the course of her dating this guy, she takes Ziva to yet another party where Zee is introduced to Bob. But Bob doesn't remember that.

Nor does he remember that eventually Fruma's husband-to-be tries to fix up Sheckley, who is separated and living in the free-fire cockroach zone by this time nicknamed Del Rey's Hell, and he asks Fruma if she has any friends, and Fruma says yes, my friend Ziva, and they set up this blind date, and *that's* how it happened, Sheckley, you idiot!

(There is this case Oliver Sacks discusses, where a man suffered from a peculiar malaise the chief symptom of which was that he awoke each day with no memory of the day before, and had to reinvent himself afresh each morn. Like the guy in the Gene Wolfe novels. Sheckley is like that. His memory seems periodically flensed. Tabula rasa. Clean slate city.)

This is really terrific. He doesn't remember shit. You can tell him anydamnthing and he'll believe you. Watch:

Hey, Sheckley! When you gonna pay me back the hundred you borrowed when you were editing at *Omni*?

Moving right along. On April 8, 1956, Robert Sheckley and Ziva Kwitney had their first date. Slightly less than a year later on February 22nd of 1957, Sheckley divorced

Barbara. Now this date is of incidental interest for the following reason: February 22nd was Barbara Sheckley's birthday. Helluva gift-giving sensibility you've got there, Sheck! What makes it even *more* interesting is that February 22nd is also Ziva Kwitney's birthday. When Bob realized the connection between Zee and Barbara, he paled significantly. Let us not suggest he's superstitious, but to this day he will not unleash his deadly member without first he's checked a woman's natal day. Not that it's prevented him from getting into dutch in non-22 February venues.

On April 7, 1957 Bob married Ziva. For the next eight years they lived in Greenwich Village. Alisa was born in 1964. In mid-1967, a few months before they moved to Majorca for a year, I stayed with Bob and Zee and the two-and-a-half-year-old Alisa at their West End Avenue apartment for about two weeks. We all bummed around a lot, I inhabited the back room and sat with a towel wrapped around my waist, writing a story called "Worlds to Kill" which I sold to *If* or *Galaxy* or one of those.

I thought they were golden. Zee particularly.

Well, it all came to an end. More or less amicably after fourteen years together, including the year they lived together before they were married.

(By the way: when Bob was staying with me out here in L.A. earlier in '67, we co-wrote one of the stories in this volume, "I See a Man Sitting on a Chair, and the Chair Is Biting His Leg." Ziva was back in New York with Alisa, getting ready for Majorca. According to superior academic sources, this story is the finest piece of work Sheckley has ever done, including IMMORTALITY, INC. from which the film *Freejack* has been made. *The New York Times* said of this short story, "Sheckley is dragged screaming to new heights of literary excellence by Ellison's inspired chivvying." *The Boston Globe* inhaled, "At last! Sheckley has found his soul's missing engine." *Harpers* ventriculated, "Was there ever a more glorious duo? Gilbert and Sullivan? Troilus and Cressida? Burke and Hare? Hurray for Ellison and Sheckley!"

(But I digress.)

So finally Sheckley blows it with Zee, which I have always taken to be a major stupid move, but maybe it was just the end of the natural life of the relationship, who knows? And who's the hell to say. None of our business, really; not that any of *us* has been so goddam smart ourselves.

Anyhow, he went off to live on the island of Ibiza, where he met this judge's daughter from New Jersey, sunning herself on vacation. Name of Abby Schulman. And that was something like 1970, and they hung out for a while, and then they got married because Sheckley seems to have this need to be linked with a strong woman, but as soon as the marriage enlarges with kids he gets twitchy and has to step out for about three years to get some air. There's nothing mean about it, it's just that he seems to need to forget it all, go off and reinvent himself. Or something.

(Zee is the psychotherapist. In private practice in New York. She writes pop-psych articles for magazines and newspapers, as well. Be interesting to see what she'd write about Sheckley. Particularly now, because Alisa—who is some terrific young woman, an assistant editor at DC Comics and author of a first novel coming from HarperCollins in the Fall of '92—just got married, and Sheckley went to the wedding, and he danced with Ziva, and he seemed pretty happy, and there was genuine affection between them after some years of acrimony because Bob was, well, how shall we put it delicately, less than forthcoming with support money for Alisa's upbringing.)

It occurs to me that this may not be precisely the sort of introduction the publisher (or my friend Bob) was expecting. Well, to tell you the truth, gang, it ain't precisely what I'd intended to write, neither. But here it is; and ain't that odd.

Now I'm starting to get nervous. I may be testing the tensile strength of a valuable friendship. Yeah...well...

He married Abby. That went on from around circa 1970 to 1981. Ended not so well. I haven't got a lot of good to say about Abby. She stiffed me for some royalty money, and put Bob in a bad way. But then, I don't know the inside story, so let's just say it was the Bride of Frankensheck #3, and move on to Sheckley's return to the States, his ascent to the fiction editorship at *Omni* in New York, something like mid-1981, and his meeting-up with a lady named Jay Rothbell, who had previously been wed to Billy Oskay and then John Shirley, and who, since being divorced from Sheckley, has married a very fine man named Jack Rems, and they live up in the San Francisco area.

He was with Jay from 1982 to 1986, approximately. For a while they lived in a trailer park in Florida, approximately.

You can understand that there are a lot of "approximately this and approximately that and circa this and circa that" as we descend into my and Sheckley's twilight years. Of late, I've been a lot more concerned with my travail than his. After a while the plight of starving children in Ethiopia becomes less persistently compelling than that one gets out of bed with fresh aches and creaks each day. Hardly noble, but a sad and inescapable truth about the human condition.

Which brings us full tilt back to Sheckley, and the imminent arrival of the Bride of Bobenstein #5, a lady I have not met, name of Gail Dana, who I'm told is far too good for wretched old Robert. Now Ms. Dana, a Portland resident, has apparently undertaken to wed the Demon Prince on October 12 of the year 1991, as I sit writing this in July.

If it works, it needn't work for long. Neither Sheckley nor I can possibly hope to hang on for more than another ten, twenty years at most. So all Ms. Dana needs is a little fortitude and the foreknowledge that most of us liars-for-hire die as poor as our predecessors, thus preparing her for a vanishing act when Sheckley goes to his just reward, because of all the creditors who'll be looking for his assets. Which, of course, won't exist.

So here's the ending. In which an introduction is supposed to sum everything up, with some sparkling metaphor, and the one-punch belief that all will be well. Wish I knew how to do that. But I don't. Sheckley and I have come down through a lot of years, if not exactly lashed together like a potato-sack race, then certainly passing the baton to each other as we caromed away into individual and idiotic adventures.

If you cannot quite perceive it, let me tell you that I love my friend Bob Sheckley. Love him for being a pal who has never treated me with anything less than seriousness and respect. Even when I was a teenaged kid intruding on his private life. He's older than I, by six years, and that ought to have set up a younger-brother-older-brother thing; but it didn't. We were both too immature for that. Too wild and too irresponsible. For me, Sheckley has always been a pal. We both seem to be the same age, which is roughly about seven or eight, with runny noses and banged-up elbows. Both of us seem to have gotten out of life precisely what we contracted for; and if I may be so presumptuous to answer for him as well as myself, we have only barely perceptible regrets. If you want to learn who the *real* Robert Sheckley is, I suggest not this book of wry phantasms, nor any of the others. I commend to your attention (if you can ever lay your hands on a copy) a very fine thriller titled THE MAN IN THE WATER, which Sheck wrote when he was living with Zee in Majorca, and which Ayjay published at Regency Books after I left for California in 1961. Truly swell piece of writing, and therein shines the real Sheckley.

Beyond that, it is only this remaining to be said:

This is a wonderful book of stories and Robert Sheckley is an important writer.

# I, Felon

Not that it's any of your damned business, but the first time I went to jail was in 1945. I was eleven years old. In 1958 I wrote a story about it. The title was "Free With This Box!" I was twenty-four. Now shuddup and leave me alone.

There are three sections in this group of homages to the pulp writers of a dear and departed era in popular literature. One of them, I'm told, is *The Crimefighters*, the third will be *The Dames*, and this one, dealing with the villains. As I am not a woman, it is manifest why I was not solicited by the *éminence grise* of this project, the esteemed editor Mr. Otto (we calls him "Slow Hand Poppa") Penzler, to pen the introductory exegesis for the book about the broads; and as you will understand in mere moments, selecting me to front a book extolling the virtues of cops, pseudo-cops, hemi/semi/demi cops, and P.I. cops is about as apropos as a piñata at a paraplegics' picnic.

I was importuned by Penzler to write a foreword for a book of stories about *crooks*. We're talkin' here thieves, thugs, knaves, poltroons, bilkers, milkers, murderers, arsonists, liars, blackmailers, footpads, cat burglars, shakedown artists, pigeon-drop and three-card monte swindlers, bloodthirsters, and backstabbers...in short, criminals.

Now, you may ask, what is this delicate flower of advanced age, this pinnacle of society, this world-famous and multiple-award-winning credit to his species, getting at? Is he, heaven forfend, suggesting that it is right and proper, even condign that this Penzler fellah thinks Ellison is *as one with* this fictional cadre of creeps and culprits, similar in spirit or outlook or past experience? Is that what we are to believe?

What is it witchu? Didn't I tell you to shuddup and leave me alone?

First of all, I grew up *reading* the pulps. I was born in '34 and, unlike most of the

Jessica Simpson-admiring twerps of contemporary upbringing, for whom nostalgia is what they had for breakfast, I actually *remember* what a hoot it was to plonk myself into the Ouroboros root-nest of the ancient oak tree in the front yard of our little house at 89 Harmon Drive, Painesville, Ohio, with the latest issue of *Black Book Detective Magazine* or *The Shadow*. Ah me, those wood-chip-scented, cream-colored pulp pages dropping their dandruff onto the lap of my knickers...

(Those were corduroy boys' pants, here in America. In England, as I later discovered to my priapic delight, the same word is used to designate female panties—ah yes, in the aphorism of G. B. Shaw: "The United States and England are two countries divided by a common language.")

...and while Jack Wheeldon and his cronies yelled "kike" as they rode their Schwinns past my eyrie, I went away from that place and that time with the adventures of masked riders, square-jawed crimefighters, mightily-thewed barbarian warriors, spacemen accompanied by gorgeous women in brass brassieres, and culprits too smooth and sagacious to be nobbled by some cigar-masticating flatfoot from the Central Office. There was something called "escapism" in the pop lit of those days. It's too bad that word has fallen on such hard times. Escapism now, I'm told, is Not A Good Thing. Yet in its place we have "entertainment" that deifies the idle, the infamous, the egregious, and the shallow. In place of Raffles and Flambeau and Jimmy Valentine we have rapper thugs for whom human speech is not their natural tongue, a morbid fascination with those missing and presumed buried or drowned in the Bahamas, the need for a daily fix of tabloid ink infusion anent the presumed grotesqueries of child molesters, serial killers, televangelist alarmists, racists and ratfinks and raucous riffraff. We have been led down the societal garden path to a place where an honest crook who carries no firearm and would not stoop to such ignominious behavior as a carjacking or ballbatting of an ATM is no-price, and we are surfeited with "entertainment" that cheapens us, distances us, turns us into an unworthy people who accept no responsibility for our bad actions, and fills us with a sense of *American Idol* entitlement that has no substance in reality.

If I seem to be extolling the chimerical "virtues" of felons and crooks, one might assume in much the same way as the naïve and gullible praised Dillinger, Capone, Ma Barker and her boys, back in the day, well, I live in the real world and I do truly *really* understand that Billy the Kid and Murder, Inc. and even Bonnie & Clyde were way less than icons to hold up to one's children...*but*...nonetheless...

I would rather spend time reading about Boston Blackie and Fantômas and Harry Lime than have to put up with one more pelvic twitch of Christina Aguilera or pelvic piercing of Pink. What used to be a necessary and even enriching, innervating, if not ennobling retreat to the made-up worlds of high crimes and low misdemeanors in the pulps, has been relentlessly, ceaselessly, tirelessly bastardized by corporate and advertising thugs (far worse than the Bad Guys you'll find in this volume), into a pounding, remorseless assault of empty trivial crap that fills the air, saturates our perceptions of the received world, and turns us away from ourselves and our true values and our important pursuits. Distractions that make the tomfoolery and toughtalk of the pulps seem as rich and golden as the Analects of Confucius or a paraphrasing of Lao Tzu. In the stories in this book, taken from the heart and core of that popular entertainment engine of the '20s, '30s, and '40s, you will experience an escapism that steals nothing from you, reduces you not one scintilla, pleasures and distracts you the way a tall champagne flute of good, tart lemonade does on a blistering August afternoon.

The fictions may creak a bit in the joints, some of the writing may be too prolix for modern tastes (don't forget, they were writing for ½¢ to a penny-a-word in those halcyon days of post-Depression America), and we have been exposed to an electronically-linked world for so long now, that some of the attitudes and expressions in these fables may seem giggle-worthy, but this is a muscular writing that sustained us through some very tough times, and their preserved quality of sheer entertainment value is considerable. So be kind.

As for me, well, I come to this book with credentials that are not trumpeted in the "official biographies" or in a WHO'S WHO or the ENCYCLOPEDIA OF AMERICAN AUTHORS. But mine is exactly the proper vita for a book'a'crooks.

As I said, I grew up *in situ* with the pulp detective magazines. And in my earliest days as a professional I *wrote* for the metamorphosed hard-boiled pulps in digest-size (which stick-in-the-mud Penzler has trouble perceiving as equally valid cred for "pulp" as the larger-sized magazines). I wrote for *Manhunt, Mantrap, Mayhem, Guilty, Sure-Fire Detective, Trapped, The Saint Mystery Magazine* (both U.S. and U.K. editions), *Mike Shayne's, Tightrope, Crime and Justice Detective Story*, and *Terror Detective Story Magazine*, just to glaze your eyes and bore yo ass with a select few of the rags for which I toiled. So that's a *second* good reason for me being the one who stands here at the prow of the ship, urging you aboard.

But the cred that stands, the one that beats the bulldog, is that I *was* a felon. I mentioned my first incarceration at age eleven, a spree of petty theft involving comic character pinback buttons concealed in boxes of Wheaties; but that was just the first. Age thirteen, ran off and wound up in a huge free-standing cell in the old (now-razed)

Kansas City slam, all alone save for a carny geek who went nuts without his bottle of gin a day, and impressed me forever with the stench of rotgut sweated out via armpits. Booted out of Ohio State University in 1954, in part, for shoplifting. Saw the inside of the Columbus jail on that one.

U.S. Army brigs of various venues, 1957–59, mostly for insubordination. 1960: I'm in New York, living down in the Village, guy I had a beef with phones in bullshit charges of "possession of firearms" to the cops, they bust me, toss me in The Tombs (see my book MEMOS FROM PURGATORY), and finally the Grand Jury looks at it, the D.A. knows it's bullshit so he urges them to return No True Bill, and that was that.

Civil Rights days. I was in jails in Mississippi, Georgia, Alabama with Martin, and on and on. In Louisiana, a couple of redneck cops grabbed me on a back road in Plaquemine Parish, hauled me in, stripped me to the waist, cuffed me behind my back, lifted me up between them, hung the cuffs over a meat hook turned into the top-half of a Dutch door, and took turns walloping me across the belly with a plastic kiddie ballbat, careful to leave barely a mark on the outside. Did that till the Boss of Plaquemine, the infamous Leander Perez showed up, thumbed through my wallet full of I.D. and credit cards, discovered I was from Hollywood, knew there'd be a *geshry* (as we say in Yiddish) if I vanished, had his boys take me down, and redeposited me: in a ditch somewhere out on a dark back road, with this admonition, which I recall with telephonic accuracy more than four decades later: "Nex' tahm you show yo ass in Plack-uh-mun, jew-boy, we gonna jus' kill you."

Is it appropriate that Otto picked me for the introductory remarks about crooks and felons? You better believe it, dawg. Now go thee hence, inside farther, and enjoy yourself.

Tell 'em Harlan sent you. And now, just shuddup and leave me alone. A tired old felon slumped and maundering about his days on the other side of the law.

Editor's Note: Much of the pulp material Ellison recalled writing in the preceding piece has been collected in HONORABLE WHOREDOM AT A PENNY A WORD and AGAIN, HONORABLE WHOREDOM AT A PENNY A WORD, both available from HarlanEllisonBooks.com.

# Clark Ashton Smith:
## Out of Space and Time

He never wrote a complete novel, though a twelve thousand word fragment of his intended full-length work, "The Infernal Star"—begun and abandoned in February of 1933—lies unpublished in darkness, possibly in some dank subterranean crypt beneath stygian waters and flooded ebon caverns through which crawl thick, white worms whose semblances of countenance are the hideous, cilia-festooned simulacra of the expressions of the human corpses on which they have fed. Or maybe just in a safety deposit box in a San Francisco branch of The Bank of America.

(One bite of the forbidden fruit of his lapidary prose, and I find myself overwhelmed, engulfed, supersaturated; I find myself tipsy with language, uncharacteristically emulating; indulging in an unashamedly baroque attack on the idea at hand in a syntax so rich and steaming with visual evocations that it borders on logorrhea. A style so purple it sloshes over into the ultraviolet. A writing style that would make Hemingway break out in hives.)

He was a poet, a painter, a sculptor of the bizarre, and a recluse; and though he wrote in excess of a hundred stories in a canon spread across more than a dozen collections, he produced almost all of them in less than a decade of furious activity, from the beginning of the Depression in 1929 till he inexplicably deserted fiction in 1938; and though his work is solidly in the traditions of Poe, Bierce, Flaubert, and Baudelaire, and though he was one of the towering triumvirate that dominated *Weird Tales* in its most fecund period—the other two being Robert E. Howard and H.P. Lovecraft—he is virtually unknown today beyond the rarefied venue of those who love obscure horror stories.

Even his name, like those of his characters, seems to echo with intimations of Omar Khayyám and the silken opulence of ages beyond Time, of places beyond Space: Clark Ashton Smith. The magical lands he created bear in their syllables resonances with dreams of the faraway we have carried with us since the Flood: Zothique, Hyperborea, Poseidonis, Xiccarph, Averoigne, Phandiom and, of course, Atlantis. Now his stories, like silent songs in stone, are beyond the reach of modern readers condemned to the paperback illiteracies of a bumbling horde of "horror" writers who have pilfered the cache of Smith's work, but who dash widdershins between their word-masticators and the *Oxford Universal*, forlornly and ineptly trying to unearth less-precise and commercially-acceptable words for *ossuary* and *innominate* and *bitumen-colored cerements*. Purveyors of the recycled cliché and the *mot unjuste* and language so inelegant it could stun a Visigoth.

And so, even as we have had our critical abilities systematically bastardized by motion pictures cut like rock videos, so that we cannot go fifteen minutes without a car crash, thus disabling us for the paced symmetry of a Kurosawa or Resnais, we have likewise been bludgeoned by decades of commercial writing below the level of Dr. Seuss, on the theory that simple is best. (Einstein once pointed out: "Everything should be made as simple as possible, but no simpler.") The stunned, the bastardized, and the bludgeoned cannot enjoy Clark Ashton Smith, more's the pity. His convolute style and sybaritic, depraved fantasies are to them as Vivaldi is to a teenager googly over Run DMC: it is merely white noise, at best impenetrable.

More's the pity, because Smith's was a voice singular and compelling. I have written elsewhere of the epiphany of my initial encounter with his remarkable fantasy, "The City of the Singing Flame," an encounter that profoundly influenced my own writing, and influenced my life. It was 1950, I was sixteen, I found it in an August Derleth anthology in a school library in Cleveland, Ohio...and it was such a powerful icon that I stole the book, and own it to this day. As Frederic Prokosch's SEVEN WHO FLED and Kafka's THE TRIAL mercy-killed my innocence about what it took to be a writer worth reading, so Clark Ashton Smith's stories thrashed out of me my ignorance about the limits of language.

I would very likely not be writing films now, had I not learned lesson after lesson from Smith about writing visually. He has an eerie way of making mimetic in the mind even the most arcane scenes. (Oddly, however, there is very little aural and tactile freighting in his work. I can see it all, but in a disembodied, fingerless silence.)

Take, for instance, this snippet from "The Last Hieroglyph." An old, and not very talented astrologer has been commanded by the auguries to follow a terrifying guide, a mummy, through a "region of stifling vaults and foul, dismal, nitrous corridors." Overcome with fear, the astrologer breaks away from the mummy, and tries to retrace his steps, through the catacombs:

> *Presently he came to the huge, browless skull of an uncouth creature, which reposed on the ground with upward-gazing orbits; and beyond the skull was the monster's moldy skeleton, wholly blocking the passage. Its ribs were cramped by the narrowing walls, as if it had crept there and had died in the darkness, unable to withdraw or go forward. White spiders, demon-headed and large as monkeys, had woven their webs in the hollow arches of the bones; and they swarmed out interminably as Nushain approached; and the skeleton seemed to stir and quiver as they seethed over it abhorrently and dropped to the ground before the astrologer. Behind them others poured in a countless army...*

Even those addicted to rap music and car crashes can *see* that horror in the dark passageway. Let Judith Krantz or Sidney Sheldon try to plow *that* field.

The passage above is from one of the twenty stories in OUT OF SPACE AND TIME, Smith's first major collection, published by the specialty house, Arkham, in 1942. Because of the rules of the game passim this book, I was allowed to pick only one title by Clark Ashton Smith. That's tough. It's representative, the one I selected, but by no means an adequate primer. I picked it because it contains "The City of the Singing Flame." One of my all-time favorite stories, as I babbled earlier. But that eliminates GENIUS LOCI and LOST WORLDS and THE ABOMINATIONS OF YONDO and a fistful more that delight and mystify. I go with OUT OF SPACE AND TIME because it remains with me, after more than thirty years since I first read it, as emblematic of what we mean when we say, "It created worlds and feelings I never knew anywhere else."

A pure wonder, especially in a time filled with white noise.

---

Editor's Note: The preceding was Ellison's 1988 contribution to HORROR: THE 100 BEST BOOKS, an anthology edited by Stephen Jones and Kim Newman, in which 100 writers were solicited to contribute essays on their favorite volumes of horror. Craig Spector chose Ellison's DEATHBIRD STORIES as his contribution to the book.

Smith's "The Infernal Star" was finally published in 1989.

# Tolerable Terror
## or, To Read Him Is to Fear Him

Now here's the peculiar part. The part that now, sixty years later, I *remember* as being odd, being peculiar. In retrospect.

Both of them were smart, my mother and father. Very nice people, you'd have liked them. They may or may not have been well-read; I was too young to make that value-judgment; I was eleven, twelve, something like that. But they were hardly what anyone would call uninformed or ignorant of the World War II milieu in which they existed. We're talking mid-Forties.

Understand: I taught myself to read when I was two or three, very precocious. I'd read anything. I read *every*thing. But here's the peculiar part. Other than in *my* room, where there were all manner of books and comics and *Mechanix Illustrated* and *The Sporting News* and reading material from everywhichwhere, there were very few books in our house. In Ohio, in the Forties.

There were two narrow bookcases in the living room, built in as sort of curio cabinets on either side of the fireplace, what my Aunt Maxine used to call *tchotchkeh* repositories; and there were a few books on those shelves; but they seem to me now—as I guess they did back then—a disparate congeries of not-too-notable titles.

There was a Maugham or two, THE RAZOR'S EDGE and ASHENDEN; a couple of Frank Yerby historicals; one or two Clarence Budington Kelland potboilers, one of which was SCATTERGOOD BAINES; a book I now understand was quite a popular title back in the day before My Day, weird title: HELL FER SARTAIN; an Ellery Queen mystery and ONLY YESTERDAY by Frederick Lewis Allen; Louis Bromfield, Hervey Allen, Hilton's

GOODBYE, MR. CHIPS; and Pocket Books #1, Hilton's LOST HORIZON. There was a copy of the famous BURMA SURGEON autobiography by Gordon Seagrave...

(And what strange linkages Destiny forges for us: years later I became friends with Seagrave's son, Sterling, and we almost lost our lives together on a snowstorm-swept highway outside East Chicago, Indiana. But that's a story for another evening.)

...and there was one other. A thin 49¢ hardcover, a fourteen-story collection that the World Publishing Company of Cleveland and New York (in that order) assured me contained "weird and ghostly tales by a master of the supernatural, selected & with an introduction by" some guy named "August Derleth."

Apart from a previously-published paperback containing only five stories, this inexpensive cheap-paper hardcover was the first publication of a selection of the tales of Howard Phillips Lovecraft. I stood in front of that *tchotchkeh* repository, a little boy not yet in his teens, in the heart of the post-Depression lower-middle-class America wherein lay all I knew of the universe, and I plucked forth:

BEST SUPERNATURAL STORIES OF H.P. LOVECRAFT.

The first story in the book was where I started. It was "In the Vault." It scared the bejezus out of me.

The second story in the book was "Pickman's Model." It scared the crap out of me.

Then I read "The Rats in the Walls" and threw the book from me as if all the name-less wraiths and grotesqueries of the Stygian depths were slobbering and keening in my wake, squamous and gibbering with the stench of a thousand opened graves rising above their eldritch spawn!

I kid you not, Chief: I didn't go near that book again for three months. It conjured in my restless nights' sleep thereafter, the template for nightmares that not even sixty years, and having lived a life, and growing up a little, have been able to usher to quietus.

Before Poe, before Bierce or William Hope Hodgson, before even O. Henry and Mark Twain, I was reading Lovecraft. So all this current foofaraw about him being "rediscovered" is a bit jejune to me. And to the spirit of Augie Derleth, who was there before all of us.

I'd never read him in the pulp magazines—that all transpired before I was born—and by 1937 when he died, he was yesterday's fishwrap. But I had been exposed to HPL in the most plastic, unformed moments of my youth, and I knew he was remarkable, and something to be feared.

To see the cosmos through his eyes was scary.

Edgar Allan Poe was a strange, troubled man. The poet laureate of the decadent, Arthur Rimbaud, was a pathologically sensitive, deeply secretive dreamer. Woolrich, Octave Mirbeau, Huysmans, Capote, Faulkner, Bierce, Robert E. Howard, avatars of the darkness in the human spirit all and each. Twisted lives, lived uneasily; ill-fitting in their skins. Each and all, teetering on the lip of the abyss.

"Odd" does not encompass it.

"Weird" discredits it.

"Peculiar" is, at its noblest, *reductio ad absurdum.* It suggests they tricked us, duped us; not greatness, merely *fichu.* Jean Cocteau: "You are always concentrated on the inner thing. The moment one becomes aware of the crowd, performs for the crowd, it is spectacle. It is *fichu.*"

Lovecraft was a semi-recluse, and the audience, if any, for which he wrote was one he never saw. Thus, no spectacle. He more than concentrated on "the inner thing." It was, it must have been, just read the stories migawd there it is, he *lived* in the inner thing. A number of recent reviewers have been drawn to a particular passage in his groundbreaking and exemplary essay "Supernatural Horror in Literature" (written in 1926–27, revised in the 1930s, but never published in its final form till 1939, two years after his death; and not in separate book form till 1945): "The one test of the really weird is this—whether or not there be excited in the reader a profound sense of dread, and of contact with unknown spheres and powers; a subtle attitude of awed listening, as if for the beating of black wings or the scratching of outside shapes and entities on the known universe's utmost rim."

This was his intent. To scare you. He scared me, long those many years ago, and does still...so why not you, too? The "inner thing" that gnawed like rats in the walls of H.P. Lovecraft's daily existence could only be calmed, borne, tolerated, by the codifying of all that black mist in story form.

To read him is to fear him. But it is a tolerable terror, a spectrum of fear that casts new and different shadows, but does not abominate us, does not turn us away. He seeks to scare us, nothing more.

And for doing the job in loneliness and obscurity, at last the snobbish world of "serious" literature has found him. When I was approached, in November of 2004 by Max Rudin, publisher of the prestigious Library of America, to contribute a "brief comment" about Lovecraft, I found myself once more before the curio bookshelf at 89 Harmon Drive in Painesville, Ohio, at age eleven, reaching for my first Lovecraft, and I wrote for the Library of America these words:

"H.P. Lovecraft was, is, and very likely will *always* be, the irregularly beating heart of darkness of American fantastic literature. If there is a more obstinately terrifying story in the genre than his 'Rats in the Walls,' even the bravest soul should be too petrified to read it."

And I saw those words in magazines by the dozens, saw them on book dumps and pr releases. Saw them, and smiled. He was getting the attention of the Academy and *hoi polloi*, the readers of true lit and the browsers of book-club crap. He was now out there, long dead but suddenly mighty, and all the king's English and all the king's men would make of him a Jacques Derrida *Festschrift*, decomposing this and explicating that.

But at the final moments, one need only stand before the bookcase of imagination, withdraw the dusty volume of fear, and read the first lines of the longest story in this collection:

From "The Dream-Quest of Unknown Kaddath": "Three times dreamed of the marvelous city, and three times he was snatched away while still he paused Randolph Carter on the high terrace above it."

He may be the new flavor for the *poseurs* and parvenus, but for those of us who ran trembling from Nyarlathotep and Shub-Niggurath and the rest of them there Great Old Ones in the *R'lyeh Text*, back when we weren't old enough to cross Euclid Avenue, he was the one who took us by the throat and made us cross vast obsidian spaces to confront alien ideas and paralyzing fright.

That's what great storytellers do.

And all the rest is merely spinach.

# THE STREETS

Editor's Note: *The Streets* ran for three installments in *Buzz* magazine, but the intended initial column did not appear in that venue, and was instead published as "The Road You Walk Is Thorny, My Son" in the program for the 1990 Georgia Fantasy Con.

# The Road You Walk
## Is Thorny, My Son
### Intended for *The Streets* 1: 21 June 1990

Years ago there was a phrase in common use all across America that made a terrific impression on kids, and they heard it a lot: "You go to your church, and I'll go to mine, but we'll walk along together."

Always thought that was the kind of righteous, kindhearted, and humane thinking that was the essence of a civilized, democratic society. Now, I'm sure it didn't have nearly the same meaning for a black kid and a white kid in Alabama, both of them scuffling through the red dust toward their houses of worship; but I was a kid in Ohio, and it *seemed* to be the way matters were handled back then.

It's a different kettle of icons these days.

No matter to which creed one subscribes, the concept of god has fallen on hard times.

One should always try to judge a movement or a belief or a nation's ethics by the example of its *best* adherents, not its weirdest or loudest or most reprehensible. That rule of thumb notwithstanding, god seems to be getting a lousy rap these days as thugs, liars, degenerates, and tv preachers who owe more to three-card monte hustlers than to Mother Teresa take god's name as endorsement for brutal if not outright lunatic behavior.

Slope-browed, prognathous-jawed skinheads spray-paint swastikas here and there; homophobic halfwits declaim from pulpits and the floors of state legislatures that AIDS is "god's punishment" against gays and lesbians; Son of Sam talked to god through his dog, and the pooch said, "slaughter the bitches"; Islamic fundamentalists are so uncertain in their faith that they chase into hiding—and put out a contract on—a mere writer of

111

fiction who dared to voice a few satirical questions about god's nature; and in Jerusalem a few months ago an Israeli Arab poet was placed under house arrest because the government was certain his "blasphemous" verse would incite riots. In Northern Ireland, in the name of god, Protestants and Catholics continue, after 500 years, to butcher each other vowing that any minute now one or the other side will locate the stolen Holy Grail. In South Africa, militant apartheidists justify tyranny with the familiar excuse, "god is on our side."

And televangelists haven't yet caught on to the real reason their coffers are depleted. It's not so much that their point-men have been caught getting it on with women who look like Texas roadhouse jukebox queens, or have been busted with love donations in satchels as they waited at the Varig ticket counter for a flight to Rio. It is that they can no longer maintain the level of benighted hysteria necessary to keep their flocks doling out the cash to help god stop rock music, Saturday morning cartoons, novels by Salinger, the use of condoms, the progress of science, and the burning of the American flag. That level of terror having been abandoned, the faithful have moved on to worship at a new altar: the Church of the Home Shopping Network. Same fervor, same intensity, same dedication to the old tried-and-true "traditional values" of greed and elitism. The *700 Club* of spending. Why send bucks to Brother Jerry or Brother Jimmy or Bro' Jim Bakker (who'll only squander it on a new Waterslide for Christ) when that same fifty dollars can be sent to QVC or HSN, brightening one's faith and knickknack shelf with a genuine Capodimonte porcelain figurine of the Madonna (modeled after Madonna, including the little mole), hand-painted by third world artisans chained to their worktables in boiler-room operations run by entrepreneurs in silk shantung suits. The response to the gospel of "god loves a consumer" is putting the fire-and-brimstone crowd out of business faster than a spate of States' Attorneys.

So here we are, this "one nation under god"—and when *I* learned the Pledge of Allegiance, back in Ohio, that "under god" business wasn't part of the litany—and I'm not sure just which god that's supposed to be.

Is it the god who says it's okay to pump up with Jack Daniels, put the pedal to the metal, and centerpunch some old lady crossing the street in Tustin, knock her sixty feet into a stop sign, open her up like a casaba melon, and then speed away looking for an Earl Cheib shop to cover the dents and spattered brains?

Is it the god who tells a yotz like ex-Secretary of the Interior James Watt that it's okay to give all that watershed land in the Parks Bill to American Plywood so they can build low-cost housing along Mulholland Drive at two-million a unit, on the strictly rational theory that, "When the Apocalypse comes, those who believe will be lifted up anyway, so what does it matter if our grandchildren never see a tree?"

Is it the god invoked by Jesse Helms when he tells us that the National Endowment for the Arts condones "ungodly and evil works of trash?"

Or is it the god who had nothing better to do than make the ball stick to the fingers of a running back who, after he's done his gyrations in the end-zone, drops to his knees and does a little male-bonding with that Great Coach in the Sky?

Is god really in favor of our retaining control of the Panama Canal, but against abortion? I tried reaching god last week, in hopes of getting a few answers. I mean, if Brother Jerry and Brother Jimmy and Bro' Jim Bakker get these frequent communiqués, why not a few words for a sincere journalist?

I'm given to understand that "it is not for us to know the mysterious ways of the lord" but I figured, whatthehell, I'd give it a try. So I tuned in to the J.C. Penney channel, got down on my woven pastel area rug ($39.95) in my Dick Tracy jogging suit ($54.95) and I called on god to say a few words to me.

Well, imagine my delight when god appeared to me, in a Burning Bush, right there in front of my Sony ($456.75). And god spoke to me. Yes, s/he did.

Unfortunately, I didn't understand a word, because I don't speak Bush.

And if you think I'm being frivolous, that I'm not being absolutely sincere about all this, let me assure you that I am exactly and precisely as sincere, not one whit less sincere, than Brother Jerry and Brother Jimmy and Bro' Jim Bakker.

Or: to quote from George Orwell, "There are some situations from which one can only escape by acting like a devil or a lunatic." Have a peachy day.

# 1: 19 July 1990

Finally figured out what's Wrong With America.

It's not only that we suffer from the worst case of cultural amnesia since the eradication of the Cherokee Nation was deified in history texts as Manifest Destiny. It's not just that we've aspirated our own endless hype about how John Wayne we are, how Jack Armstrong we are, as Japan kicks our fundament economically, intellectually, imaginatively. Nor is it simply that we've gorged ourselves on the Forbidden Twinkie from the Tree of GimmeGimme in the Garden of Greeden.

One could shudder, I suppose, when confronted by a stat from the National Assessment of Educational Progress that shows 70% of 8000 17-year-old students queried didn't know what the hell the Magna Carta was—but according to a survey taken by the National Science Foundation, between 64–65% of the 2000 respondents believed lasers work by focusing sound waves and that the earliest human beings lived at the same time as the dinosaurs. (Ah, but don't tremble! According to a recent Gallup Youth Survey, at least 95% of the representative national cross-section interviewed believed in the existence of angels, ESP, Bigfoot, ghosts, the Loch Ness Monster, and the efficacy of astrology in predicting the solutions to daily problems. Now don't that make you breathe easier?)

Sure, it's easy to take the line of accepted wisdom that says we're a nation of know-nothings, with a national average of intelligence on the level of something that makes its home in a petri dish. Yeah, we could go along with all those fuzzy-minded intellectuals who tell us that continued exposure to slasher films and the laissez-faire floating ethics of Michael Milken, Pete Rose, and Marion Barry has unraveled the fabric of our ethics

115

to the point where news of the homeless makes us yawn. We could buy into that knee-jerk liberal codswallop, sure we could.

But that isn't what lies at the core of our National Malaise.

The answer lies not in Washington D.C. or Sacramento, cannot be codified in the canyons of Wall Street or the underground missile silos near Denver, escapes explanation at the Harvard Business School and in the halls of CBS where decisions are made about the national character. What's wrong with us is Yorba Linda.

Now, I know this is going to go down smooth, like a demitasse of warm hair and Drano, but Yorba Linda is this nothing sort of burg about twenty-five miles northeast of Disneyland, appropriately enough, where pop. 30,000 is currently experiencing the galvanic twitch of a frog-leg with a live wire in it. On July 19th, Yorba Linda got itself finally on the map as something other than a running joke about being so dead that for a hot time you gotta go portage to Fullerton on a wild Saturday night.

On July 19th, Yorba Linda dedicated the $21 million Richard M. Nixon Presidential Library & Birthplace, on the same day that Pete Rose got sentenced in Cincinnati; and if you squint your eyes very hard and masticate about six pages of Thoreau's ON MAN AND NATURE you can discern a dismaying connection. For on that splendiferous day of 50,000 red white & blue helium balloons and "peace doves" let fly, a hero went down to disgrace, and a lying, treacherous paranoid was feted as having "repaired his image."

Hundreds of acres and a 52,000 square foot library (filled with Xerox copies of papers Nixon already sold for big bucks) have been dedicated to the greater glory of the man who said (in the Washington *Star-News*, 9 November 1972), "The average American is just like the child in the family."

And everyone makes a big who-struck-John about how the money to build this Parthenon of the Putrescent came not from the taxpayers, but from the pockets of private citizens, most of whom rode Nixon's gravy train to financial fecundity. Yes, indeed, the 21-mil was raised by Maurice Stans, and who should be surprised? For, if we recall correctly, and we do, Maurice Hubert Stans was Dick Nixon's Secretary of Commerce from '69 till '72, at which point he became Finance Chairman for The Committee to Re-Elect the President (meanspiritedly referred to as CREEP). And though he managed to get through the Watergate minefield reasonably intact, he's the upstanding citizen who was indicted for conspiracy to suppress a federal investigation of Nixon's chum Robert Vesco; he's the fund-raising whiz who, in March of '75, was convicted in Washington Federal Court of five counts of violating campaign fund-raising laws. Yessir, Maury Stans is a name beloved in Yorba Linda these days and nights.

Because they are days and nights filled with the tinkle of tourist coins. San Clemente—which had a chance to be the situs of the Nixon Memorial Apologia Atrium—must be kicking itself these days. They opted for slow growth and being able to look in a mirror without seeing the Swamp Thing. But think of all that lost revenue: hotel and motel business, conventions, trinket shops and souvenir doodads, guided tours, four-color pamphlets explaining how Nixon "opened" China.

Just think how much Yorba Lindoids will derive from this paroxysm of self-delusion and grotesque rhetoric, as 25,000 braindamaged visitors to the opening ceremony queue up to buy videotape knockoffs of the Checkers Speech at $39.95 per cassette. Think what a future lies just beyond that rough-hewn little hut where Dick was born! They can expand. They can build out and up!

The Milhous Theme Park, featuring the trickle-down water-slide; the House of Fiscal Mirrors in which civil rights and patriotism get their reflections warped beyond recognition; the Pirates of the Pentagon ride, featuring Agnew, Haldeman, Haig, and Westmoreland; the Pat Buchanan forelock-tugging pavilion; the Kissinger Small World attraction, in which the endlessly repeated themesong turns nasty gang kids into brainwashed consumers. Pin the tail on the Ellsberg, throw a pie at a clever lookalike of Helen Gahagan Douglas, shoot a peacenik at the Tet Offensive shooting gallery. It's Yorba Linda, America! Home of the Library extolling the ability of one man to make an entire nation ashamed of itself.

And then they can erect ancillary attractions, just as Anaheim has done. The Charles Manson Waxworks and Chamber of Slaughter. The Benedict Arnold Hall of Shame. The Wounded Knee Frontier Village. And perhaps later, maybe, a life-size replica of Babi Yar, as part of the Josef Stalin Spa and Fat Farm.

You know what's wrong with America?

It's not that we're stupid, or that we forget the past, or that we have all the sophistication of a turnip-truck hayseed playing three-card monte on a streetcorner.

The trouble with America is that we don't hold a grudge long enough.

## 2: 25 September 1990

Like Swaggart and Meese, he used the name of the Lord to good advantage.

There's no knowing what might have happened by the time you get to read this—he may well be out there sucking the necks of gullible octogenarians again—but as I write these words, the ass of Charles H. Keating, Jr., the multimillionaire who got fat off the backs of more than 22,000 investors of American Continental Corporation and the Irvine-based Lincoln Savings & Loan, is developing hemorrhoids sleeping on a hard metal bunk in the L.A. County Jail.

And how do I feel about this? Picture, if you will, a panel from a Marvel Comic, in which Dr. Doom is standing over a map of the world, laughing demonically, head thrown back, arms spread wide, and shouting, "Today, Latveria! Tomorrow, the World!!" And then lots more of that demented villain laughter.

That's how I feel about Keating's butt being in Durance Vile.

Right, right, I know: one should be gracious and not delight in the fall of one's enemies. Be a good winner as well as a good loser. Don't be like Bush, who kept running off at the mouth about The Death of Communism and How We Finally Won, Hurray Fer Us...until his advisors said, "George, fer chrissakes, cool it, willya! The Wall's coming down, Gorby's got reorganization problems up the ying-yang, and you wandering around going, 'Nyah nyah nyah' isn't helping matters."

But I remember when I was ten years old, back in 1944, and there was this semi-scandalous novel called LEAVE HER TO HEAVEN by Ben Ames Williams, that sold more than two million copies in hardcover; and I sneaked a reading of it under the covers, with a flashlight, having liberated my mother's Literary Guild copy; and it made a strong case for God, or the Universe, or Cosmic Justice, or somesuch, always zapping evil *momsers* with a bolt of lightning, the way Salman Rushdie is fried in that popular Iranian film *International Commandos*. And I really and truly believed in that "leave them to heaven" nonsense, until I got old enough to see things like Nixon not being clapped in irons, and white collar thugs getting a slap on the wrist and then retiring to their villas at Cap Ferrat, and Anita Bryant actually dying and being reincarnated as Phyllis Schlafly.

I came to understand that if you are a big enough crook you can always weasel out of the worst of it.

Which is why I am running around like Dr. Doom, laughing demonically, and proclaiming all's right with the world.

Because it's not just that Keating seems to be a crook and a liar and maybe even an embezzler with about as much morality as Abu Nidal, it is that I lived long enough to see Keating, with whom I had a run-in in 1959 in Evanston, Illinois, shorn of his sanctimonious, bible-thumping, mendacious hypocrisy and left to stand naked before America as the ethically-arid heir to the mantle of Cotton Mather, Torquemada, and Joe McCarthy that I always knew him to be.

This whited sepulcher, this paragon of the virtues, this lean and distinguished pillar of the community who masterminded the hustle of uninsured, high-risk junk bonds that will cost taxpayers more than $2 billion, is the guy who, for the last thirty-four years, has been running around the country making sure we understand the perils of "moral anarchy." That is to say, Mr. Keating has been a highly-vocal, highly-visible foe of the demon, *Porn*-Ography!

So, yeah, sure, he's a loathsome blob of ambulatory phlegm, something that leaves a sticky trail when it passes, a hustler utterly despicable in the eyes of honest cat burglars and car thieves, because he screwed so many "weak, meek, ignorant" old people, whose remaining years have been blighted by the loss of what little they had to sustain them... but his fall is all the more a subject for unbecoming glee because of his endless crusade to dictate right and wrong from the most gussied-up float in the Purity Parade.

Like Swaggart and Bakker and ex-Attorney General Edwin Meese, this protector of public innocence never took the name of the Lord in vain. He took it as cover-up for his own marked-cards, loaded dice, bait-and-switch corruption. From 1956, when he started Citizens for Decent Literature in Cincinnati; through his public pronouncements that hot pants and Bermuda shorts "provide the occasion of sin" that would stamp a demerit in the spiritual ledger for girls who wore them; past his attempt to control the morality of residents in a Phoenix housing project called Estrella, by insisting they sign covenants that permitted the board of directors to enter any home they chose, to remove what they considered "pornographic material deleterious to the community," and gave these petty *Oberstgruppenführers* the right to boot out anybody who had shaken hands with the devil by having had an abortion; to his shrieking minority objection to the findings of the 1969 Presidential Commission on Obscenity and Pornography—on which sanhedrin he sat—when they concluded there was no demonstrable connection between violence toward women and pornography, that adults have a legal right to own that kinda stuff, and that national sex education was a worthwhile endeavor...Keating has always used the name of the Lord to good advantage. His own.

"One who wallows in filth is going to get dirty. This is intuitive knowledge," Keating said, when he tried to drive a stake through the heart of the Commission's report. He also said it in 1959 in Evanston, Illinois, at a town meeting he had engineered through his Cincinnati-based Citizens for Decent Literature. He said it as he stood before a jam-packed hall of god-fearing, decent folks; and behind him was a long table stacked high high *high* with smutty magazines and redolent novels and brain-destroying obscenity in every printed form.

He looked like Andy Hardy's dad, the Judge. He was slim and charismatic, well-spoken and passionate. And he strode around the front of that hall, now and then picking up one or another icon of sexual idolatry, riffling its pages, shaking it like a shaman's rattle at the goggle-eyed citizens who could damned near see the steam of perversion rising off that mound of unspeakable filth. He was good.

I was in that audience. I was there at the request of the publisher who had hired me straight out of the Army to edit *Rogue* magazine, a coat-tail imitation of the then-fledgling *Playboy*, whose offices were just over the line in Chicago. The offices of *Rogue* were in Evanston.

At the break, Keating invited everyone to come up and paw the degrading smut piled hurly-burly on that table. "Perhaps we should issue rubber gloves," he said. More than thirty years since he said it, and I heard it: never forgot the smug little smile he wore as he got that one off.

So I went on up there, and I looked through the goods. We're talking 1959 here. Long before *Last Tango in Paris* and string bikinis and *Hustler*. Lemme tell you, the raciest item on that table was maybe the blinding sight on pulp paper of Bettie Page's left breast. No nipple showing.

And there was, among that congeries of trivialities, the one odd item that served as catalyst for my lone encounter with Charles H. Keating, Jr., the Masked Rider of Rectitude. And I smiled. As I smile now, thinking of Keating in the pokey.

When the meeting was called to order again, and the floor was thrown open to questions, I bided my time through a couple of queries, and then I raised my hand, was noticed by Keating, and stood. I was in the second row.

"Mr. Keating," I said, "during the break I went up there and examined some of the materials you've called pornography. You told us earlier that you had personally selected this stuff to show us. Is that correct?"

He acknowledged that I was quoting him accurately.

"And—correct me if I'm wrong—you said earlier that exposure to this material would plant evil thoughts in innocent minds, that it was corrupting, malevolent filth that would pollute our precious bodily fluids, strike us blind, grow hair on the palms of our hands...am I pretty close to what you said?"

He smelled a rat. "Well, sir, I certainly wouldn't have used *those* words—"

"But that's the general idea, am I right?"

"Well, yes."

"And you've personally selected all this stuff, which I suppose means that *you* looked through the magazines, and read the books, and suchlike? That's what you said, correct?"

He nodded. I moved out of the row, into the aisle, up to the front of the room, past Keating, and yanked a paperback novel off the stacks. "Everything? Even *this* one?"

"Yes, all of them," he said.

"Well, then," I said, looking not at him but at the hushed crowd that knew something was afoot, "can you explain what there is of a pornographic or obscene nature in this novel of juvenile delinquency that has been adopted by more than a hundred Police Athletic League social workers in New York as a positive deterrent to street violence, a book that has been lauded by the Catholic Archdiocese of New York as a force for good, that was selected by the *School Library Journal* as a book espousing the highest values for young people? I ask, sir, because *I* am the author of this book."

He tried to back and fill. "Well, it's possible that one or another item has found its way into this group of materials by accident, that..."

"But you said you'd read it *all*, Mr. Keating!"

"Well..."

"So you *haven't* read it all, have you? And since what you *have* read of all this stuff has not, clearly, corrupted *you*, has not polluted *your* precious bodily fluids, are we to take from this that you are somehow closer to the Holy Spirit and can combat these noxious influences, while we poor creatures are made of such inferior materials that we would surely go straight to the devil, or the gutter, if we indulged as you have?"

Well, Keating didn't have his way that night.

But he had it plenty of other nights; and days; and months. He was a zealot who preached ethics and morality and rectitude and abstention and censorship. And while he squeezed the bible with one hand, the other greasy mitt was fast-shuffling widows and orphans. As a swell scenarist named Richard L. Breen once wrote, in a movie called *Pete Kelly's Blues*, "He's so crooked, they say he's got rubber pockets so he can steal soup."

It isn't nice to gloat, okay, I agree absolutely. And as I write this he hasn't yet been convicted of any of the charges. But it's been more than thirty years since the night in Evanston when that putz Keating tried to lift his leg on the First Amendment, and you'll permit me just one *frisson* of unbridled joy, okay?

How do I feel as I contemplate the twenty-two years that slug Keating may well draw down?

O frabjous day! Callooh! Callay!

# 3: 23 July 1991

It's now alarmingly clear: everyone in the city of Los Angeles was scared of \89 Gates. Cops were scared they were losing the most unassailable revetment between them and a long-overdue examination of their bunker mentality. Politicians up and down the ladder were scared he'd release those "secret files" he kept hinting existed, that he'd fasten his choppers in their throats, and take them down with him. The Mayor was scared his lack of control over Gates and the cops would show the constituency that he's impotent when it comes to big bangs. The minority communities are scared that whatever little protection they get from the boys in blue will vanish out of spite as Gates is deposed. The fat white Wonderbread crowd is scared of the guaranteed instant invasion of The Dreaded Lower Classes when their big stick Gates is broken over the knee of Rodney G. King. The average citizen is just plain scared at Gates's sly threats (noted by Councilman Mike Woo way back on March 20th) that if he goes down, his troops will stand idly by, picking their teeth, as you and I are beaten to death by ball bat and ball peen hammer-wielding thugs and gangbangers who lie in wait for us when we stop to use ATMs after sundown. Gates had everybody scared witless.

It is also clear, even to such dopey supporters of Gates as Erik Estrada's ex-wife, that what it finally took to get the *Oberstgruppenführer* out of power was nothing less than his having made fools out of his toadies on the City Council. Hal Bernson continued, in the face of overwhelming evidence to the contrary, to maintain that the Chief was doing a helluva job, that the beating of Rodney King was (in Gates's circumlocutious forage through the dictionary) "an aberration," that the public's love and admiration were the basis for support of this evil troll, and that we should ignore Paul Conrad's scathing political cartoons in the *Times* that took Gates's own words—"These cops were just a few bad apples in the barrel"—and used them to show the rancid barrel with a rancid-apple-headed Chief beside it. Joy Picus was a female Angeleno version of Josef Goebbels or Saddam Hussein's minister Tariq Aziz, rationalizing each new affront, depredation, and display of strutting hubris as if she were Daryl's own invested Stepford Wife on the City Council. And as for "the deal" allegedly struck, after long negotiation, between Gates and those two poor yokels Joel Wachs and John Ferraro, which they announced so triumphantly (along with the sidebar notation that Tom Bradley hadn't had squat to do with it)...well, if one had a quart of Baskin-Robbins French vanilla, one could have enjoyed an *à la mode* dessert eating off their startled faces.

No sooner did they begin puffing up like pouter pigeons that they had solved the problem, than Gates held a press conference essentially saying they were blowing smoke, that he'd check out when he was damned good and ready. At that point, looking like schmucks, having been betrayed to Gates's overweening ego as the entire community, the LAPD rank and file, and all the Rodney Kings for the last thirteen years had been betrayed, enlightened self-interest was jettisoned, the commonweal was served, and the politicians abandoned their bully-boy. Fear of *our* wrath, in the final analysis, overcame their cowardice of what Gates could do to them.

He was our own local version of J. Edgar Hoover.

He had the same sort of *apparat* deeply entrenched as that which served the late, unlamented FBI monarch who held half a dozen presidents in thrall. Gates and Hoover: secrecy, coverup, internal authority, autonomy, jingoistic public relations, black bag jobs, retaliation, intimidation, free-floating fear of the organization's ability to "get" anybody. Over time—no matter how laudably each began his career—Gates, like Hoover, had become drunk with his own sense of self-importance and indispensability; Gates consciously adopted the *sub rosa* m.o. of Hoover's crisis management: ADMIT NOTHING/DENY EVERYTHING/MAKE COUNTER-ALLEGATIONS; and he wickedly polarized our own police department against us. Not just the crooks and polluters and felons and drive-by shooters...all of us. The citizenry. Anyone who dared to suggest that what we have known for decades—that the LAPD attracts more than a few unstable personalities that should *never* be gifted with authority—became an intolerable certainty. Anyone who dared to suggest that cops cannot be trusted to police themselves. Anyone who dared to suggest that there is a hollow irony to that slogan painted on the door of every squad car: *To Protect and To Serve.*

Gates self-servingly manipulated the institutionalized paranoia of cops to his own ends. He turned the men and women who supposedly *work for us* into a palace guard dedicated to keeping him in office, no matter the heavens fell and the earth split and the populace rose in wrath and demanded the despot be dethroned! (He ought to be driven out of office, if for no other reason, because he gets some of us so pissed off that we write in ridiculously purple prose!)

We may even yet be nothing more than saps, believing as we do that his announcement on July 22nd was cast in stone, that he will be just a bad memory by next April. We have been told by the City Attorney's office that the "letter of intent" (which he promised the LAPD rank and file they would hear about first, and which he then released to the press before the cops knew what was happening, thus lying to them again) has no legal weight. Gates can change his mind. He can weasel and obfuscate and dissemble and say, "Well, I can't retire just yet, because I'm not satisfied a proper replacement for my wonderful self has been selected." Hell, he could declare a state of civic emergency and throw the City Council into concentration camps in the name of "public safety." Who knows *what* this guy is capable of, all in aid of proving how macho he is?

Yet saps that we are, for the moment we accept that Gates will pass through our system and out the other side like strained bananas through a baby's backside come next April.

And the deeper lesson that will surely pass unlearned is that Daryl Gates was merely the latest in a long line of whacky and too-powerful police chiefs that Los Angeles has had to endure, from the thoroughly corrupt 1930s, when you could buy police protection for union-busting or thug patrol, or even a job on the force, through the days of "Hang 'Em High" Bill Parker, who conspired to vanish and alter the evidence at the site of Marilyn Monroe's death, through the brief tenure of Tom Reddin, who spent most of his time getting cross-eyed about "dissidents, trouble makers, anarchists, militant criminals (chiefly Black Panthers), and revolutionaries," to ex-Police Chief, now State Senator, Ed Davis who, until recently, won the hands-down title as Most Demented Head Cop in L.A. History.

(My favorite Ed Davis story is not the one in which he asked the City Council to buy him a submarine so he could thwart drug-running into San Pedro, it's the moment I saw, on tv, a press conference during which Davis announced that "as everyone knows, Women's Lib is the cause of juvenile delinquency." At which point the camera operator panned the assembled media reps, and it was like that great shot in Mel Brooks's *The Producers*, where they do a long pan of the audience watching the "Springtime for Hitler" dance number full of goose-stepping Nazis, and the entire audience is in slack-jawed shock, eyes bulging, disbelief steaming out of their ears. And finally, one brave newspaperwoman raised her hand and asked, "Er, uh, could you, uh, sort of explain how that is, Chief?" And Davis, mad as a mudfly, but as seemingly bolted together as Gates in *his* regular sound bites, responded [as if the questioner had missed school the day that was covered], "Well, *everyone* knows that women are out making careers, trying to 'fulfill themselves' or something like that, and they aren't staying home and taking care of the housework and the kids, so the kids are out running around the streets, causing delinquent behavior, and that's why Women's Lib is the cause of..." And everyone just glazed over and nodded patronizingly, the way you do when Earl Long says *Vote for me, I am not a nut!*

(In all conscience, and much to my bewilderment, I must admit that Ed Davis has been a startlingly effective senator. Don't ask me how that happened. Maybe when one becomes chief of the LAPD a brain miasma settles, turning one into a demento; and the minute one's ass is kicked out of office, sanity returns, along with a freightload of chagrin, and one spends the rest of one's days in abject public service. Maybe.)

Since 1978, when he was appointed, Gates spent his best efforts solidifying his power base. Check out news-clips of those zombie chanting audiences at pro-Gates rallies. "Gates must stay! Gates must stay!" (And wasn't it a sweet sip of *déjà vu* to have seen Gates in Jesse Helms country, out there in redneck North Carolina, being cheered in just the same way, suggesting that them crackers ought to move to L.A., where he could use their All-Amurrican support against the vile forces of ACLU darkness.) Consider that one of the Chief's biggest defenders was Council President John Ferraro, who just happened to be President of the L.A. Police Commission, which didn't do shit to implement the findings of the *last* big probe into police brutality, the McCone Commission report on the Watts riots of 1965. And he has continually sent the scintillant message from on high, to the ranks, "It's Us against Them, boys!"

If you were going to cast a film and you needed someone to play the chilly, soft-spoken, amoral basketball coach who forces the star player to get out there despite the certainty that the kid's arrhythmic heart will explode, a guy who uses threats of revoking the kid's scholarship (the sort of role usually assayed by G.D. Spradlin), you couldn't do better than to cast the late Daryl Gates.

If you were looking to fill the role of the smooth, high-verbal corporate executive covering up the midnight dumping of toxic waste by sacrificing his puppy-faithful vice president, you would be dead on target casting the recent Daryl Gates.

If you needed a player for the role of the CIA liaison in a war-torn Latin American banana republic, explaining to the wife of a missing dissident that "the government is looking into this, just trust me," you would have a shot at glory come Oscar time if you gave the role to the former Daryl Gates.

His endless performances on television, down to those last videotapes shown in the precincts, were an unparalleled demonstration of duplicity, hubris, and weaseling that finally nauseated even the most loyal, resulting, at the end, in a slippage of his public support to the tune of 83% negative get the hell outta there Gates opinion. Yet it still seemed, through May, June, July that the only thing that could make him go away was an enema with a thermite bomb.

He was the gargoyle that had taken possession of the cathedral.

This arrogant, swaggering petty dictator had so terrified the 8345 men and women who make up the LAPD that all they could think of was hatred for George Holliday, whose videotape (at first offered to the cops, who chose to reject it, thereby causing their own exposure) denied them the usual obfuscation of lack of smoking gun attendant on such past depredations as the beating of blues singer Jimmy Witherspoon in 1952, the six days of Watts riots in 1965 during which 34 were killed and 1004 were wounded, the still-suspicious death of Chicano activist and journalist Ruben Salazar, smashed flat by an LAPD tear gas cannister in August 1970, the shooting of Eulia Love in 1979, and the dozens and dozens of other instances of extreme force applied by psychopaths masquerading as police officers, as authenticated by the Christopher Commission report.

*This* time we saw it.

*This* time it wasn't just that lawbreaking, PCP-crazed, gun-wielding, officer-resisting nigger bastard's word against the frosty, well-mannered, I have it all written down here in my report officer. *This* time we saw what we've all known for a long time: There *are* LAPD officers who ought to be off the streets.

A writer named Theodore Sturgeon once wrote that because they are forced to deal with criminality all the time, cops begin to behave like the prey they pursue. He suggested that the only way to make it possible for decent law enforcement personnel to keep their heads straight, to stay in tune with the people they've been hired to protect, would be for cops to serve five days on duty, and then five days working on a farm, or tending children in a day care center. Well, that may be rose-colored glasses; but what are we to do with a system that produces Sgt. Stacey C. Koon and all the cops on whose behalf we taxpayers have paid out more than $35 million during the past decade in judgments and awards due to police misconduct?

What are we to do to demonstrate that the Gates mentality will no longer be tolerated?

Cops always justify their behavior by telling us that there are people out there with guns trying to kill them.

My response is like that of Sam Kinison yelling at starving Ethiopians that, yes, of course they're starving: *you live in a goddam desert!* Move to where there's water, like Minneapolis, and you won't be starving in a desert.

Of *course* there are people trying to shoot at you, Officer! That's what happens when you're a cop. Even granting all the nut-cases running loose, the chances of getting shot are a lot less if you've decided on being a reference librarian or a garage mechanic or a chimney sweep, than working on the SWAT team. But if, like Daryl Gates, you conceive of everyone not in LAPD uniform as someone out to get you, someone out to kill and debase you, then perhaps you shouldn't have been gifted with the power and authority of being gun-hipped, badge-protected, prowl car-armored. Maybe you ought to go work on a farm for five days, or take care of kids whose fingers are too small and weak to pull a trigger.

And having written all this, I would not want you to get the idea that I am anything less than fearless. Nonetheless, let me add that I do not use drugs, and as anyone who has read my books knows, I have never been able to drink alcohol, even as lightweight as a beer. So when you get up one morning soon after this column is published, and you tune in KNX for the news, and you hear that writer Harlan Ellison was arrested and thrown in jail for driving under the influence, and that half a dozen officers of the LAPD were forced to kick the shit out of 5'5" Ellison who resisted arrest, and that they found $150,000 worth of street-quality cocaine in his glove compartment, would one of you out there call my attorney, Henry W. Holmes, Jr., and let him know that I've been set up?

On the other hand, if Ellison was shot dead resisting arrest, just chalk it up to another smartass who didn't know when to keep his yap shut.

Until then, however, I'll accept (like the rest of you saps) that Gates will be taking a hike by April, or sooner. Not only will I believe that Daryl will be getting out of our face, I will also believe that Ferraro and Picus and that crowd will select, for the first time in fifty years, a police chief who gives a shit about the people he's sworn to protect and to serve.

Oh, and I'd also like Santa to bring me a cure for my herpes, and a choo-choo train, and…

Editor's Note: Daryl Gates finally left the LADP on 28 June 1992.

# T'anks but No Tokes

Basically, fuck dope. No offense, dude, but: fuck dope.

This has virtually nothing to do with the subject at hand, but as deep background permit me this brief preamble:

I ran away from home at age thirteen. I'd already been earning my living for three or four years prior to that, apart from mooching off my parents in Painesville, Ohio. I mean, I was nine or ten, fer chrissakes, so when I say "I was earning my own living" I *mean* I was paying for everything a kid of nine or ten in the early Forties would need money for: 10¢ admission every Saturday afternoon to the Lake Theater, the latest issue of *Big Shot Comics* featuring Skyman and Tony Trent as The Face, an occasional Grosset & Dunlap hardcover of a Lone Ranger novel ($2 each) bylined Fran Striker, who had created the radio show and the character, but actually ghostwritten by the unsung Gaylord DuBois, a new pair of U.S. Keds hightops with the big red ball on the side, a Tom Mix "nuclear bombardment chamber" radio premium ring for ten cents and two Ralston Purina box tops, a bottle of Teel tooth drops, some Fleer's Double Bubble...I earned the money for such staples by selling the Sunday edition of the Cleveland *Plain Dealer* every Saturday night at the corner of State and Main Streets, by shining shoes at that same excellent location, by mowing lawns raking leaves shoveling snow catching flies cleaning garages and attics.

Back in the days before the discovery of Cultural Guilt and the advent of the Victim Society, that was how us lower middle-class white boys paid our way. It was a hardscrabble existence for Clark Bars.

And then I ran away. And began to earn my keep *for real*. No mommy bargaining that if I'd eat my peas and carrots I could stay up an hour later to hear *Big Town* or *The Hermit's Cave*. No father saying if I cleaned my room, I could come downtown after he closed the store on Saturday night and we'd have hot roast beef sandwiches and french fries at Jerry & Bert's. It was *La Strada*, dude. I was on the road, sans bucks, sans mommy/daddy, sans even Kerouac—who wouldn't be published yet for another decade.

I worked farms and orchards, picking crops. I bluffed my way into truck driving jobs on construction sites. I worked in a lumber camp, on tuna boats, door-to-door salesman, short order cook, printer's devil and slag-bucket carrier in a lithographing plant, garbage collector. I worked in a carnival, on a road gang, in a quarry, standing by the side of the road selling bouquets of flowers. I lied to farmers' wives and told them I could repair the busted washing machine (or mangle, or stove, or hot plate) out there rusting in the side yard, in exchange for a meal. I rode the rods, I drank gypsy coffee out of a tin can with Princes of the Road under railroad trestles in ten different states, I had my ass saved a hundred times by men of many other colors, and I was locked up in the old Kansas City slam with a carny geek who had gone "wetbrain" so long ago that the scent of rancid sour mash came out of his pores when he sweated. I saw what liquor and dope had to offer.

I have been around drugs all my life.

I came back with Chinese food one night, to a sleazy railroad flat I was sharing with a beautiful girl, and found her dead, naked, o.d. in the tub. The water was still warm. I actually heard Charlie Parker blow, one night, at a $1.00 admission rent and spaghetti party up on 101st and First Avenue in Harlem; and he went into the can, went Charlie "Bird" Parker, and he fixed, and he came out, and he blew...crap. Discordant shit. I heard the great legend Bird blow, only that once, a year or two before he died, and he sounded like shit. From the dope.

Here is the subject at hand:

I have been on the street since I was thirteen. I have learned important stuff about staying alive.

I have learned that sneaky bastards and kindhearted slobs come in all colors. I have learned that you're never as smart as you think you are. I have learned that love is rare but cowardice is plentiful. I believe that anything not nailed down is mine. And anything I can pry loose...ain't nailed down.

All through the Sixties and Seventies, going to parties and just hanging, this one or that one would offer me a hit of this or a lid of that. Drop one of these, stick this in your instep, shove this spansule up your ass, honk a line of this, inhale a vape of this...

I always said, no thanks.

I wasn't afraid. Ask anyone who knows me. I don't scare. Simply put, I didn't want any part of that crap. When someone would thrust a doobie the size of a Macanudo under my nose and intone the magic word, "Toke?" I'd reply, with a sweet smile, "Not till I come down."

Theodore Sturgeon (if you don't recognize the name, go look it up, you ignorant asshole) once wrote that he'd seen studies of people who allegedly produced psilocybin in the bloodstream. He opined that I was like that...always high. Otherwise, how to explain all the weird stuff I've done in my life?

The subject at hand is Krassner asking me to write my "dope story" for his idiot book. Here it is. Fuck dope, oh, and...

Have a nice day.

Editor's Note: The preceding piece served as the introduction to *High Times*'s POT STORIES FOR THE SOUL, edited by Paul Krassner. One can only assume Ellison was commissioned to introduce a book for purposes of irony.

Theodore Sturgeon, whose opinions have been featured in the two preceding pieces will return in...

"Abiding with Sturgeon: Mistral in the Bijou" originally appeared in the May 2007 issue of *Interzone* before serving as the introduction to North Atlantic Books's THE NAIL AND THE ORACLE: THE COMPLETE STORIES OF THEODORE STURGEON, Volume XI, edited by Paul Williams. This antepenultimate volume of the sixteen-year publication of Sturgeon's *oeuvre* contained both 1967's "If All Men Were Brothers, Would You Let One Marry Your Sister?" (which Ellison commissioned for DANGEROUS VISIONS) and 1970's "Runesmith" (the Ellison/Sturgeon collaboration first collected in the former's PARTNERS IN WONDER).

## Abiding with Sturgeon:
## Mistral in the Bijou

It is unlikely that I could have worshipped him more, the day he came to live with me, had his knock on my door been accompanied by thunder and roses. Let us get this clear between us, right from the git-go: I admired Ted Sturgeon more than words can codify. Not just the writing, but much of the man. Not just the art and craft, but the flawed weird duck who schlepped them.

We both smoked pipes, but Ted tamped his bowl full of a *grape*-flavored tobacco so sweetly and sickly redolent it could stun a police dog. I was a little over thirty-five years old when Sturgeon came to live with me. Ted was just fluttering his wings around age fifty.

Herewith, the (by actual count) eleventh time I have started to write this recondite introduction to Volume XI of the North Atlantic Books collected *oeuvre* of the iconic H. Hunter Theodore Waldo Sturgeon, simply a Great Writer of Our Time. In preparation for this day—one I had foolishly hoped would never come—I have worried this exercise as would a pit bull with an intruder. But now it's here, and now I have dawdled and postponed and evaded to the point where I got put in the hospital for a couple of days. Evaded? As would the helot duck the knout! Ten times before I sat down here, put my two typing fingers on the keyboard of the stout Olympia manual office machine (that Ted sometimes usurped when he was here), and ten times I have said awfuckit and torn out the paper. Ten times. Now eleven. And everyone is screaming at me for my seemingly dilatory behavior.

And here's the flat of it, friends.

And Ted would understand.

Most of what I know about Ted Sturgeon, I cannot tell you.


In preparation for this endeavor, I have gone back and done my homework: I have reread all the guest forewords in the ten previous volumes: all twelve in ten big fat wonderful congeries of Ted's phantasmagoria—twelve in ten? Yeah, there were three in volume one—and let me assure you: this will not be a learned, long-bearded exegesis such as Chip Delany's, even though both Chip's and Ted's beards have inspired awe. Ah, but that's just splitting hairs. Nor will it be a charming and pop-pastoral reminiscence overflowing with the chirrups of songbirds reeling through Disneyesque delusions courtesy of LSD, à la Dave Crosby's piece that leads off Volume VI (though both of these friends of mine downed more acid than your local neighborhood hiatic hernia)...


a pause, if you'll indulge me. I never did drugs. Probably because I was on the road at an early age and saw what it could do to the creative process. But Ted did stuff, and I have neither the inclination nor the information to comment on what effect it had on him. But what I wanted to tell you was a sweet little moment tangential to the whole substance thing, and it was this:

Ted and I were at a party thrown by a brilliant young poet named Paul Robbins; something like 1967. Everybody was toke'n and somebody passed me a doob the size of a stegosaurus coprolith, and I passed it on to Ted, sitting next to me. And, naturally, some yotz, whose paranoid orientation conned him into a sense of an ill wind blowing in the room, snarked at me, "Whassamatter, you don't want a hit?" And before I could tell him to mind his own, Ted said (in that lovely tenor), "Harlan won't use till he comes down."

I couda kissed him. And years later, Ted, commenting on how my stories could seem so hallucinatory when I'd never done drugs, told an interviewer, "Harlan is the only person I know who produces psilocybin in his bloodstream." Couda kissed him again.

Uh, for the record, Ted and I never kissed.

Although two men kissing is fine, just fine. Just saying.


...and this foreword will not be a well-intentioned and elegant homage to someone never met by the Introducing Entity, such as Jonathan Lethem's nice piece of Volume X; and it sure as hell isn't going to be a noblesse oblige accommodation such as the one my old chum Kurt Vonnegut proffered in Volume VIII.

It will no doubt upset the faithful, dismay the shy, outrage the punctilious, and get both Publisher and Series Editor to get off the trolley at downtown nose-outta-jointville. Complaints; oh yes, there will be complaints. I get a lot of complaints about my manner.

Yeah, well, if Ted or I had ever given much of a foof about the penalties pursuant to living our lives by our own manner, we sure as hell wouldn't have behaved the way we did, and still do.

But it is the eleventh attempt to climb this Nanga Parbat, in for a penny is in for a pound, either I do it or I don't. Had I my druthers, I wouldn't. But since Ted called me before he died to say he wanted *me* to do his obit...

...since we're in it together at this point, let me pause again to reprint some words. This is what I wrote for *Locus* an hour and a half after Ted died. It was on the first page of that "journal of record" of the science fiction world, June 1985, issue #293 if you care to check.

### Theodore Sturgeon Dies

It began raining in Los Angeles tonight at almost precisely the minute Ted Sturgeon died in Eugene, Oregon. Edward Hamilton Waldo would have cackled at the cosmic silliness of it; but I didn't. It got to me; tonight, May 8th, 1985.

It had been raining for an hour, and the phone rang. Jayne Sturgeon said, "Ted left us an hour ago, at 7:59."

I'd been expecting it, of course, because I'd talked to him--as well as he could gasp out a conversation with the fibrosis stealing his breath-- early in March, long distance to Haiku, Maui, Hawaii. Ted had written his last story for me, for the MEDEA project, and we'd sent him the signature plates for the limited edition. He said to me, "I want you to write the eulogy."

I didn't care to think about that. I said, "Don't be a pain in the ass, Ted. You'll outlive us all." Yeah, well, he <u>will</u>, on the page; but he knew he was dying, and he said it again, and insisted on my promise. So I promised him I'd do it, and a couple of weeks ago I came home late one night to find a message

on my answering machine: it was Ted, and he'd come
home, too. Come home to Oregon to die, and he was
calling to say goodbye. It was only a few words,
huskingly spoken, each syllable taking it out of him,
and he gave me his love, and he reminded me of my
promise; and then he was gone.

Now I have to say important words, extracted from a
rush of colliding emotions. About a writer and a man
who loomed large, whose faintest touch remains on
everyone he ever met, whose talent was greater than the
vessel in which it was carried, whose work influenced
at least two generations of the best young writers, and
whose brilliance remains as a reminder that this poor
genre of dreams and delusions can be literature.

Like a very few writers, his life was as great a
work of artistic creation as the stories. He was no
myth, he was a legend. Where he walked, the ether was
disturbed by his passage.

For some, he was the unicorn in the garden; for
others, he was a profligate who'd had ten hot years as
the best writer in the country, regardless of cat-
egorizations (even the categorization that condemned
him to the ghetto); for young writers he was an icon;
for the old hands who'd lived through the stages of
his unruly life he was an unfulfilled promise. Don't
snap at me for saying this: he liked the truth, and he
wouldn't care to be remembered sans limps and warts
and the hideous smell of that damned grape-scented
pipe tobacco he smoked.

But who the hell needs the truth when the loss
is still so painful? Maybe you're right; maybe we
shouldn't speak of that.

It's only been an hour and a half since Jayne
called, as I write this, and my promise to Ted makes
me feel like the mommy who has to clean up her kid's
messy room. I called CBS radio, and I called the
Herald-Examiner, and that will go a ways toward
getting him the hail-and-farewell I think he wanted,
even though I know some headline writer will say SCI-
FI WRITER STURGEON DEAD AT 67.

And the kid on the night desk at the newspaper took
the basics--Ted's age, his real name, the seven kids,
all that--and then he said, "Well, can you tell me
what he was known for? Did he win any awards?" And I

```
got crazy. I said, with an anger I'd never expected
to feel, "Listen, sonny, he's only gone about an hour
and a half, and he was as good as you get at this
writing thing, and no one who ever read THE DREAMING
JEWELS or MORE THAN HUMAN or WITHOUT SORCERY got away
clean because he could squeeze your heart till your life
ached, and he was one of the best writers of the last
half a century, and the tragedy of his passing is that
you don't know who the fuck he was!" And then I hung
up on him, because I was angry at his ignorance, but
I was really angry at Ted's taking off like that, and
I'm angry that I'm trying to write this when I don't
know what to write, and I'm furious as hell that Ted
made me promise to do this unthinkable thing, which is
having to write a eulogy for a man who could have
written his own, or any other damned thing, better
than I or any of the rest of us could do it.
                                    —Harlan Ellison
```

...and since Noël won't spill the beans in *her* tureen, yet expects *me* to do it—"Get in there and suck up them bullets!" she said sweetly—even though she knows most of what I know—though not even between us can we seem to make the dates properly coincide—at least I have a living witness that what I write here is true. Ted's daughter and the Trustee of his Literary Estate; she has read this and vetted this.

Other forewords in this series have brilliantly dissected Ted's style, analyzed his widening circle effect on other writers...

When I encounter the encomia of other writers about Sturgeon, and they gush something like, "I learned so much from him," or "his work taught me how to write," I think they are either fools, or they're lying. No, wait, that's unfair: not lying...deluding themselves; so stunned by what Ted could do seemingly effortlessly, oblivious to what agony accompanied the doing of it, that they've become tropes of what Stephen King noticed about writers, if you leave sour milk open in the refrigerator, pretty soon *everything* in the box takes on the smell.

Yes, he certainly laid down a new architectural elevation every time a story left his nest (onward, madly onward flew the farraginous metaphors); and to be sure, any scribbling idiot can perceive his facility with language, like a pizza chef whirling that expansible crust aloft; and no question that there are glimmers of Ted's auctorial seminar *every*where these days; nonetheless, you *cannot* learn to write from Sturgeon any more conveniently than one could learn how to dance by studying Fred Astaire.

Ted was among the very best there ever were. And the way we're going, he may be among the very best there ever *will* be. He loved the sound of words the way trees love the wind, the way yin loves yang, the way the halves of Velcro love their mate (and Ted often contended that he had "invented" Velcro in one of his stories). Ted played and sang not only with the guitar, but with words like the best chum you ever had, like dopey kids drunk on the summertime, careering through an empty lot. Words were, to Ted, the best chums possible.

Inspirational, but out of reach. What he did, he did like Blackstone or Houdini, with lock-picks and escape engines from flaw-free fetters under his tongue, in his butt, up his nose. Ted was, in the purest sense of the word, a runesmith.

Anyone who misbelieves that they learned to write by deconstructing a Sturgeon story—try it with "A Way of Thinking" in Volume VII, I double-dog-dare you!—is not only building castles in the air, he or she is trying to move furniture *into* it. Sturgeon was what he called me once: *rara avis*. Weird bird, existent in the universe in the number of one.


Do I interrupt myself? Very well then, I interrupt myself. I am large, I contain multitudes.

Here's what Ted wrote in 1967 as an introduction to my book of short stories, I HAVE NO MOUTH & I MUST SCREAM. It goes here, correctly, because it was one of the spurs that moved and shook him to come stay with me. I was in deep anguish in 1967, some of the toughest times of my life, and Ted wrote this, in part:

> *...You hold in your hands a truly extraordinary book. Taken individually, each of these stories will afford you that easy-to-take, hard-to-find, very hard-to-accomplish quality of entertainment. Here are strange and lovely bits of bitterness like "Eyes of Dust" and the unforgettable "Pretty Maggie Moneyeyes," phantasmagoric fables like "I Have No Mouth, and I Must Scream" and "Delusion for a Dragon Slayer"...*
>
> *There are a great many unusual things about Harlan Ellison and his work—the speed, the scope, the variety. Also the ugliness, the cruelty, the compassion, the anger, the hate. All seem larger than life-size—especially the compassion which, his work seems to say, he hates as something which would consume him if he let it. This is the explanation of the odd likeli-hood (I don't think it's ever happened, but I think it could) that the beggar who taps you for a dime, and whom I ignore, will get a punch in the mouth from Harlan.*

*One thing I found fascinating about this particular collection—and it's applicable to the others as well, once you find it out—is that the earlier stories, like "Big Sam," are at first glance more tightly knit, more structured, than the later ones. They have beginnings and middles and endings, and they adhere to their scene and their type, while stories like "Maggie Money-eyes" and "I Have No Mouth" straddle the categories, throw you curves, astonish and amaze. It's an interesting progression, because most beginners start out formless and slowly learn structure. In Harlan's case, I think he quickly learned structure because within a predictable structure he was safe, he was contained. When he got big enough—*confident *enough—he began to write it as it came, let it pour out as his inner needs demanded. It is the confidence of freedom, and the freedom of confidence. He breaks few rules he has not learned first.*

*(There are exceptions. He is still doing battle with "lie" and "lay," and I am beginning to think that for him "strata" and "phenomena" will forever be singular.)*

*Anyway...he is a man on the move, and he is moving fast. He is, on these pages and everywhere else he goes, colorful, intrusive, abrasive, irritating, hilarious, illogical, inconsistent, unpredictable, and one hell of a writer. Watch him."*

*Theodore Sturgeon*
*Woodstock, New York 1967*

And as I wrote for Ted's attention in a 1983 reprint of the book, for which I refused any number of Big Name offers to supplant Ted's 1967 essay: "Ted Sturgeon's dear words were very important to me in 1967 when they were shining new and this collection became the instrument that propelled my work and my career forward. To alter those words, or to solicit a new introduction by someone else, would be to diminish the gift that Ted conferred on me. This book has been in print constantly for sixteen years... Only this need be said: I have learned the proper use of 'lie' and 'lay,' Ted."

"Watch him," he said. That was the lynch-pin of our long and no-bullshit, honest-speaking friendship. We were a lot alike. (Noël's son, age 16, has also read these pages and he declares I'm "a fantastic writer, and arrogant as hell." You just described your grand-father, kiddo.) A *lot* alike, and we watched each other. Avis to avis, two bright-eyed, cagey, weird birds assaying a long and often anguished observation of each other— Ted, I think, seeing in me where and who he had been—me, for certain, seeing in him where I was bound and who I would be in my later years, which are now. We were foreshadow and *déjà vu.* We were chained to each other, in more a creepy than an Iron John way.

I had watched him from afar, before I met him, when I reviewed the just published MORE THAN HUMAN in the May–July issue #14 (1954) of my mimeographed fanzine, *Dimensions.* I was an extremely callow nineteen, Ted was only thirty-six and married to Marion, living back East in Woodstock, I think; Noël still had two years to go before she could get borned.

With all the imbecile *sangfroid* of, oh, I'd say, an O-Cel-O sponge mop, I pontificated the following comment on Sturgeon at his most exalted best:

```
Book reviewers, like Delphic Oracles, are a breed of
individuals self-acknowledged to be authorities on
everything--including everything. Thus it is with some
feelings of helplessness that a reviewer finds he is
totally unprepared or capable in describing a book.
    It happens only once in every thousand years or so, and
is greater tribute to any book than a word of praise for
each of those years. So enjoy the spectacle, dear reader.
    Theodore Sturgeon has expanded his Galaxy novella
"Baby Is Three" into a tender and deeply moving chronicle
of people, caught in the maelstrom of forces greater
than any of them. The book, in case you missed it above,
is MORE THAN HUMAN, and insures the fact that if
Ballantine Books were to cease all publication with
this volume, their immortality would be ensured.
    We have dragged out more than we thought we could.
Sturgeon is impeccable in this novel. Unquestionably
the finest piece of work in the last two years, and
the closest approach to literature science fiction has
yet produced.
```

We watched the hell out of each other. After we met, if I remember accurately, in the autumn of 1954, I remember taking offense at a remark the late Damon Knight had made about Ted's story "The Golden Egg" (he opined, the story "starts out gorgeously and develops into sentimental slop"), and Ted just snickered and said, "Damon can show a mean streak sometimes."

Later in life, one day I remembered that and chuckled to myself and thought, "No shit."

Ted called me one time, before he lived here, and sang me the lyrics to "Thunder and Roses." I wrote them down, ran them in *Dimensions*, in issue #15, and when next Ted called me, we sang it together. Ted wrote quite a few songs. They were awful, just awful. What I'm trying to vouchsafe here is that in terms of songwriting, both Pindar and Cole Porter felt no need of stirring in their respective graves at the eminence of Sturgeon's lyricism. He was superlative at what he did superlatively, but occasionally even Ted pulled a booger.

Oh, wait a minute, I have just *got* to tell you this one...

...no, hold it, before I tell you *that* one—Ted and the guy reading THE DREAMING JEWELS—I've got to tell you *this* one, which Noël just reminded me of, he said ending a sentence with a preposition.

One early evening, I was rearranging a clothes closet, and I unshipped a lot of crap that had been gathering dust on a top shelf. And Ted was just hanging out watching, for no reason (we used to talk books a lot but I don't think on that particular evening he was again driving me crazy in his perseverance, trying to turn me on to Eugene Sue's THE WANDERING JEW or THE MYSTERIES OF PARIS). And I pulled down this neat tent that I'd used years before, when I was a spelunker; and Ted got interested in it, and he unzipped and unrolled it, and of a sudden this nut-case says to me, "We should go camp out."

Now, two things you should know, one of which Noël remarked when she reminded me of this anecdote. "The two *least* Boy Scouts in the world!" And she laughed so hard her cheek hit the cancel button on her cell-phone, and that was the end of *that* conversation. (Which is a canard, because I was, in fact, an actual Cub and Boy Scout, Webelos and all, with merit badges, when I was a kid, so take *that*, Ms. Smartass Sturgeon.) And the second thing you should know is that my home, Ellison Wonderland, aka The Lost Aztec Temple of Mars, sits at the edge of two hundred acres of watershed land and riparian vegetation, high in the Santa Monica Mountains, facing what is known as Fossil Ridge— two million year old aquatic dead stuff in the rocks   now part of what the Santa Monica Mountains Conservancy has designated Edgar Rice Burroughs Park because the land that Carl Sagan and Leonard Nimoy and I saved from developers is *exactly* where the creator of Tarzan and Barsoom used to have picnics, back in the early 1900s.

Okay, so now you know that, and now you know why this resident nut-case Sturgeon is saying to me, "Let's go and camp out."

Which—don't ask me why, it *seemed* like a good idea at the time—is why I found myself the next night in a tent, outdoors, in the middle of a very humid spring night, with semi-nekkid Sturgeon, eating gypsy stew out of a tin can that fuckin' exPLOded, festooning the inside of the tent wherein I slept till the mosquitoes and no-see'ms gorged on my flesh and I crawled moaning back to the house at three AM...

Here's the one I was going to tell you before I got feetnoted: Ted had a surfeit of hubris. Every *good* writer has it, especially those who scuff toe in the dirt and do an aw-shucks-ma it weren't nothin'. (John Clute, the critic, just calls it "shucksma.") False humility is bullshit or, as Gustave Flaubert put it much more elegantly, "Modesty is a kind of groveling."

But Ted had that scam down pat. He could act as shy as the unicorn in the garden, but inside he was festooned with bunting and firecrackers for his talent. One would have to be in a coma to be as good as he was, as often as he was, not to revel inwardly at the power. He was selfish and self-involved, even as you and I. He was also generous, great-hearted, and loyal.

Yet in all the analyses I've read in the previous ten volumes, no one else seems to have perceived that Ted—who was touted, by me as well as others, as knowing all there was to know about love—was a man in flames. He had loathings and animosities and an elitism that ran deep. He knew genuine anguish. But he also knew more cleverly than anyone else I've ever met, that it was an instant turn-off; if he wanted to get what he wanted, he had to sprinkle dream dust; and so he filtered his frustration and enmity like Sterno through a loaf of pumpernickel, distilling it into a charm that could Svengali a Mennonite into a McCormick Thresher.

From the starting blocks, Ted had been lumbered with the words "science fiction," and unlike Bierce or Poe or Dunsany, he never got out of the ghetto. Dean Koontz and Steve King know what I'm talking about; and so does Kurt, who created Kilgore Trout, who was Sturgeon. He wanted passionately to get out of the penny-a-word gulag, and he *knew* he was better than most of those who'd miraculously accomplished the trick.

Ted had gotten into writing because he understood all the way to the gristle the truth of that Japanese aphorism: *The nail that stands too high will be hammered down.* And while I'm citing clever sources, Ted also got into the writing in resonance to Heinrich Von Kleist's "I write only because I cannot stop."

But he also knew it was a gig. It was a job. Masonry and pig-iron ingots and pulling the plough. Not a lifetime job for guys like Ted and me, weird ducks who'd rather play than labor. A kind of frenetic, always-working laziness. Tardy, imprecise, careless of the feelings of others, obsessed, and selfish. He was, I am, it's a fair cop. So he and I have produced enough work to shame a plethora of others, enough to fill more than a dozen big fat COMPLETE STURGEONS or ESSENTIAL ELLISONS. What no one ever realizes is that it's all the product of guilt and laziness, guilt *because* of the laziness.

We know what we *can* be, but we cannot get out of our own way. Ted was the king of that disclosure. He could not cease being Sturgeon for a moment, and he was chained to the genre that was too small for him.

(Ted once told me, and everyone I have dealt with since has told me I'm full of shit and lying, that he *hated* the title, "A Saucer of Loneliness," that Horace Gold attached to the story before he'd even finished writing it—because UFOs were "hot" and "sexy" at that time—and that he'd originally wanted to call it just "Loneliness" and sell it to a main-stream, non-sf market. Apparently he wrote it as a straight character study, couldn't move it—same with "Hurricane Trio," he said—and did it as Gold had suggested.)

(Had a helluva fight with the brilliant Alan Brennert over titling "Saucer" when Alan wrote his teleplay for *The Twilight Zone* on CBS in 1985 when we worked the series together.)

No matter how congenial, how outgoing, how familial, Ted knew way down in the gristle what Hunter Thompson identified as "...the dead end loneliness of a man who makes his own rules." And it made for anguish because he was imprisoned in a literary gulag where there was—and continues to be—such an acceptance of mediocrity that it is as odious as a cultural cringe. And Ted wanted more. Always *more.*

More life, more craft, more acceptance, more love, more of a shot at Posterity. Not to be categorized, seldom to be challenged, just famous enough that even when he wasn't at top-point efficiency everyone was so in awe of him that they were incapable of slapping him around and making him work better. That kind of adulation is death to a writer as incredibly *Only* as was Theodore Sturgeon. He hungered for better, and he deserved better, but he could not get out of his own way, and so...for years and years...

He burned, and he coveted, and he continued decanting those fiery ingots, all the while leading a life as disparate and looney as Munchausen's. He knew love, no argument, but it was the saving transmogrification from fevers and railings against the nature of his received world. And this anecdote I want to relate—as funny as it tells now—was idiomatic of Ted's plight.

Here's what happened.

What we were doing in a Greyhound bus station, damned if I can remember. But there we were, about five of us—I think Bill Dignin was one of the group, and I seem to recall Gordy Dickson, as well. But Ted and I and the rest of these guys were going some-where chimerical, the sort of venue my Susan likes to refer to as Little Wiggly-On-Mire. And there we sat at a table waiting for our bus, chowing down on grilled cheese and tomato sandwiches, or whatever, and one of the guys nudged Ted and did a "Psst," and indicated a guy at the counter, who was (so help me) reading the Pyramid paperback reissue of Ted's terrific novel, THE DREAMING JEWELS (under the re-title THE SYNTHETIC MAN). And it just tickled Ted, and he came all a-twinkle, and whispered to us, "Watch this, you'll love it."

And Ted got up, sidled over to the dude, slid onto the stool next to him and, loud enough for us to hear, cozened the guy with the remark, "Watchu readin'?" and the dude absently flashed the cover, said it was something like a fantasy novel, and Ted said archly, "How can you waste your time reading such crap?"

And we waited for the guy to defend his taste in reading matter to this impertinent buttinski. We held our breaths waiting for the guy to correct this stranger with lofty praise for what a great writer this Theodore Sturgeon was.

The guy looked down at the book for a scant...

Shrugged, and said, "Y'know, you're right," and he flipped it casually across the intervening abyss into the cavernous maw of a huge mound-shaped gray trash container. Then he paid his coffee tab, slid off the stool, and moto-vated out of the Greyhound station.

We knew better than to laugh.

Ted came back; and he had the look of ninth inning strike three. None of us mentioned it again.

It seemed funny at the time. Not so funny when I write about it.


Here's a funny one. I don't have this authenticated, that is to say, I (thankfully) have no photos, but I sort of always knew that Ted had an inclination toward, well, not wearing clothes. *Your* doctor would call it nudity. Now, as I say, I don't know if Ted was a card-carrying *nudist* at any time in his life, but around here he started walking around *sans raiment.* I could not have that. Not just because we had studio people and other writers and girl friends and the one or two people who made up my "staff" also *in situ,* but mostly because bare, Ted was not any more divine an apparition than are each of you reading this. He had blue shanks, scrawny old guy legs, muscular but ropey; he wasn't inordinately hairy, but what there was...well...it was *disturbing*; a little pot belly that pooched out, *also* mildly distressing; I will not speak of his naughty bits. But there they were, wagglin' in the breeze. I am, I know, a middle-class disappointment to Ted's ghost, that I am thus so hidebound, but I simply could not have it. Particularly, especially, notably after The Incidents:

Primus: he decided to make *Paella* for me and a select group of dinner party favorites. So we got him this big *olla*, and amassed for him the noxious ingestibles (did I mention, I not only *hate* this olio, would rather have someone hot-glue my tongue to a passing rhino than to partake of *Paella*), and off into the kitchen went the naked Sturgeon. A day he took. A whole day. No one went near the kitchen. I sent *out* for my coffee. And here's what is the Incident aspect of it: as he mish'd that mosh, he used his hands, alternately digging into the heating morass and then occasionally *scratching his ass*. I am not, I swear on the graves of my Mom and Dad, not making this up. I have no idea if others in the house saw it, but I did, and I got to tell you, had I not loathed *Paella* out of the starting-gate, that tableau from The Great Black Plague would have put me off it at least till the return of the Devonian.

(Another footnote within an anecdote inside a reminiscence: Ted was impeccable. Clean. This was a clean old man I'm talkin' here. Not obsessive about it, not some pathological nut washing his hands every seven minutes, but *clean*. So don't get the idea that the horror! the horror! of The *Paella* Incident stemmed from Sturgeon uncleanliness, it was just straightforward here-is-a-dude-slopping-his-claws-in-our-dinner-and-then-maybe-skinning-a-squirrel-who's-to-know.)

Secundus: he liked being helpful; little chores; nice short houseguest strokes that won one's loyalty and affection. Did I mention, Ted used charm the way Joan of Arc used Divine Inspiration. He could sell sandboxes to Arabs. Charm d'boids outta the trees. Devilish weaponry. So: little aids and assists. Such as answering the doorbell every now and then. Which was all good, all fine, except most of the time he forgot he was *bare-ass nekkid!* Capped as Incident on the afternoon, as god—even though I'm an atheist—is my witness, he answered the door and the Avon cosmetics lady in her Ann Taylor suit and stylish pumps gave a strangled scream, dropped her attaché sample case, her ordering pad, her gloves (I think), and flailed away down the street like a howler monkey.

Tertius: after the cops left, I laid down the law. No more Incidents. Put the fuck some *clothes* on, Ted! I don't care if it's SCUBA gear, mukluks and a fur parka, a suit of body armor, but you *will* henceforth go forth *avec* apparel!

So he started wearing a tiny fire-engine red Speedo.

I cannot begin to convey how disturbing *that* was, mostly because the li'l pot belly overhung that *sexe-cache* the way the demon Chernabog overhung the valley in Disney's *Fantasia*.

Avon has never sent a rep to my house since that day, decades ago. Also, Pizza Hut will not deliver. Go figure.

And so it went on with us for more than thirty years. Ted growing more ensnared by a received universe that was both too small to contain him while simultaneously telling him he was a titan. It is hideously bifurcating to go among one's readers, many of whom look upon you as the mortal avatar of The Inviolable Chalice of Genius, having had to borrow the bus-fare to get cross-country to the convention. He grew more and more careless of what his actions and life-choices would do to those he left behind, yet to those who met him casually he was more charming than a cobra at a mongoose rally.

And we continued to watch each other; sometimes to watch *over* each other. I have a letter I'd like to insert here. It was written during that very tough time in 1966–67 I mentioned earlier in this jaunt.

Thought it may not seem so, this long in the wind, this exegesis is not about me. It is about the trails Ted and I cut with each other. The other guest introductions are variously great, good, okay, and slight; but this one is the only one that minutely tries to codify the odd parameters of an odd friendship, a human liaison. So I'll not go into particulars about the shitstorm under which I went to my knees in '66–'67, save to tell you true that I was neither feckless nor freshly kicked off the turnip truck.

Nonetheless, I got hit hard, and Ted wrote this to me, dated April 18, 1966:

> *Dear Harlan:*
>
> *For two days I have not been able to get my mind off your predicament. Perhaps it would be more accurate to say that your predicament is on my mind, a sharp-edged crumb of discomfort which won't whisk away or dissolve or fall off, and when I move or think or swallow, it gigs me.*
>
> *I suppose the aspect that gigs me the most is "injustice." Injustice is not an isolated homogeneous area any more than justice is. A law is a law and is either breached or not, but justice is reciprocal. That such a thing should have happened to you is a greater injustice than if it happened to most representatives of this exploding population.*
>
> *I know exactly why, too. It is an injustice because you are on the side of the angels (who, by the way, stand a little silent for you just now). You are in the small company of Good Guys. You are that, not by any process of intellectualization and decision, but reflexively, instantly, from the glands, whether it shows at the checkout in a supermarket where you confront the Birchers, or in a poolroom facing down a famous bully, or in pulling out gut by the hank and reeling it up on the platen of your typewriter.*
>
> *There is no lack of love in the world, but there is a profound shortage in places to put it. I don't know why it is, but most people who, like yourself, have an inherent ability to*

*claw their way up the sheerest rock faces around, have little of it or have so equipped themselves with spikes and steel hooks that you can't see it. When it shows in such a man— like it does in you—when it lights him up, it should be revered and cared for. This is the very nub of the injustice done you. It should not happen at all, but if it must happen, it should not happen to you.*

*You have cause for many feelings, Harlan: anger, indignation, regret, grief. Theodore Reik, who has done some brilliant anatomizations of love, declares that its ending is in none of these things: if it is, there is a good possibility that some or one or all of them were there all along. It is ended with* indifference—*really ended with a real indifference. This is one of the saddest things I know. And in all my life, I have found one writer, once, who was able to describe the exact moment when it came, and it is there-fore the saddest writing I have ever read. I give it to you now in your sadness. The principle behind the gift is called "counter-irritation." Read it in good health—eventual.*

*...and in case you think you misheard me over the phone, I would like you to know that if it helps and sustains you at all, you have my respect and affection.*

*Yours, T. H. Sturgeon*

Accompanying the letter was number 20 of TWENTY LOVE POEMS based on the Spanish by Pablo Neruda, by Christopher Logue, from SONGS (1959). And then, quickly, DANGEROUS VISIONS was published, Ted's marriage to Marion underwent heartbreak, Ted and I talked cross-country virtually every day, and in the wake of the notoriety of DV and his story, "If All Men Were Brothers, Would You Let One Marry Your Sister?" which I had chivvied him into writing after a protracted writer's block dry spell and financial reverses, Ted came to live with me.

It was 1966, '67, and at various times I think it was for a full year, at other times memory insists it was longer, but separate inputs staunchly declare it was only six, eight, ten months. I can't recall precisely, now more than forty years later, but it seemed to go on forever.

I have all of Ted's books, of course, but the only two he ever signed were my copy of DANGEROUS VISIONS with *all* the authors logged on—a rare artifact existent in the universe, as I've said, in the number of one—and my personal library copy of his first collection, WITHOUT SORCERY, Prime Press, 1948, for which I paid a buck fifty (marked down from $3.00) in 1952. Here is what he wrote on the front flyleaf in May of 1966 during my birthday gathering:

*To Harlan Ellison —*

> *Who has, at an equivalent stage in his career, done so much more—so much better.*
>
> *Theodore Sturgeon*

That's gracious crap, of course, but what I *did* do was get Theodore Sturgeon writing again.

In the wake of my own day and night hammering on one of the half dozen or so Olympia office machines (never mind how many Olympia portables I had stashed), Ted grew chagrined at his facility to *talk* new story-ideas but not to *write* them, and I rode him mercilessly. The phrase "your fifteen minutes of fame has drained out of the hour-glass" became taunt and tautology. I showed him no mercy; and with so many other younger writers passing through the way station of my home, all of them on the prod, worshipful but competitive, Ted ground his teeth and set up shop in the blue bedroom, and began writing.

I'd long-since gotten him inside *Star Trek,* but now—for the fastest money in town—I opened the market at *Knight* magazine. Sirkay Publications. Holloway House. The low-end men's magazines: *Adam, Cad, Knight, The Adam Bedside Reader.* Two hundred and fifty, three hundred, sometimes a little more, each pop…paid within 24 hours. Sometimes we'd kick the story around at the breakfast table; sometimes he'd come into my then tiny office at the front of the house, dead of night, as I was pounding away under the unrelenting pressure of studio or publication deadlines, and we'd noodle something out. Sometimes it was a snag in one of my stories, sometimes it was a glitch in his.

And we wrote "Runesmith" together. And he wrote or plotted or set aside a snippet of the following, here at Ellison Wonderland: "The Patterns of Dorne," "It Was Nothing— Really!" and "Brownshoes," "Slow Sculpture" and "Suicide," "It's You" and "Jorry's Gap," "Crate" and "The Girl Who Knew What They Meant." Maybe others, I can't remember. But most of the stories that he finished when he was living with Wina about a mile away from me down the hill at 14210 Ventura Boulevard, La Fonda Motel, he plotted and started here before I threw him out.

Here's the flat of it, friends.

And Ted would understand this.

Most of what I know about Theodore Sturgeon I cannot tell you.

We watched each other. He looked after me. I tried to help him. And then came out STURGEON IS ALIVE AND WELL...

Many of the stories from that last, final collection of (almost) new fictions, got born here. Right downstairs in the blue bedroom. And I harassed my buddy Digby Diehl, the now-famous editor, who was at that time the editor of the *Los Angeles Times Book Review* section, to let me review ALIVE AND WELL. And he did, beneath the copy editor's headline "Sturgeon's Law Overtakes Him."

No good deed...

Here, reprinted for the first time, is that review, from the April 18th, 1971 *Los Angeles Times*.

You will kindly note the cost of this 221-page hardcover in the early Seventies. This will give you an idea of the kind of money a writer as excellent as Sturgeon had to subsist on, it will also inform your understanding of the love-hate attitude even as lauded an artist as Sturgeon had with his work environment.

```
          STURGEON IS ALIVE AND WELL
       A new collection of stories by
              Theodore Sturgeon
           (G.P. Putnam's Sons—$4.95)
```

```
Alive and well, yes definitely. But up to the level of
his past brilliance, no I'm afraid not.
     Theodore Sturgeon, you see, is without argument one
of the finest writers--of any kind--this country has
ever produced. His novels MORE THAN HUMAN, SOME OF
YOUR BLOOD, and THE DREAMING JEWELS stand untarnished
by time and endless re-readings as purest silver. His
short stories have so completely examined the
parameters of love in a genre of imagination woefully
shy in that particular, that the words love and
Sturgeon have become synonymous. The word syzygy also
belongs to him.
     He is also much-quoted as the author of Sturgeon's
Law, a Deep Thought that suggests 90% of everything is
mediocre...puddings, plays, politicians; cars, carpenters,
coffee; people, books, neurologists...everything. A
realistic assessment of the impossibility of achieving
perfection that, till now, has applied to everyone and
everything save Sturgeon. Sadly, and at long last, his
own Law has caught up with him. Ninety per cent of
this new collection of stories is mediocre.
```

After a long and painful dry spell in which the creative well seemed emptied, Sturgeon began writing again three years ago, and eleven of the twelve stories herein contained date from this latest period of productivity. Only two of them approach the brilliance of stories like "The Silken-Swift," "A Saucer of Loneliness," "Killdozer," or "Bianca's Hands." It has been said time and again about Sturgeon, that had he not suffered the ghastly stigmatizing ghettoization of being tagged a "science fiction " writer, he might easily surpass John Collier, Donald Barthelme, Ray Bradbury, or even Kurt Vonnegut as a mainstream fantasist of classic stature. Yet here, freed of that restriction, the fictions seem thin and too slick and forgettable; stories that could have been written by men not one thousandth as special as Theodore Sturgeon.

"To Here and the Easel," a 1954 novelette printed here in hardcover for the first time (and the only story to have a previous publication), is the longest, and the dullest. A fantasy of schizophrenia in which a painter who can't paint swings back and forth between his life as Giles, helpless before his empty white canvas, and his life as Rogero, a knight out of ORLANDO FURIOSO, this overlong and rococo morality play seems embarrassingly reminiscent of the kind of pulp writing typified by L. Ron Hubbard's SLAVES OF SLEEP, a novel bearing almost exactly the same plot-device Sturgeon employs.

Of the remaining eleven tales, five are straight mainstream, four are clearly s-f oriented, and two are borderline. However, only two crackle with the emotional load aficionados have come to revere in Sturgeon's work. In "Take Care of Joey," a man whose world-view is built on the concept that no one performs a seemingly unselfish act "without there's something in it for him," finds just such a situation operating. A nasty, troublemaking little bastard named Joey is watched over by a guy named Dwight, who obviously hates the little rat. He goes way out of his way to keep Joey from getting the crap kicked out of him, up to and past the point where Dwight himself gets stomped. The narrator of the story has to find out why, and he does, and he finds out something else that makes this eleven-page short a stunning example of Sturgeon's off-kilter insight and humanity.

"The Girl Who Knew What They Meant" is the other winner and it is so carefully-constructed, so meticulously-spun that not until the last twenty-seven words, the final three sentences, does the reader know he has had his soul wrung like the neck of a chicken. It is Sturgeon transcendent. And if Martha Foley's BEST AMERICAN SHORT STORIES overlooks it this year, surely there is no justice.

On sum, though the book is weak and for the most part a terrible disappointment, merely having Sturgeon writing again--and being able to prove it with slugs of type--is a blessing. And even with typographical errors rampant (a felony heretofore difficult to charge to Putnam's) it is a book well worth having done. Not just for those two incredible little short stories but by the same rationale that insists we preserve every letter and laundry list written by a Lincoln, a Hemingway, or a Melville.

What I'm trying to say, is that Sturgeon is one of our best. He will be read and enjoyed a hundred years from now. So we <u>must</u> see it all, even the least successful of it.

This has been a difficult review to write.

Ted never told me what he thought of that piece. We had no bitterness over it but we never sat down to bagels and lox about it, either. We were friends, and both of us knew that meant unshakeable trust in the truth that we loved each other, that we respected and admired the best of each other's work in such a way that to blow smoke and/or sunshine up each other's kilt would have been to poison that trust. Unlike many writers who expect their friends to write blurbs and dispense encomia on the basis of camaraderie rather than the absolute quality of the work, Ted and I understood that we could lie to others that way, but never to each other.

So. Enough.

I have more, endless more that I could set down about Ted, about abiding with Ted, about the chill wind blowing through the burlesque houses of both of our lives, but enough is enough.

Noël has suggested that I take the eulogy I wrote for Ted in 1985, that appears near the beginning of this essay, and move it back here, because every time she reads it, she cries.

And she thinks it is a proper end for this love letter to my friend now dead more than two decades.

No, dear Noël, it has to stay where it is; and I'll tell you my thinking here.

Ted wanted me to write his eulogy. He made me promise. And I did it. But I was so wracked by loss at the time, it was brief, far briefer than *this* eulogy. And thus I left out most of what's set down here in print for the first—and last—time. It is the for-real eulogy Ted probably wanted, and which I have perceived is being read over my shoulder as I've written it, by Ted's ghost. Not for you, Noël, not for any of Ted's other kids, not for Marion, not for the publisher who is herewith getting a major piece unexpectedly, and sure as hell not for admirers, fans, readers of Ted's work.

I have written this because Ted needs to read it, and because it is a picture of The Great Artist that cannot exist via *hoi polloi.* It had to be done by me, kiddo; and if you think this is all of it...

*Most* of what I know about Theodore Sturgeon I cannot tell you. I haven't told you about the two times we fought, the first being the imbroglio over that meanspirited pissant, the toweringly talented British novelist Anthony Burgess, who was a nasty little shit; and the second time subsequent to Ted doing one of the most awful things I've ever known of a human being doing to others, resulting in my telling him to get the fuck outta my house, now, tonight, this minute!

I haven't told you about Ted and the Meatgrinder; Ted and the Tongue-Tied Germans; Ted and the Apollo Trip; Ted and Chuck Barris in Movieland; Ted and the Wing-Walker; Ted and the Naked Monkey. Oh, trust me, I could go on for days. But...

Enough.

I would have liked to've written more extensively about how Ted and I wrote together, but Paul Williams has covered some of that in the story-notes, and the rest is whispers and memories. So, at last, after more than twenty years, Ted, I've kept my promise. In full.


To say, at finish, only this. I miss my friend. I miss Ted's charm, his chicanery, his talent, his compassion. I miss them because they will never, not ever, not embodied in anyone or anything, never ever exist on any plane we can perceive. Those of you who never met him, who have only read him, can know what an emptiness there will forever be in your life. Because I know the emptiness in mine.

An Untitled, yet Antagonistic,
Essay of Approximately
2700 Contumelious
but Logical Words

So let's assume you can pry your bloated eyeballs off that pc screen long enough to flex your brain around a couple of pablum-digestible concepts. The general idea is Peaceful Co-Existence, as in "you do your thing, and I'll do my thing, and don't be comin' to my house on Sunday morning when I'm unlaxing, just so you can tell me I'm a sinner and I'm goin' posthaste ASAP to the 9th and inner circle of Hell because you're a True Believer and I'm a goddam Luddite because I don't schlep around the same obsessive beliefs in which *you* wallow."

Now that we're off on a charming note, masticate these two propositions, in aid of the general idea:

1. One should work at the level of Technology that best produces the Art or Artifact, with the understanding that pumping up to employ all the latest toots and whistles is merely "keeping up with the Joneses" and is useless crap guaranteed only to put money in Bill Gates's pocket.

2. Is it possible that you are a semi-mindless lemming, straight out of *Night of the Living Dead*, who would buy chocolate-covered goat turds if the tv advertising was dumb and dynamite enough to con you...the way McDonald's toadburgers and The Gap and smash-eyeball trailers for garbage SFX movies directed by Roland Emmerich (*Independence Day*, *Godzilla*) turn you into a quivering mass of consumer jelly, ready to have your brain churned into *purée* of bat guano,

155

ready to have your wallet vacuumed, ready to do Their bidding just so's you'll be *kew*-ell? Whaddaya think, is it possible? Can you give it the barest?

What I'm talking about is this:

According to every single survey, study, perusal, review, statistic, overview, investigation, analysis, or epicrisis, the average American of primetime-tv demographic desirability age is getting bone-stick-stone dumber by the nanosecond. When it takes some yotz two lifelines to deduce that the governing legislature of Japan is called the diet (a fact that is in the press only every other day), and he wins a hundred grand for backing into the right choice between *diet* and *bidet*...well, Cap'n, what we got here is a species infected with terminal Cultural Amnesia, upping the percentage of free-range assholes to a Columbine Shootout level, and beyond.

Now understand something: I ain't cranky when I take my portable typewriter through the security kiosk at LAX or O'Hare or La Guardia, and some poor doofus getting four-fifty an hour, but all puffed-up like a pouter pigeon because s/he has a uniform and a pair of handcuffs, doesn't have a clue what that infernal-looking device in the case is, and makes me open it, and makes me explain it, and makes me roll a piece of paper around the platen and type THE QUICK BROWN FOX JUMPS ALL OVER YO MOMMA...I ain't cranky. Nor do I get upset when I'm in the middle of a college lecture and I mention Dachau or Buchenwald or Auschwitz, and I get back blank stares from the giant intellects sitting out there chewing gum and picking their noses. I don't get upset. Nor do I scream and drool and tear my hair when I call down to the front desk at a famous hotel in Chicago, and tell the manager that I'm doing a book signing in an hour, and I need a blotter, because I like fountain pens and use them when I'm auto-graphing, and the word *blotter* is as foreign to her as the word *mulligrubs*, which is what I am up to here with. Nosiree, I do not spew spittle. I am sanguine in the path of the onrushing tsunami of dumb that threatens to turn this country into an intellectual abbatoir fit only to elect an empty suit like Bush or Gore.

Einstein once wrote that "Things should be made as simple as possible...but no simpler." It seems to me that goes for the level of technology one should use to do a job, as well as for repairing a car, removing the plaque from an artery, or telling a story. But that proposition flies in the face of what most advertising spends its frenetic moments trying to do, which is getting us to buy something new that is no better than what we already own. Except that to buy it, we have to give them money, *and* be convinced we cannot live without it.

Thus, the pc and the uncritical yet illicit love affair with the internet.

As I write this sentence, the stock market has at last emerged from its Ecstasy-drugged stupor and realized all these idiot e-commerce sites—flensed of their overhyped dazzle—are sucking money pits that ain't making a buck. Overcapitalized by poor schlubs who went for the okeydoke, like yokels from Chitling Switch, Idaho playing three-card monte on a street corner in Manhattan, being gulled and conned and scammed and taken by electronic hustlers using words they don't understand (such as calling "customers" by the word "eyes" as in "we'll have ten thousand eyes a day at this site"), the dawn finally came. And everyone understood that *someone has to spend money* at these e-venues. There have to be customers, folks, just plain old brick&mortar style customers, like you and I. Who find it just as easy to buy a Barbie doll at a store!

Per Einstein: as simple as possible, but no simpler.

The form of this argument is commonly known in the rigor of Aristotelian syllogisms, the world of forensic debating, as "arguing from the lesser to the greater." Which is to say, I clarion trumpet the equality and humanism of Peaceful Co-Existence, but to codify the general climate I propose, I must machinegun you with anecdotal f'rinstances.

Know this: I do not own a computer. By choice. I have no access to the internet. By choice. I do not visit chat rooms; do not engage in colloquy with total strangers who need to foist off their feelings and opinions about my writings; do not shop for cars or furniture or stocks on the web; do not look up "facts" or reference material from unknown and usually quixotic sources; do not overpay by ten times their value at eBay for collectables I might desire (tried it once; once was horror enough); do not waste endless hours responding to meanspirited attention-seeking superannuated adolescents who, in times past, would have had only fanzine or letters-to-the-editor access to the eyes of the world for their pitiful kvetching. None of the above. By choice.

I receive about two hundred pieces of mail a day. I look at all of it. Much of it I respond to. Not *all* of it, because Life's Too Short, but *much* of it. Most of it is the sort of casual conversation that gluts the e-mail chute. The kind of thing that we used to write in a brief letter or postcard—and because we actually had to do the job in a finite space, we tried to keep the imbecile blather to a minimum. And we actually had to think about what we wanted to say, rather than firing off projectile rodomontade, misspelled ranting, unexamined and irrational vomit of the moment. And we actually took in hand a pen or a pencil, or even a Crayola if we were institutionalized, and made it a personal, traceable missive. As opposed to a cold screed on a screen, sent by some coward with a "handle," too chickenshit or demented to stand behind the words. Sent from who-knows-where by who-knows-who. Blather and misinformation and gossip and innuendo and evil trickery...and all of it adding not one whit to the store of human wisdom.

And here's the kicker.

All of that crap *has* to be sent NOW NOW NOW!! Has to be read NOW NOW NOW! Not good enough that it might take 48 hours from one end of the continent to the other. I need you to read my self-centered gibberish NOW NOW NOW!

Like greedy babies to whom ratiocination and careful speech are anathema, the *marabunta* horde of e-mailers, crazed and starving ants denuding a grove of teaberry bushes, rush to print and tie up every phone line in the world, just so they can "express their opinions." NOW NOW NOW! Gimee, gimee, gimee!

And like good little Quislings, intellectual Fifth Columnists, you serve the ends of the corporations who batten on this farrago of insensate codswallop, by helping them alter the terminology. You call the U.S. Post "snail mail." *Snail Mail?!?* One or two days from coast-to-coast? Gimme a break. Don't tell me that 98.6% of all that e-mail crap can't survive a posting with a 33¢ stamp! (Yeah, there are exceptions, *always*. A piece of big business, a note from one surgeon to another, a request for money in an emergency... don't sidetrack us with that logical fallacy known as an argument *ad ignorantiam*. I'm talking about 98.6% of what you send and receive every day.)

But now I get letters from people with no return address, and no phone number. Just a website. As if it never occurred to them that I might *not* have lurched into the webworld as frantically as have they.

I am no Luddite. I do not drive a horse and buggy. I have two cars, one a 1947 Packard more beautiful than any object has a right to be, and a ten-year-old Geo that gets 58 miles per gallon in the city, 62 in the country. I am no Luddite. I have an Elektrodex for my phone numbers, a fax for instant paperwork, a Canon photocopier for my business, a microwave, an actual literal quarter of a million book library, a phone in just about every room of my 5000-square-foot sanctuary, a bunch of tv sets, Beta *and* VHS recorders, CD player and—as I write this—I sit in my office with an Ennio Morricone film score cranked up to a hundred and eighty decibels, listening to it through a pair of Quad Electrostatic Screens, not cone speakers, but Quads, the state-of-the-art 3-mil thick Mylar foam, electrostatically charged to catch the highest highs and the lowest lows, not only of the CDs I play, but also of the five or six thousand LPs that I spent twenty years reviewing. I am no Luddite.

But I have spent over fifty years writing as a professional. Seventy-four books published, dozens of teleplays and movies, over 1700 stories and articles and essays and reviews and columns of opinions just as dumb as yours (except I get paid for it, eat your heart out, you e-mail junkie). And I've done all of them on a typewriter.

I own several dozen typewriters.

All Olympias, the best machine ever made. Eight or nine office machines, a dozen or so portables, and even a few of what they used to call the "wafer," a very thin, but accurate machine that used to be the tool of choice of foreign correspondents under fire. I've carried those Olympias through race riots, insurrections, strikes, brushfire wars, *Star Trek* conventions, and a short stay at Cedars-Sinai, where they split me open like an ancient tome, spilled out my innards, and rewired me with a zipper in my chest. I use typewriters. And oh, yeah, not to be too snotty about it...they're all manuals. Not even electric.

I've got nothing against electric typewriters, but they're no good for me. Too slow. I type too fast. Two fingers, at 120 words a minute, virtually no typos. (That's because I learned how to spell, you morons; didn't need to depend on an idiot Spell Check device that scratches its diode and can't decode the word *reify*.) So I go through Security at JFK and the doofus thinks I've got a Doomsday Device in the case. Ah me.

But I don't get online and chivvy *you* for needing a pc and a Spell Checker to write a simple thankyou note. I don't write infuriated letters to the magazine in which this essay appears, screaming bloody murder because that Creep Geezer Shit Ellison doesn't wanna wallow in our obsession. Like a gaggle of MTV Spring Break philistines harassing some dude who won't get as shitfaced and wasted as they are, calling him a "party pooper." Join in my delusion or be called "snail mail."

And so, at long angry last, we come to the point. Peaceful Co-Existence.

I don't give a flying fig newton if you want to spend your days and nights online. I care not that you choose to write or bargain or buy or belittle via the web. You do your thing, and I'll do mine. But if you don't want me to come to your house and nail your goddam head to a coffee table, knock off this singleminded assault on *my* choice NOT to be a mind-slave of the e-commerce bloodsuckers.

Get it, kiddo: I love music, almost every kind of music. But I cannot turn on the radio today and hear Scarlatti or Monteverdi or even Gershwin; I cannot hear Glenn Miller or Artie Shaw or Jackie Paris singing "Skylark"; I cannot hear Stevie Ray Vaughan or Carl Perkins or Joe Tex; I cannot hear Erroll Garner or Bix Beiderbecke or Jack Teagarden; I cannot hear the equivalent of *I Love a Mystery* or *The Shadow* or *The Great Gildersleeve*. All I can hear is what has been pre-sold to teen consumers who are, as we all know, the most astute and discriminating judges of Artistic Value in our little sphere of attention. I may or may not be able to pull in the white-noise phantom sound of some far-off esoteric university station playing Bach, or the lone jazz station at the ass-end of the dial, oh sure there we are with that argument *ad ignorantiam* again, but for the most part all I'll get of music is—as of today—Britney Spears or The Backstreet Boys or (if we don't spurt blood from our ears) Garth Brooks—that stuff, and hip-hop. Which may or may not be an oxymoron, like "rap music." But I cannot hear much of *any*thing that I, or millions of others who've abandoned commercial radio, can derive a moment of musical pleasure from letting into my head.

I deny no one the right to listen to anything they choose, as long as it doesn't proceed from skinhead or right-wing religioso lunacy, but I ask politely...politely...to let *me* and my kind have a little something.

Peaceful Co-Existence.

Use the pc if you choose. Use a goddam raven's-quill pen as you stand on one leg before a fumed oak lectern. I do not give a fig. But stop trying to justify *your* having been suckered into Slavery to the Machine by demanding all the rest of us trundle on behind you into the fire.

Stop being a shill for the merciless creeps who only want to make you buy updated garbage. Understand that we all derive our joys sipping different brews. You do your thing, and I'll do mine, sitting here like Captain Nemo at the grand pipe organ, boogie'ing *Toccata and Fugue in D Minor* with my trusty Olympia.

*We* are the gods, folks. Not the machines. They're supposed to serve *us*, not we serve them to the greater exchequer of commercial interests.

Not all change is progress.

Things should be made as simple as possible.

But no simpler.

Have a nice day.

---

Editor's Note: The preceding essay was written in 2000, but was never published. It was found in a stack of unfiled papers while this volume was being prepared, but there was no evidence of the commissioning entity's identity. The author fully appreciates the irony of it debuting in a print-on-demand publication distributed exclusively via website.

# Arthur 'n' Me

"Ah, yes; well, good luck with that, Harlan," Arthur C. Clarke said to me, while standing barefoot in his pajamas, smiled and closed the door.

This is how that happened. Not my friend Arthur's first remarks to me, nor his last—but auspicious for their context, nonetheless. This is how, why, when and where it happened.

1956. An upper hallway in the old Biltmore on 42nd Street in New York City. Fifteen minutes earlier I had been apprised (thus confirming suspicions even the dullest schmuck would have long sustained) that my wife-at-the-time, my first wife, Charlotte, had been cuckolding me with a bronzed and heroically-statured SCUBA diver named Mike Wilson, a diving companion of Arthur's off the Coast of Coral. They had collaborated on several books.

I am reminded that Wilson was somewhere over six feet tall and I, at 5'5", could have been snapped like a used Q-Tip. Nevertheless, as Robert Silverberg has written, "Harlan is fearless," and I went looking for the cad.

He and Arthur were traveling together, in NYC for the 14th World Science Fiction Convention (see photo A), and since I did not know *his* room number, I went stalking Arthur's. It was, perhaps, midnight or even slimmer on the clock. I whanged and banged on Arthur's door until the Great Author I had originally met in 1953 shambled to open the door.

Photo A

Blearily, and standing in pajamas the cut and illustrative pattern of which memory cannot, this far removed from the event, summon up, Arthur goggled at me and said, in his gentle and urbane way, "Whuh...whuh...izzit, Harluhnnn...?"

I blurted. In a *tsunami* foaming over with such words as sonofabitch and adultery and death and defenestration and, possibly, transfiguration, I demanded of poor innocent Arthur the immediate whereabouts of his poltroon sidekick. Arthur, of course, had been dead asleep, and had no slightest knowledge of the scapegrace's venue at that moment, and I fulminated anew for a few moments, came to my bloodied senses to understand that not only was it none of Arthur's concern, but that my friend was still half on the nod; and I begged his pardon for waking him; and—thoroughly chagrined and ashamed at myself—started back down the corridor.

Arthur closed his door, paused a beat, reopened the door, stuck out his head, and said to my slumped, retreating back, "Ah, yes; well, good luck with that, Harlan." Smiled. Closed the door.

I thought that was awfully nice of him.

Arthur and I met in the Spring of 1953, as I've said. At a resort hotel just outside Beliefontaine, Ohio. Beatley's On-The-Lake Hotel, actually Indian Lake, Ohio. Arthur always referred to it as "Beastley's-On-The-Bayou."

He, I, Bob Tucker, Jerry Bixby, Robert Bloch, Lee Hoffman (and other famous names no one reading this will remember) were all friends. Back in The Day. A simpler, more generous time, kinder of heart. We were all science fiction fans, and some of us were struggling professionals, and some of us were still in high school. You may sort among those names (and note photo B) to ascertain who was which, or whom; whatever.

It may be difficult for those encountering these words to think of the Great Author aka the Great Futurist aka the Knight of the U.K. aka the Great Extrapolator as mere a man (as Lee used to call him, paraphrasing Pogo), but Arthur started out mere a human being not unlike each of us. What I did not know then, in 1953, but what I was to learn many years later, is that as sharp-edged and too-often meanspirited as American writers can be to each other—usually behind their back—we are as parvenus compared to the Brits, who savage each other with an unending onslaught of ignoble calumny that can justly be termed *vicious*. And so it was, back then, that the first thing I learned "about Clarke" was that he was called Ego C. Clarke.

(I pass along this snippet not for any value save that when a Great Man has died, *every* snippet takes on heft and curiosity value. So that *this* snippet is not lost, I drop it here, with the attendant footnote:

(I knew Arthur for more than fifty years. Never once, in all that time, did I *ever* encounter even a scintilla of *argumentum ad baculum* that would speak to Arthur properly being thus monickered. Either the canard was a jealous snipe from those floundering professionally in the wake of his vast success...or he was a whiz at playing courteous, gentlemanly.)

What may also be difficult for those who have lived in a world where the Great Man has always existed, is that when Arthur first flushed with success, he'd only had two books published. The first was INTERPLANETARY FLIGHT in 1950 but though he had been a Fellow of the Royal Astronomical Society and became Chairman of the British Interplanetary Society in 1949, this was half a decade before Sputnik, and people who talked about Interplanetary Flight were only a smidge-cut less certifiable than those who frequently see portraits of Jesus in their Mexican food. INTERPLANETARY FLIGHT was not a great commercial success. So strapped was Arthur that he accepted a commission tendered by his then-literary agent, Scott Meredith, to write an original novel slanted for young adults. ISLANDS IN THE SKY. It was one of the Winston series packaged by the Meredith Agency, and it came out not long before Arthur and I became friends. But it was with the publication of THE EXPLORATION OF SPACE in that same year, 1951, that he suddenly became not just another Brit scrivener trying to crack the big U.S. market, but a sudden sensation.

Now, fifty-seven years later, it may be difficult for some of you to fathom how genuinely B● I● G●! was the appearance of THE EXPLORATION OF SPACE.

It was the very first ever book even *remotely* associated with science fiction, or the core interests that formed the nucleus of that genre...to be selected for The Book-Of-The-Month Club. In these days of "franchise" authors who crank out dumpsterful of proscribed crap—one a year like crazy clockwork—writing so pallid and ephemeral that it is ennobled by the insult "creative typing"—stories so instantly forgettable they go through you like beets through a baby's backside—to have One of Our Own reach the pinnacle of the game in 1951 was *beyond* breathtaking.

Arthur did that. To us, he was a Great Man long before most of you even knew he walked this planet he loved so deeply.

Soon after all the foofaraw about how soon-to-be-*Sir* Arthur had predicted communications satellites and blahblahblah, he and I found ourselves by chance sans dinner plans simultaneously, on West 47th Street, Arthur was in from Sri Lanka, I was in from

Photo B

Photo C

Los Angeles, and we bumped at the corner of Sixth Avenue.

So we said whatthehell, and decided to go to dinner without letting anyone on either side of us know where we were, and we hiked over a block to the old, famous, Steuben Tavern, and we had a swell evening. It was nifty, and it was swell; and sometime in the middle of the schnitzel, ribbing him about his new Great Fame, I asked him, "Hey, kiddo, I know you're famous for extrapolating all these great advances, but tell me the biggest boner you ever predicted."

And Arthur, who ribbed me in a completely different Brit way than I did as a Yank, thought about it for a few moments and answered, "I was smart enough to know we'd see the moon landing in my lifetime, but I wasn't smart enough to know we'd be watching it as it happened, in our living rooms, on the telly."

Look at photo C. It was taken as an *hommage* to photo B, more than a quarter century after the former. In 1953, at Beastley's-On-The-Bayou the great fantasist Robert Bloch has his arm around a pipe-smoking smartass me, age eighteen. Next to me was standing the awfully beautiful Evelyn Paige, who was the wife of the editor of *Galaxy Science Fiction*, H.L. Gold (who published many of Arthur's best stories), and there at the end of the progression is Arthur, quite tall. In 1980 Arthur came to Los Angeles for a signing, and at Barry Levin's old shop on Westwood Boulevard we gathered the group redux.

Bob is where Bob was, I've been moved over a space and the place Evelyn held is occupied by the estimable Dr. Jerry Pournelle. And there, again, was my friend Arthur, now not so tall. I consider this a treasure because...

As time, space and gravity had their way with us, we spoke less frequently. The years slipped by in shadow, but three years ago or so, Arthur sent me a birthday card (I usually called him on *his* natal anniversaries) and a photo from Sri Lanka. It is a spiffy photo of Arthur in a well-starched, untucked blue Hawaiian sport shirt festooned with leaping dolphins. The shot was taken from slightly above, at a descending angle so he's looking up at me with that smile that age never altered; and hugged to his side with his left hand is a baby-blue *T. Rex* that is wearing, I swear, *exactly* the same grin.

It is my smug secret suspicion that the saurian felt overcome with honor and camaraderie, at being permitted to have his photo taken with such a Great Man.

# THE PITCH

Editor's Note: Two installments of this
column were written for *Written By: The
Journal of the Writers Guild of America, west.*
A third column, promised in the second, never
appeared.

# It Goes in Neat,
# but It Comes Out...

So these three suits from the production company schlep me over to, I think it was CBS, in the middle of an afternoon; and as we're going up in the elevator, having been full-body-cavity strip-searched and irradiated by the golem working security at the reception desk in the lobby, one of these guys says to me, "Don't pick a fight."

There wasn't anything to say to that, but I gave him the look. It was my *I'll suck out your eyeball for a Jujube* look. This was my third pitch get-together with these gents and the resident hemorrhoids currently calling themselves VPs of Development. It was my certain belief that human speech was not their native tongue. These jamooks were so dense they'd drown in a Think Tank.

Nonetheless, I was "involved" in the project; in for a penny is in for a pound; and so I kept letting myself be dragged over to Fairfax, to CBS, for these bone/stick/stone-stupid pitch meetings. I was younger. I was doing social work among the intellectually deprived.

After the demeaning heel-cool in the outer office, we were shoveled into the conference chamber where the great old wizard Shazam sat with his Sanhedrin of post-pubescent yes-folk. After the traditional seeking for gnats and lice in the fur of the VPs, after the traditional puckering and posturing, we got down to work. *Work*, being the following: "Well, fellahs, we think we've finally got the kinks worked out, think we've really got some *wonderful* ideas to bounce off you, think we're finally on the right track and *take it, Harlan*!"

At which juncture all simulacra of intelligence in that chamber fastened on me. So, like a tap dancing ten year old out with Mommy at an audition, I began to do my number.

(I'll save you the specifics. Same crap each of us has had to do. But, for continuity, here's what the basic idea was: guy from Atlantis; nasty humans polluting the crap out of his undersea world; he comes up to enlist the aid of a crack *Mission: Impossible* sort of team of variegated stock-personality specialists to stop the ravagers of the natural world; he walks among us like a latter-day aquatic Jesus, or maybe just a moist Michael Ovitz.)

When I completed, having done the triple somersault with a full twist and nailing it on the landing, there was universal acclaim. Loved it. *Luh*-ved it!

That is, till the great old wizard Shazam (we're talking about thirty years old here) steeples his manicured paws and looks down the table—not at me, mind you, I was just the writer who was gonna do all the goddam work—but the head suit from the production company—and he says, "But who gets punched?"

Let me drive that one past you in low gear.

"Who gets punched?"

The company dude bites his lower lip and turns to me. So, now, do all the others. I look at Shazam and I ask, though I know, "What do you mean: 'Who gets punched?'"

He amplifies, demonstrating the value of an education at the Wharton School. "Who gets hit? Where does the action land? Who gets punched?"

...

There is a timeless moment in all events.  In Indonesia they call it *djam karet*, the hour that stretches. And in that gelid instant of infinite possibilities, if one is attuned, one may hear the rocking of the Earth, that great egg that beats in the stillness of eternity. Who gets punched?

...

"Yo Momma," I said,  "Yo *Momma* gets punched!"

There was, then, a silence one encounters only at the deepest beneath of the Cayman Trench. A hush that would make an itch nervous.

And, finally, eons later, one of the yes-nerds blurted, "How *dare* you speak to Shazam like that?!? Who the hell d'you think you are?"

And I stood, and I said, "I *think* I am a writer. I *know* that you-all ought to be out on a hillside, planting trees and serving the commonweal, instead of squatting here pretending to be adequate to the conception of ideas when you ought to have your IQs taken with a rectal thermometer. I'm a writer, you buncha bozos, I don't know *what* the hell *you* are."

And I walked. Slowly, in a stately fashion, hoping one of them would make a move on me. That series went on the air...briefly. I didn't write it. I didn't watch it.

Next time, Unca' Harlan will tell you *another* pitch story.

## ...but It Comes Out Spinning, Like a Flying Saucer

What it hadda be—in some previous incarnation—maybe Phoenicia or Atlantis as an heir to the throne, but more likely as the court jester in some Kansas City slaughter-house in the early 1800s—I must have pissed off the local deity; and so, for my sins, in *this* life I was forced to work with Chuck Fries. The well-known producer and universe-class ballbuster, Charles W. Fries.

We're talking 1975 here. The project was a movie-for-tv called *The Tigers Are Loose*, based on the murder of the eight student nurses in Chicago by that sick fuck Richard Speck, 1966. This sweet guy named Barry Kirk had brought me in to do the two-hour script, and Fries was the "producing entity."

Entity, in the sense of a necromantic being from some stygian underworld. An entity who, to call him up from below, required the use of pentacles and the blood of ebony goats and the ability to chant mystic verses in a guttural tongue. We suggest a resonance of Lovecraft when I call Chuck an entity. Lovely man. Ate flies.

So after the first few meetings with Barry and Fries, at the latter's offices in what is now CBS Studio Center, I came to develop a "working relationship" with Chuckie-ChuckieChuckie. (Ask Ray Bradbury or Stan Lee: they'll tell you this was an inspired way to liaison with Charles W.) And here's how it worked—

I'd come into Fries's office, with whatever revision to the script he'd visited upon me during our previous session in the Abattoir of Ideas he called a story conference, and he'd look over the changes I'd been thumbscrewed into making (all the while trying to keep my gorge from becoming buoyant), and he'd cluck to himself like a Water-Pik run

169

amuck, and then he'd look up, fiercely, his beady little marmoset eyes flashing…and he'd start to scream.

Let me amend that. He would start to SSSSCUH-REEEEM!!!

(Trust me on this. I come from a good Jewish family in which no one but my dear, long-gone father ever spoke in anything less nerve-shattering than a 180-decibel warwhoop *geshry*. I am a scream expert, a maven of mind-shattering noise. Hitler exhorting the mobs was a mute by comparison with Chuck Fries. The man's voice, at full measure, could shatter cardboard.)

Don't ask me what the hell he was so apoplectic about; at this happy, far remove from that season in development hell my memory of inconsequential specifics is fuzzy. But it was usually something so petty, so minuscule, so cosmically trivial—but always in support of his well-muscled yet turbid delusion that he knew how to Discuss Ideas in Human Congress—that even if you *could* figure out what he was fulminating about, it would inevitably be something you didn't give a fig about anyway. (Please excuse my harsh language.)

What it was, was that Chuck Fries, I'm dead certain, just stayed in the Industry so he could intimidate people. Making movies and selling tv series was a serendipitous accident. He did, in fact, manage to turn out some exemplary material over the decades (and is still at it, I guess), but no delight could the production of even an Oscar or Emmy winner have brought him that would rival the blasphemous rapture he experienced when he was howling like a demented fruit-bat at some galley slave of a writer. A look of such beatific ecstasy suffused his ruddy, chubby countenance when he was at full foghorn efflorescence, that one couldn't help but feel privileged, uplifted, nay…*honored* to be in the line of that ultrasonic tongue-lashing!

But while plaster was crazing and windows were shattering, and the Golden, Colorado Seismic Center was registering 6.7 on the Richter, one found oneself in some personal distress, because blood would start to spurt from nose and ears, and one would have to think with warmth of a THX Sound System in a truly tiny Cineplex screening room for its mellifluous and calming qualities. By comparison.

(There are members of the Writers Guild who are, to this day, able only to eke out a living by selling used 8-track cassettes at rock concerts, while collecting High Hazard Medical Benefits from the health-&-welfare program of the Guild's swell insurance scheme. These dismal creatures all worked for Chuck and are now, in technical terms, referred to as the Legions of the Dumbstruck, or, Chuckie's Kids. Telethon this weekend, channel 11. Give till it hurts.)

So what I would do, when he commenced bleating at me, was to get up from the chair in front of his desk, walk quickly but with dignity to the farthest venue of the room, turn my face into the corner like an errant child, and begin speaking to him in a *very soft* voice. Barely above the level of audibility. Now get this: he's way over there, on the other side of the office, howling and pounding the desk, shattering the eardrums of the potted plants on the window ledge, and I'm way over here, see, way over here in this corner, talking almost to myself. But low. Very soft. Nice. A cute kid.

A couple of moments of this, and here comes Fries, all the way across the office to scream at me from close up behind me. But do I turn around? I do not, nosiree. I keep talking quietly, sweetly. And in about a minute he torques down to mere air raid siren level, then to that of a passing locomotive, and eventually to a normal tone of voice. I use the word *normal* in its most transmogrified manifestation.

And when he'd calm down enough that his eyeballs receded to their original situs, I'd turn, smile sweetly, what a cute kid, and I'd say, "Now, you beast of the fields, you wanna talk story?"

And you know what…it worked every damned time. But here's the problem: this was only the preamble to The Pitch story I *wanted* to tell you, in which I took the screenplay of *Tigers* to Steve Gentry at ABC. Well, maybe next time Unca' Harlan will delight you with the denouement of this heart-rending saga. We'll see. If you eat all your vegetables, and stop making excuses for Roland Emmerich movies.

Editor's Note: The following essay and subsequent letter concern the pin-up icon Bettie Page. The first appeared as the introduction to *The Betty Pages Annual*, the latter in the letter column of *Outré* magazine.

# The Queen of Guilty Pleasures

Go ahead, burn down the farm! Put my barn to the torch, slaughter my brood mares, rape my chickens, and pour salt on my silo! I *will* speak the truth, having been cursed with a truly anemic tolerance for bullshit; because we all know the time has come to end this duplicity, mendacity, and doubletalking. And commonsense protect us from the endless parade of forelock-tugging, mealymouthed, tremulous dissemblers who seek to avoid the scorpion sting of the censors with gibberish about her identity as a mythic cultural icon. What the hell is the matter with those people?!? Have they no understanding that *nothing* can deflect or assuage the self-righteous, stick-up-the-ass bluenoses? Just look at what we seek to honor: a creature of flesh and blood whose turn of ankle and pertness of breast can reduce a man or boy to Silly Putty.

There's no way on Earth that the direct lineal descendants of Cotton Mather who sniff out "turpitude" in Teenage Mutant Ninja Turtles and Madonna and *Playboy* centerfolds could ever be turned away from trying to paint a crimson A on the forehead of anyone foolhardy enough to sigh publicly at a poster of those naked buttocks.

I refuse to join that legion of dithering apologists.

I'll tell you the simple truth.

I never met her; I have no idea if she was a bright and cheery person or an empty-headed tart; was she inordinately intelligent or a dumb bunny; was she a virgin till the day she vanished from our ken or did she make her living in shadier ways than merely posing for those naïve cheesecake shots? Given my choice of an evening in conversation with her, or Albert Einstein, or even Eleanor Roosevelt...well, she'd come in third.

My most intimate contact with her was in the examination under a magnifying glass

173

of hundreds of sheets of contact prints trying to select half a dozen photos for a layout in *Rogue* magazine, when I was an editor on that publication in the late Fifties. But like every male I've ever met who has seen a picture of her, I cannot to this day see a photo of Bettie Page without getting an erection. And that is the simple truth; and that is what it's all about.

For all the sweetness of her glances, the innocence of her most exotic poses, the ineffable quality that shines out of every muzzy, scratchy still printed on magazine paper of blotter quality that swallowed clarity and definition...she was (and reportedly still is) one of the sexiest women who ever lived.

I have no idea if the correct spelling is *Betty* or *Bettie* (though it was the latter I first encountered, and the one I choose to use, because it's part of the litany for me), and I have no desire to track her down in modern times, to learn to my sadness that she is no longer the ingénue that lives in my memories. It is enough for me—and clearly enough for the thousands who buy all those posters and magazines—that she remains young and smoldering on glossy paper and in a few remaining movie shorts. Bogart is alive and well in Casablanca, Garbo is without wrinkle or shadow as Mata Hari, and W.C. Fields can still shoot one hell of a game of eight-ball with that meandering pool cue. Like a saber-tooth tiger flash-frozen in a block of ice, the wonder of Bettie Page is preserved forever in the photographs taken when she was a young woman.

She turned me on then, when I was a teenager; and she turns me on now, as I caper through my middle fifties. Sitting on a plane at 36,000 over the Grand Canyon, on the way back to L.A. from an adult journey to New York, where I lectured at an institution of higher education, just like a real grownup, and I get to section D of *USA Today* (the journalistic equivalent of Pringles) and I'm looking at Bettie in mesh hose and tassle-festooned panties, and I'm a teenager again. There's that curtain of dark hair, the erotic bangs that only she and Ella Raines could wear with impunity, the sloe-eyes, that great butt thrust back and out as if she's about to jump your bones; and she's posed with one of the two best ways she formed her mouth: the lower lip dropped in something like a half-snarl. And I coulda kissed the photo editor who picked that still for the June 5th, 1991 *USA Today*, because it was obvious that s/he was also a love-slave of Bettie Page. A parvenu would've picked one of the lousy poses, where her nose looks lumpy, and her expression is sappy.

*That* was her magic gift: the ability, even forty years down the line, to crank back your puberty clock so you're just a horny, drooling, simpering adolescent, wishing you could melt as one with the tachyons in the time-stream and rush back to a moment when she was in her early twenties and might have given you a tumble. She is simply pure fantasy. A dream girl in all the nicest ways, in that undiluted human passion way that we all shared at some point in our innocence. She is lust in an ice cream cone (two scoops), enthusiasm in the whisper of nylon, postpubescent rambunctiousness in the back seat of a Studebaker Commander. Like maybe only a handful of American women who gave themselves to public adoration, like Fay Wray and Jinx Falkenberg and Barbara Eden and Suzy Parker and Joi Lansing and the usual group of suspects spearheaded by Marilyn (who couldn't compare to Bettie for inciting lust-dreams), Page transcended mere mortal flesh. She was icon, Venus on the spike-heel, the goddess Astarte come again, smoother and sleeker and possibly available.

She didn't have Dietrich's legs or Marta Toren's cheekbones or the young Liz Taylor's waist, but whatever congeries of parts and measurements were hers, they were hers alone; and when Madonna and Amy Grant and Sean Young are names as flensed of resonance as Ella Raines's, there will still be golden hordes of dopey guys like me who tremble at the sight of Bettie Page jerkily doing her hoochie-koochie on one of Klaw's peekaboo films.

Wherever she is now, staying out of the spotlight of all this new-found attention, she need never try to hide her past from Jesus or her grandchildren. She was something special; and just by *being* she has brought more undiluted joy into the universe of drabness than a thousand senators and do-gooders and religiosos. Bettie Page got the gift we all seek:

She got the gift of Forever. Posterity knows her. And *that*, gentle readers, is a trick almost *nobody* pulls off.

## An Open Letter to *Outré* and Its Editors: *J'accuse*

Like me, you have been duped...you have been used...and like me, you have aided and abetted a disreputable, distasteful and (in its purest definition) basically evil enterprise. I refer to the exploitative "commentary" by John Michlig in *Outré* number 12 concerning Richard Foster's vile book about Bettie Page. As I am desolate at my own naïveté, as I am frustrated that I was unable to stop publication of this loathsome tome through legal channels, so am I equally disappointed in you—Michael, Ted, and *Outré*—that you gulled yourselves into believing *any* attention paid to this crappy dishonoring of an innocent woman was, in any way, "in the public interest."

It doesn't matter if what Foster dredged up from the sewers of human behavior is true or false. Doesn't matter. Who cares!?! Who the hell cares that Pee-wee Herman frequented porn movies, or that Robert Mitchum smoked marijuana, or that Dalton Trumbo once sent a letter in solidarity to oppressed Communist writers, or that King Kong had dandruff, or that Princess Diana had extramarital affairs!?! The only ones who care about this kind of cheaptrash garbagemouth minutiæ are the scum who work for the nasty tabloids, and all the knuckle-dragging, slope-browed, prognathous-jawed troglodytes who slaveringly *read* those crappy little journals. The kinds of people neither you nor I want to have anything to do with, right Michael, right Ted? We're better than that, ain't we? Knowing the pustulant anecdotes that Richard Foster dredged up does not, by even a scintilla, improve our state of existence, or tell us anything that we needed to know. It is someone's private life, served up to make a filthy buck, by a writer and a publisher utterly empty of decent ethic or restraint of human compassion.

177

That you gave aid and comfort to their enterprise, is a sad thing, no matter *what* chirping self-exculpatory rationales you cobble up. You did a bad thing, you did a wrong thing, and if I were your mommy I would say, "Shame on you!"

But just so you can feel even *slightly* exonerated for your behavior, I will put myself in the same 9th and inner circle of Hell with you, by advising you that Foster is a duplicitous, out-of-the-bag liar, who conned me into an involvement with this wretched book that I find sticks in my craw like a gobbet of uncooked polecat.

Way back early in 1997, Foster contacted me. He said he'd read my *hommage*-introduction to Bettie that appeared some years ago in Greg Theakston's *Betty Pages* annual. He said he wanted to use it in a new book he was writing about Bettie Page, and he wanted to interview me about my "association" with Ms. Page, in addition to reprinting my already-published essay. I expressed some head-scratching curiosity about it, because the Karen Essex biography of Bettie seemed more than sufficient. (We are, after all, and this is a large part of the point to be made, talking more about an *icon*, an *image*, a *cultural trope* than a human being. Bettie, as person, is *her* business; Bettie, as public persona, as vision on a printed page, is what *we* are correctly allocated.)

I said to Foster that I thought such a project was probably redundant, chewing the meal twice, coals-to-Newcastle. That is, unnecessary. Oh no, he assured me, rushing into the vacuum of my trepidation, this is going to be a much more *elegant* tribute to Bettie Page. Filled with fascinating new material about how wonderful she was and is, and blah blah blah. At no time did Foster even remotely hint, suggest, imply, or fore-shadow his intent to make a scurrilous buck off this elderly and reclusive woman through the dredging-up of inconsequential yellowjack ancient history. Never once did he let on that I was being asked to participate in a kind of foul non-literary graverobbing that would cause Bettie Page misery. He was, in short, a lying creep who twisted my affection for someone I'd never even physically met—nor do I care to intrude to do so—to get me to help legitimatize an act of meanspirited callousness.

On 16 April 97 he thanked me by letter for giving him the telephone interview. He also thanked me—and here's the emblematic element that sums up Foster and what sort of excuse for a human being he is—for allowing him to reprint my essay for a token ten dollar fee. (When he'd solicited the piece, he did a tippy-toe worthy of Fred Astaire, assuring me that the Carol Publishing Group had limited finances, and so he could only pay me a "token honorarium"—his phrase—though he knew I received fees much larger for reprint rights to my material. In this case, a piece of this length, anywhere from $700 to $1500 usually.) All through April I corrected faxes of the copy relating to me, and then I heard nothing again until I saw page proofs in August. I updated the essay, corrected typos, added bits of revised copy, and sent it back. August 22$^{nd}$, he advised me the book would be out the week of 20 October. And still, no advisement of what gossipy, drooling nastiness the book would proffer. Still innocent, like a country bumpkin, I waited to see this new "tribute" to that lovely lady.

On Tuesday 21 October 97, I received the Bud Plant Catalogue of art books and allied titles. For the first time I saw the cover of Foster's book, and though the image was tiny, I was able to make out—with utter horror—the alleged mug shots of Bettie Page. I was furious. "The truth about the queen of the pin-ups" said the blurb, and the come-on copy guaranteed to get those pruriently fascinated to order the book added tasty phrases about Bettie's "descent into violent obsession and madness" and on and on.

If Foster had been within arm's reach, I'd have done him a grievous bodily harm. I know he'll be wise enough never to put himself within arm's range of me. I called the wretch at *Style Weekly*, and told him I wanted to yank my contributions from his filthy little hustle, on the grounds that he had lied to me about the purpose and slant of the book. He tugged his greasy forelock like Uriah Heep, and drywashed his hands like Pontius Pilate, and mealymouthed like the *paparazzi* whose lizard heads emerge from your toilet as you're taking a dump, who snap a photo of your ass, and then shyly explain that "the public needs to know" and they're only reporting the news as they see it.

That is to say, basically he told me to go fugg myself, that he wasn't removing one word he'd mulcted out of me. I told him I'd sue him and Carol. Anyone knows me, knows I don't do empty air.

You'll love *this* part. Foster, who had been slavishly grateful to me for my cooperation, who had imposed on me evenings and weekends to revise and correct his idiot writings, who couldn't express enough sincerity and gratitude...sent me the following letter by fax on 22 October (bear in mind that great line from *A Streetcar Named Desire* that crops up in Neil Simon's *The Goodbye Girl*... "I happen to have this lawyer acquaintance downtown..."):

> *I spoke with Carol Publishing today and they instructed me to tell you that any further questions—legal or otherwise—that you have about my book and/or the use of your essay should be directed in writing to the publisher, Steven Schragis, and not to me.*
>
> *Schragis, who is also a lawyer, can be reached in care of the Carol*

*Publishing Group* (address followed).

    *I'm sorry, but that's all the information I have to offer regarding your demand. Sincerely...*

Weasel. Bow and scrape and beg for freebies, dupe well-meaning people into serving your filthy little endeavor, then when you get caught with your knife bloody, scamper for cover and offer the paralyzingly scary specter of Schragis—whose name and previous reputation echo tinnily—instead of standing up to what you did. Walk like a man, Foster, don't crawl like a slug.

I consulted my New York counsel, Patrick Lyons, Esq. (I happen to have this lawyer acquaintance downtown...) Pat sought a restraining order, or an injunction, or whatever the hell it's called when you seek to enjoin *rodenta* from dropping their diseased pellets. Pat made it clear it would cost me many thousands to get such an instrumentality issued. I told him I didn't care. I don't have that many thousands that I can toss them around frivolously; but I respond badly to realizing with chagrin that after all these years, as smart as I like to think I am, that I can be conned by someone as transparently disreputable as this Foster.

Pat got back to me a day later. They'd pushed up the date of publication, apparently to make certain that if I wasn't just a blowhard, that I wouldn't actually be able to embargo their little putrescence, that I'd be left standing on a windy hilltop with my dick in my hand, as we of the Culturally Elite put it.

The book was already on press. I couldn't stop it.

So I got in touch with Dave Stevens—he of *The Rocketeer*—and Bettie's good friend—and told him what had gone down. I begged him to tell Bettie, when next he saw her, that I had been an unwitting tool of these miserable back-alley miscreants, I asked him to ask her please to forgive my gullibility and my lack of proper investigation of Foster before I ever accommodated him.

And now, *Outré* serves as Foster and Schragis's hand-maiden. I cannot fathom the thinking of you guys, or of Mr. Michlig, who wrote the piece, that would permit you to dupe yourselves into thinking you could possibly be doing anything but *harm* to this woman who never hurt anyone, who has lived her later life in serious reclusion. The disclaimer that "well, it would all come out, anyway, and *somebody* had to write it" is bullshit! Even if it came out in Foster's book, there was no need to add an *additional* venue by bringing *Outré's* readers, who might have missed being tainted by the knowledge, into it. You spread the gossip one more wave. You now refuse to cop to your morbid need to run yet another exploitative Bettie Page feature, with more opportunities to show her sexy self, and you rationalize it with the indefensible apologia that Mr. Michlig was trying to be "supportive" and "sympathetic." Bullshit. It's yellow journalism, and it's even less honest than what Foster and Schragis did. They, at least, are media whores without any heart. They don't care how tainted a buck they make with their minimal talents and their hyena business ethics. But you guys...you didn't need to buy into it. Michlig could've been told to peddle his second-hand "sympathetics" to a journal less stately than this one that I'd come to admire so much.

You, me, the bunch of us. We did Bettie Page a dirty. I'm a dumb schmuck. But what name do you guys give yourselves/and the magazine? And have you maybe learned a valuable lesson about how easy it is to be dragged into the mire of vileness and bad journalistic practices that has become the sickening norm in this country?

Have you at least the balls to drop Bettie Page a note, to apologize?

Harlan Ellison
6 April 1998

Editor's Note: "He Speaks, and the Angels Sing" originally appeared as liner notes for *Benny Goodman and His Orchestra: Let's Dance*. It was subsequently reprinted in *Musical Heritage Review* Vol. 10, #2. The author and editor wish to thank David Jessup for his correction regarding the date of the gig in question.

# He Speaks, and the Angels Sing

The minutiae of the memory is fuzzed, like the second hundredth replay of one of those heavy vinyl lp's from the early Fifties, sans filter; but the important parts are as fresh as the sounds that came through the wall that day.

Since it was just before I got drafted, it had to be some time in 1956. We're talking here about an apartment on West 82nd Street between Amsterdam and Columbus Avenues in New York, during the first full year of my writing career as a professional; an apartment in which I spent most of every day, hammering away on a typewriter: at a penny a word, one could not grow weary. Being a pulp writer in those days was, I always think, the equivalent of doing endless one-nighters with the big bands in the Thirties and Forties. Different beat, same end result: lots of product turned out.

On that afternoon in 1956 I was having a hard time working. Not for lack of inspiration—the rent was due and I'd taken to swiping bottles of milk from in front of a neighbor's door two floors below—but because the guy in the next apartment kept playing the same damned tune on the piano. Hour after hour, never really running through the number completely, but stopping, starting, playing a series of chords again and again. And I knew that song.

Finally, less out of annoyance than curiosity, I went next door and rousted him out. "Don't for a moment let the fact that my career is going down the drain because I can't concentrate on what I'm writing because you're driving me up a wall," I said cheerily, "but what's the name of that piece you've been eviscerating?"

He grinned at me, and said, "Stealin' Apples."

So I grinned back. "Benny Goodman."

And we stood there grinning at each other like a pair of lemurs. After a moment he invited me in, and I learned he was doing some rescoring for a gig Goodman was soon to play out in New Jersey. We chatted a while, he ran through the number in its entirety, just to make me smile, and I went back to work. And since I always write to music, I removed the Scarlatti from the turntable and put on the Goodman 1938 Carnegie Hall Concert. Funny how fast and how easily the writing went.

It's been, what, about ten years since we last heard new cuts from Goodman? A lot longer since we've heard Benny with the big band. (There was that terrific session along about '58, with charts by a kid named Bobby Gutesha, a Yugoslavian composer-arranger Benny met when he was working the Brussels Fair, a session that featured one of the juiciest jazz numbers Benny ever recorded, "Batunga Train"…and then the band he led at Basin Street East with Red Norvo and Flip Phillips and Russ Freeman and just a *mess* of great players; that was 1960.) Yeah, there's been totally too much Goodmanoid silence this last decade.

But current evidence proves the old man's still got it. At seventy-six years of age, now looking like a warmhearted, cherubic, Great Hornrimmed Owl, Goodman is back with a full complement of sidepersons (there's a female up there in the horn section now), and the joyous sound is with us once more.

One tends to forget, if one is continually exposed to what passes for popular music today, that it is possible for music to make you smile. One need not wish to stuff one's head in the oven or drink Lysol after having spent an hour listening to music. There is a panacea available for the logorrhea of Top 40 babble. It comes as an over-the-counter medication packaged under the trade name Goodman.

On October 7th, 1985, at a thousand dollar a seat, by invitation only concert in New York's Marriott Marquis, Benny and the big band played a sensational date to be aired on PBS on March 15th. *Benny Goodman: Let's Dance! A Musical Tribute* is the listing. And though it is strange to look at all these giants on whose work I grew up— Teddy Wilson, Red Norvo, Louis Bellson—and see them lined and gray, if you close your eyes and unfetter your heart and just listen, there they are…still young, still tough, because it's young, tough music. There is happiness in the performance; young, tough, unfettered happiness.

The range of numbers, newly-charted and dust-free, is heavenly. "Blue Room" and "Down South Camp Meeting;" "King Porter Stomp" and "Memories of You;" "After You're Gone" and the 1939 Martha Tilton stunner, "And the Angels Sing" with its echoes of the *hora*; and "Don't Be That Way" and "Goodbye;" and even a new version of (wait for it) "Sing, Sing, Sing."

There is also the singing of Carrie Smith on "Gimme a Pigfoot (and a Bottle of Beer)" and "Ja-Da." Ms. Smith is, in the parlance of west Texas, a real frog-strangler. A natural force. Louie Armstrong died, but his throat got reincarnated in Carrie Smith. Not even Bessie could find fault with her Pigfoot.

And Louis Bellson, the last of the real drummers, right in there clipping off rimshots, enunciating for all who care to listen that the drum box and the control panel neither uplift nor sustain.

There is even a tasty new version of "Stealin' Apples," be still my heart.

What I like to do is put this new session on the machine, crank up the gain, leave the room, close the door, get on the other side of the wall in this place I now live bought by all those penny-a-word days and nights, and settle down to hearing Benny doing "Stealin' Apples." Coming through the wall again after all these years.

It ain't 1956, thank goodness, but it's nice to feel airy and happy in just the same way. To all the encomiums laid at Benny Goodman's feet, add this one: he has made the world smile for more than half a century.

I said that to Scarlatti just yesterday, and he gave me a thumbs-up and said, "You tell'm, kid."

Editor's Note: From 1990 to 2013, Peter David wrote *But I Digress...*, a column for *Comic Buyer's Guide*. David credits Ellison as the inspiration for the work, and the latter provided introductions to two volumes collecting the various installments: 1994's BUT I DIGRESS... and 2009's MORE DIGRESSIONS. In 2000, Ellison contributed a guest column, collected herein.

# But I Digress...
## Guest Column

So Todd McFarlane and Larsen walk into a building.

You'd think *one* of them would have seen it.

Erik Larsen looses the gardyloo: "Poor millionaire Toddy! If this verdict stands, o lord lord lordy lord, think of the hideous 'chilling effect' on First Amendment rights! Oh, me! Oh, my!"

Oh, horse puckey.

What we're talking about here is an amateur writer's fannish gag of naming characters after real people. They are called "Tuckerisms," after Wilson "Bob" Tucker, a science-fiction and mystery writer who was very, very big in the sf field. He was a toastmaster, a humorist, and a friend.

When Bob Tucker did his novels, he occasionally used the names of real people, such as F. Towner Laney or Charles Burbee. They were then prominent fans. He did mystery novels: THE RED HERRING, THE CHINESE DOLL, others. They're excellent novels, they're just wonderful, though now long out of print. In his sf stuff he did the same thing: He used the names of fans. So "Tuckerism" became the accepted nickname for such loving homages, and for a while a fairly widespread kind of thing. Almost every writer at one time or another has done it. It's usually done as a nod to friends, an in-joke, and no one takes it seriously.

What happened to McFarlane is a very different thing. He used a name in a malicious way, as he has done in the past with Peter David and John Byrne. A smartass version of "Tuckerism," as weapon. It is a mean-spirited, amateurish, adolescent trick used by a person with a nasty heart. A professional does not do it, ever, because pros are aware of the fact that in this litigious society, anyone can sue anybody at any time, with or without genuine grievance. And it causes ancillary damage to innocent parties: Look at the money in settlements it has forced on *Wizard* and HBO, just so Todd McFarlane could demonstrate his childish bravado.

It doesn't matter whether they're wrong or right or if they have a case or don't have a case, as when Michael Fleischer sued me. And I was praising him—*praising* him—in the interview that I did, but he didn't like the way I praised him. So he sued me and tried to make some money off it. Well, I always fight these things to the wall. At the moment I'm battling remarq.com and AOL and we're litigating a case very much like the one that a federal judge dealt with in the Napster decision last month. Copyright infringement. Mooches and punks who think they can post other people's stories for free are learning that copyright applies online as well as offline. But I digress.

Back to the dangers of Tuckerisms.

In the early days of my career, 1956, I was assigned by the editor of *Infinity Science Fiction* as one of three writers who would do a trio of short short stories, each with the title "Blank." The three writers who were picked by Editor Larry Shaw were Randall Garrett, Isaac Asimov, and me. Isaac did a story called "Blank!" Randy did one called "Blank." Mine was "Blank..." In my story, because Isaac and I were friends, and everyone called him Ike, my villain's name was "Rike Akisimov." An example of using a Tuckerism. Dopey—but I was young in the job.

Yet apart from that, I can't recall doing that kind of thing very much. When I was in the Army and I hated my first sergeant and the captain in my company, I used their names in a story. But I didn't use their first names, just their last names. I was aware that you couldn't do that kind of thing and make someone a negative character, because I was running the risk of being jumped on. I didn't do it often, and, when I did, it was just for a lark.

So I came to Hollywood in 1962 and started working in tv. After a little while, I was writing *The Man from U.N.C.L.E.*, the series produced by the famous Norman Felton. I had an office at MGM and I was their fair-haired boy, because I had written some very clever shows for them, according to the critics. And I went to *The Man from*

*U.N.C.L.E.* after having made a big splash on *Burke's Law* and I was making top dollar in Hollywood and had been, by no merest chance, dating Norman Felton's daughter. Norman was very high on me and wanted me to create my own series, since his spinoff, *The Girl from U.N.C.L.E.* wasn't doing that well. So I was building my own series at the time. On the fast track to glory.

Right around that time, the most popular novel in America was PEYTON PLACE. So I created a plot for *The Man from U.N.C.L.E.* about a woman, Jacqueline Midcult (played by Sharon Farrell), living in a small Iowa town, who finds a diary in the attic of her family home, and the diary is filled with a long story detailing the adventures of a spy. She uses the notebooks as the basis for writing a *roman à clef*, a spy novel entitled THE PIECES OF FATE. What she doesn't know is that this was her grandfather's (or perhaps it was her father's) memoirs, when he was part of the enemy network T.H.R.U.S.H. So now she's got these books, T.H.R.U.S.H. goes after her, and U.N.C.L.E. sends Kuryakin and Solo to protect her and find out where she got the info. And the script was called "The Pieces of Fate Affair." I wrote it in 1966. And it aired as the 82nd episode on Feb. 24, 1967. It aired once, was not rerun, and was not included in the syndication package. And I will tell you why. And you will understand why this relates to Todd McFarlane... and why it chills not.

In the script—and it was a silly thing to do, however innocently it was intended—I used the names of some of my friends in the SF world. I thought they'd get a kick being in-group trivia in an enormously popular primetime tv series. There was a shoppe in town called Jack Vance's Bookstore. There was a T.H.R.U.S.H. assassin named Simeon Spinrad (because Norman Spinrad was my closest friend, and he laughed and I laughed, and it was like that). Don't forget *The Man from U.N.C.L.E.* was very much parody, it was never a serious kind of program. THE COMPLETE DIRECTORY OF PRIMETIME NETWORK AND CABLE SHOWS, 1946–PRESENT by Tim Brooks and Earl Marsh describes it as a "spy spoof." And Bill Koenig's *The Man from U.N.C.L.E. Episode Guide* described that episode as one of the Season Three highlights, saying, "Ellison's script parodies small-town life, the literary world, and television. He's also witty enough to make the light-hearted approach work." (*Note:* Peter unearthed the encomium: I am far too humble to toot my own fife.)

Also in the episode was a book critic who was an undercover T.H.R.U.S.H. agent, and I called her Judith Merle. The part was played with incredible elegance by Grayson

Hall, who was that year an Academy Award nominee for Best Supporting Actress, *Night of the Iguana*. So we're talking about a very fine and very well-cast part. She played most of her scenes in silk pajamas in a circular bed that turned as she gave instructions to get and kill Solo and do the things a spy does. Elegant, classy. The show aired and everybody loved it.

Now, at that time there was a book reviewer named Judith Merril. She was also a well-known editor: THE BEST SCIENCE FICTION STORIES OF THE YEAR. She had a great deal of power but she was a very opinionated and confrontational woman. She had at one point been married to Ted Sturgeon. She was known for having had affairs with any number of writers, whose works would then be included in BEST OF THE YEAR. If, on the other hand, you invoked her wrath for any reason, such as turning down her advances (as I once did in H.L. Gold's apartment in New York), you found that your work somehow didn't make it into THE BEST OF THE YEAR collection. (Well, actually, I did achieve that singular feat without compromising myself, once; but it was years later.)

Judith Merril led a strangely bifurcated life. It was incredibly dichotomous, because on the one hand she would go to these sf cons and people would treat her as if she were the Dowager Empress of China. She was feted and lauded and catered to and curried. But in truth she was working as a waitress in a diner in a small town near Milford, PA. So most of the year, she was schlepping ham and eggs and then, Cinderella-like, she would go and become this great literary lion. She was in England at the time that "The Pieces of Fate Affair" aired. I didn't think anything of it; her name wasn't used in a bad context; it didn't do anyone any harm. I never gave it a thought, in truth. My stupid!

Judy didn't have much money; she had been Bohemian strapped most of her life. So she flies back from England, gets off the plane; and the first thing that happens is her daughter says, "You were maligned on this episode of *The Man from U.N.C.L.E.* on this show that Harlan Ellison wrote." She got her all het up about it.

Without even seeing the show, they hired a man named Milton Amgott. Amgott was a science-fiction fan who also happened to be an ambulance-chasing attorney, who'd worked for all of the destitute, amateurish sf writers of the 1940s and '50s. If they had a problem, if they got thrown in jail, if there was a drunk charge on them, or they needed a will drawn up, Milt Amgott did it. But he was basically a barrister friend to the sf indigent.

Amgott took this case and proceeded to let MGM and NBC know that he was going to sue for libel on behalf of Judith Merril who had been "horrendously maligned by Harlan Ellison." They were going to sue me for a million, MGM for a million, and NBC for a million. Even though no one could specify exactly *how* Judy had been damaged. Nonetheless, Amgott seemingly initiated the lawsuit. He advised MGM and NBC that he was gonna sue.

Well, instantly I got in touch with Judy. This was very easy to do, because Judith Merril's literary agent in New York was the same as mine: Robert P. Mills. And Bob Mills set up a meeting for Judy and me to talk face to face.

I flew to New York, I sat down with Judy and Bob in his office, and I said, "Look, Judy, you've known me for more than fifteen years, and we've been friends; and I meant no harm." We both chuckled, as longtime friends would, when I mentioned "Tuckerizing," which Judy acknowledged she had herself done a few times over the years. I asked her if she'd seen the show. She said no. I said, "Kiddo, this isn't like some frivolous fanzine feud. This is the Big Time. This is MGM and NBC. These people have no sense of humor and they don't play around. This can do me great and permanent harm, Judy. So before you jump on this thing, look at the show, we'll get you a tape, and you'll see that I meant no harm...and I did you no harm."

And she said, "Harlan, I would never sue you, honey. But we have to include you as a defendant because you wrote the show. But we're never gonna pursue it with you."

I said, "Judy, it doesn't *matter* if you pursue it with me. Hollywood is a town where they live in fear of this kind of thing. And if there is so much as a *whisper* that I have caused a lawsuit, it will kill my tv career."

"Oh, no no no, honey," she said lightly, "that will never happen."

I said, "Judy, I'm telling you, it *will* happen. Don't do this to me, for pity's sake, don't."

And Bob Mills said, "Judy, this is foolish. It can't possibly do you any harm. For anyone who knows enough to have heard that there's a Judith Merril who is a book critic, they're going to laugh. It's just friends doing a funny little thing with friends. Don't do this."

I said, "Look, Judy, I've saved $5,000, in the bank. I'll give it to you. All of it. Just take the five grand and please stop this."

She got up from the chair and she came over and hugged me and gave me a kiss on the cheek. She said, "Honey, that's the end of it. I'm not going to pursue it." I breathed a sigh of relief.

Well, needless to say, she did not drop the case. And my tv series was canceled before it ever got into the production stage, and I did not work on NBC for five years, and they never re-ran that episode of "The Pieces of Fate Affair," and I lost thousands of dollars in royalties and residuals (although it did eventually turn up 20 years later on CBN, now called The Fox Family Channel). But to this day, I've not earned one more cent from that episode.


And you wanna hear the upshot? You're gonna love this. Milton Amgott, in fact, *never even filed the lawsuit*. Judy couldn't pay him, and so all that ever surfaced was the original threat in 1967. No lawsuit, no follow up, no damage—except to me—and no one to remember the bogus attempt at reaching into MGM's and NBC's "deep pockets." And 10, 15, 18 years later, they settled out of court for something like $2,000. But in the process she blighted my TV writing career. That's what killed me. At the height of my popularity, I was cut off from one of the three major markets and the studio, MGM, where I'd been working for two years. Never spoke to her again, never saw her again; she died a few years ago. When they settled for the $2,000, the Studio or NBC (I can't remember which after all this time) came back to me on the indemnification clause and the lawyers demanded, "We want you to recoup the 2 g's for us." I said, "Screw you, I'd rather starve, never work in tv again, rather than reimburse you because it was convenient for you to settle out of court on a bogus nuisance suit!"

But I learned the lesson: "Tuckerisms," using the names of people you know or real people in fictional works, can get you clobbered. It is bad, bad, bad, bad business. And any writer who is a professional knows it. Let me say again: *Bad*! *Dumb*!

And so the *Spawn* case is no more an assault on First Amendment rights or Freedom of Speech (even though Mr. McFarlane would like to pretend it is) than I am the prima ballerina of the Bolshoi ballet. What it was was Mr. McFarlane...who seems to think he is above all common rules of social congress...who seems to view himself as some sort of wonderful rebel who performed an amateur act of adolescent spitefulness... and who—like a little baby who came down and took a leak in the middle of his parents' party in order to gain attention—has had his johnson taken off with a cheese grater by Tony Twist, who was *absolutely in the right*. Mr. McFarlane did something stupid and he has no one to blame for what happened to him but his own big stupid self. And no one should have any concern that a jury judgment like this will have even a scintilla of that much-touted "chilling effect" on writers. Being who Mr. McFarlane is, and judging him only by his past inability to cop to his own missteps, he won't "get it," he'll keep indulging his skewed view of being wrongfully accused, of being a victim, and he'll keep doing this kind of adolescent jackanapery until the *next* time he gets knobbled.

There is nothing more meaningful in this little imbroglio than there was in mine, but you see how serious such silliness can become. And if ya wanna know the bottom line for anyone with a brain in his head but a McFarlane stalking horse like the intellectually paralogical Erik Larsen, this ain't nothin' more tragic than a prankster adolescent getting his knuckles rapped with a judicial ruler. May some gods or other provide Mr. McFarlane with the commonsense to get past his hubris and immaturity to come to grips with that simple truth.

# The Misty Forward
### a cautionary tale

Be polite, I've been warned: don't piss anybody off! Apart from that being impossible in an electronic age whereat every arrogant adolescent has access to a smartass mouth available in one or another hand-held interstellar blab-device, and no matter how mildly one may venture an opinion, there are always—always—seventeen imbeciles and/or adolescents who not only think they are entitled to their opinion, they are consumed with the utter irrational conviction that they must blurt it blogwise, or the universe will blanch out from its not being heard. Well, with the admonition not to ruffle anyone's most fragile pinfeather, here is my first mantra to you: "everyone thinks he/she is entitled to his/her opinion; nonsense; you are only entitled to your *informed* opinion. All the rest is what-if, supposition, and blue smoke up your skirt."

I've attempted to edge into this politely, having been warned not to crush the tender blossoms of anyone chancing on this jeremiad unprepared, and by the way, if I employ a word beyond you...go look it up in a dictionary not wiki-inaccuracy. Are we cool so far?

There is a man named Richard Curtis; he is my New York literary agent, has been for decades; he is also one of my most trusted friends. (There is a reason I'm intruding this information—you'll get it in a moment, because it weighs prominently why I am here, now, lecturing you.) Richard had an enormously successful and prestigious agency, filled with dozens of the best, most sought-after writers in the game. Eventually, recently, he came to the attention of a large, international *apparat* name of Open Road, also brimmed full of famous and multi-moneymaking authors. Like a bedraggled dock-side beggar, I abruptly found myself press-ganged into the ranks of Open Road "clients."

195

Now, they had to figure out what the hell to *do* with me. (They seem to be very pleasant people, competent, anxious to make millions from those of us chained here to the auctorial oars in the bowels of their galleys.)

But what to do with this feral "Ellison" eventually comes top of the agenda? He has 115 books published in a wide circle of genres and popular culture…we're assured he's famous, near-legendary, an exciting personality, yet he threatens to kill each of us, our spouses, those we are sleeping with, our pets, and parents…all the way back to Phœnicia, Lemuria, and Atlantis, and our ancestors…if we carelessly, misguidedly, erroneously— having been warned repeatedly—label him as "a science fiction writer." Open Road, of course, risks the Fall of the Skies by being categorically careless in this respect. Nonetheless, Richard has indentured me to these people, so I try to be polite, as you see here, and piss no one off. My success at this endeavor is yours to quantify.

Bringing us to why you, and I, meet here. Open Road has decided to bring to play a bit of process to "push" my profile on their stalwart list of galley-slaves, and with something like 36 handsome uniform titles available, they thought they'd take a shot at moving some of the sweeter viands. (If you haven't had your ire already raised, you might want to go to [shameless self-promotion] the handsome website HarlanEllisonBooks.com— whereat I've done at least 16 new books under my self-publishing imprimatur, Edgeworks Abbey. Now, back to the task at hand.)

So Open Road gets it into its collective consciousness, why not get this jackanapes actively working for us, and they go to Richard, who naturally inquires, "to what purpose, and in what form, and for what audience do you wish this great savant to produce his *prolegomena*?" Everyone stares at everyone else. The great international multi-tasking institution spanning continents and oceans and lost continents *under* the oceans pretty much tell Richard to tell me to write whatever I choose to write. Just speak clearly, frankly, and to empty my heart.

Not the most sagacious executive editorial path to amble, yet Richard does their brainwork for them, knowing me intimately for half a century, and he sums up the excellent, gracious consideration of Open Road's Marketing Manager, Kat Sherbo of "Integrated Media," whatever that may mean…and she is very courteous, gracious, and helpful when she writes me:

"Much has been made of your opinions through the years… Yet we feel that not enough has been made of the sagacious, thoughtful advice you have to offer to a younger generation."

On consideration, this is to me like offering Jack the Ripper a job working the unsupervised graveyard shift in a Spitalfields slaughterhouse.

"Now that the generation of Millennials are coming of age, we were wondering if you would like to write an Op-Ed piece for young adults—a kind of updated, shortened version of your book TROUBLEMAKERS, which takes into account current events and your own feelings now more than 14 years later.

"Current events you may be interested in reflecting upon include:
- The Ferguson Case and police brutality.
- The legalization of medical marijuana.
- The increasing cost of education."

Called Richard, and said, "Let'm just take my introduction to TROUBLEMAKERS, it's all I had to say that was even remotely polite or sane." He said, "They don't want to use it; they think it's too rude and will get young people pissed off!"

"Well...imagine my chagrin!"

"Just do it," he said in the voice he'd been using on me for ages. "Just goddam *do* it! For your own good!"

So. Ferguson. You won't care for my observations. At core, I don't like cops. Known 'em all my life, a few are very close pals, but overall I think theirs is a very crappy life-choice to while away your years, cheek-to-jowl with criminals and deadbeats. Too close, day in and day out, too much self-identification I think, after not very long, every cop develops a "them and us" viewpoint in which anyone walking lopsidedly toward them could be a dangerous malefactor. Combine that with the raging racism that still propels American culture, and you've got all the Fergusons your widdle heart could wish for.

Marijuana? Don't use it, never have, don't give a fuck if they legalize it, embargo it, burn it, or put it in rectal suppositories. Not on my agenda. I've known dopers since I was twelve years old, and they seem to me incomplete. Like half-visible wanderers; Tinkerbells in Never-Never Land. Not just meth freaks or cokeheads or straight-shooters right into the main vein or between the toes—they're so far hanging off the cliff, just don't hook up with them, hang with them, and let them drag you under. They'll straighten or drown on their own. They're losers. You control your own life. Mantra #2.

Education. Good thing. Can't get too much of it.

That's pretty much what I had to say to "young people" in TROUBLEMAKERS, and apparently it was too harsh for their delicate sensitivities. Well, this time, as you can see, I've tread delicately, told you all that you are: without flaw and Our Best Hope for Tomorrow. I lie a lot.

Now if that doesn't shower courtesy and goodwill to all you "maturing Millennials;" then I can empty my pockets no further.

# Ellison's Folly

### or, Horrors of the House of Glass

When the moment arrives, for each of us, that moment in our lives when we have ingested the final increment of wisdom that ever we shall pack into our brain, it is as sure as day follows night that we shall realize—to our sighs and chagrin—that the core nugget of human smarts is this:

*It seemed like a good idea at the time.*

Why did you invest in such a risky stock? *It seemed like a good idea at the time.* Hey, lady, how come you entered into such an obviously brutalizing, destructive relationship with a guy as creepy as that? *It seemed like a good idea at the time.* Of all the new cars you could have purchased, all the Caddys and Camaros and SUVs, howzacum you opted for a Yugo? *It seemed like a good idea at the time.* Yo, Bonaparte, Nappy m'man, what made you think invading Russia in the wintertime was a smart move? *It seemed like...*

Well, you catch my drift.

Thus, as one with each of you poor damned souls reading this journal, having succumbed to the illogical, inexplicable, infectious obsession, several eons ago I began amassing a lovely (but nonetheless useless) cache of collectable drinking glasses. A cache that became, as has yours, a plethora.

At first, merely the DC comic character glasses, because I was then, and am now, a comic book kid. Then came the Brockway Looney Tunes *tsunami*, the Sunday Funnies set, a few Little Orphan Annie items from my childhood. The Marvel plastic cup deluge. Kentucky Derby winners. World's Fair 1939 passions. The Phantom and Ren/Stimpy from Australia. This and that. One of these and two of those. Like the little old man who kept picking up cats in that classic children's book, MILLIONS OF CATS, until he wandered home to his little old wife, trailing millions of, well, millions of cats. We're talking plethora here. Cabinets fulla glasses. Shelves fulla glasses. Display cases fulla glasses. And, of course, the madness:

Not one item out of that hundred&hundred&hundred stockpile could, heaven forbid!, ever be used to quaff a beverage. Are you kidding me? Put actual liquid in one of those glasses? Fuggedaboutit! Sooner would I permit you to lodge bamboo slivers under my fingernails.

We're dealing here with a lunacy akin to the dancing madness of the Middle Ages, the tulipomania of 17th Century Holland, the fervor of the French for the antics of Jerry Lewis. Dementia of an infamous intensity.

Until, at last, on 8 March 1999, the fever assaulted my weary spirit to a degree that could no longer be denied. We broke ground—my good wife, Susan, and I—on the NEW WALK-IN DISPLAY PANTRY for collectable glassware. Broke ground, I say, not with shovel and Garden Weasel, but with actual gifriggingantic humungus 2.6 ton John Deere tractor, street-clogging dumpster, jackhammers, and a contingent of sweaty gentlemen from at least three nations, each and all of it and them hellbent on staging a horny-handed Sons of Toil roadshow version of *Journey to the Center of the Earth*. Or at least the center of the bottom of our backyard, which rests on a mountaintop of the Santa Monica chain, here in the middle of Los Angeles.

I designed, and Don Kline, my artisan-construction guy, facilitated, the addition to our kitchen of a cunningly rounded, circular-window-adorned, skylight-topped enclosure to house my collection. The word for it is nifty. Also spiffy.

A small child of our acquaintance, who saw it at night, lit up and aglow, called it "bitchin'." Our UPS guy called it "kewl."

Construction took more than a year. Not full time, but steadily. And it was completed sometime last May.

Then Susan spent an eternity loading up the shelves. And fastening down each item with Museum Gel.

You ask why?

I tell you why. And it is this:

When we were hit with the 6.7 magnitude temblor called the Great Northridge, California Thruster of Monday, January 17, 1994 (4:31AM for the punctilious among you), Ellison Wonderland was lifted with a four-gravity thrust. It takes only six gravs to throw a rocket to the moon.

The house sits about five feet over bedrock, so the structure was not one of those you saw on television, flayed and flattened and smoldering by whim of Nature. The house went straight up, and came down…and everything in it, including Susan and I and a quarter of a million books and art treasures that will never again exist on this planet and all my glassware…all of it went up and came down, and we lost more than two hundred thousand dollars worth of Lalique and Royal Doulton and Erté and Tiffany and lots and lots of Bugs Bunny glasses.

Don't ask. Just do not ask.

Well, it's six years later, and I've replaced almost all of the collectables—but that incredible Art Deco tea set from 1921 Belgium is nothing but shards and dust and memory—and so every item in the new walk-in pantry sits on a coagulated film of Museum Gel. The shaker may come again—don't give me that look, kiddo, you've got floods or fires or hurricanes where *you* go to bed every night, and if you haven't got any of those, you've got strip malls and Blockbusters and Starbucks every fifteen feet—it's a chancy business, this living of life—but if it weren't, hell, *everyone* would be doing it—but if it comes again, we're bolted down as best one can be.

And Mark Chase of *Collector Glass News* has been more or less following our little situation, as well as Mark's wife, who tells me that a couple of you are becoming real pains in the *tuchiss* when you call in your bids late on auction closeout night, so I promised him I'd take time out of writing the new movie I'm doing for Samuel L. Jackson (he said, smugly name-dropping)(otherwise why get rich and famous if you can't show off)(because, essentially, rich and famous is wearying and time-consuming, so if you can't name-drop a little, and every once in a while build a room for displaying glasses, why bother doing all that work to get rich and famous in the first place)(but…I digress), and I'd write him a brief essay on the storehouse of glassware. More than a year. And if you've even had to put in a new shower stall you know what an inconvenience and a mess results from construction. Not to mention the cost.

Oh. Yeah. Now, I know I've given you the impression that Susan and I exist in a world of vast abundance; but I've done that only to flaunt it, baby, flaunt it, as Zero Mostel said. In truth, I am precisely like each of you: I am a working stiff. Twenty-four seven. So when I told Susan I wanted to build this "little nook" for the glassware, wanted to knock a hole in the kitchen wall right over *there*, and I assured her it was going to be a mere bagatelle, her response was reasoned and appropriate.

She hit me. She hit me very hard. She hit me in a place where it wouldn't show, if I were to go to the cops.

And now, more than a year later, we estimate that the oddly-shaped but gorgeous walk-in pantry has cost us something in excess of $29,601.22. That is a rough estimate. Don't hold me to it.

And last week we had the well-known international portrait photographer Ibarionex R. Perello come in and take some shots just for youse guys who dote on *Collector Glass News*. (Is that not one of the coolest, most magical-sounding names! Geez, with a name like Ibarionex Perello, I coulda been a star.) He charged me about a hundred and fifty bucks.

To take pictures of dopey drinking glasses from which I do not drink. A hundred and fifty bucks, on top of the $29,601.22 I roughly estimate this lunacy has cost me.

So now, here are all the photos—including some Susan took with her little clickbox— and Mark will pick what he thinks best envisions this end-result of the same obsession that torments each of you. I urge yourself to ooh; even to aaah.

And the moral of the story is this: I am you, you are me, we are both and all of us here in the same skin, but I'm the one who stands forth before you as a living demonstration of the horrors of glassware collecting, the purpose of which, when they ask you...as they ask me...is only this:

*It seemed like a good idea at the time.*

Photo by Jason Davis, because we couldn't find the originals from the article.

# The Soul of Solomon
## What *Is*, Is; Sometimes, Perhaps,
## What *Ain't*, Shouldn't Be

"Wisdom come late, is wisdom nonetheless."
PAUL SELVIN, Attorney

I curse the lesson, and bless the knowledge. An old man sits at a manual typewriter as the midwinter sun sighs beyond the horizon. He seeks what he has always sought, the right path through the story. The correct and only way to weave the spell, sense and mordant wit, adventure and recurring surprise. As with each time, all the way back to the very first one, it calls its name, finally revealing its true self, and he follows where it leads. He trusts those tiny voices. They always give up their name and their hiding place. The story tells itself.

An old man practices his craft.

But this time he hears only his own heartbeat and the empty cavern of his mind. The story hides. But he goes on, because this is the work, the work he has done all his life, and one does not leave the plough in the unfinished furrow.

It used to be so effortless, a glide, a slalom; now, there is heaviness, and the voice out there is barely audible. Time and gravity are no man's friends.

But he said he would do it, and the plough stands waiting, so he goes on. And how little the younger ones know. How shallowly they confront the work to come. A *tsunami* is coming toward them, and they perceive of it merely as a new season of *American Idol*.

Arrogance will not suffice. Nor will putting the shoulder to the wheel. No amount of dithering will shorten the heavily-trod pathway to the abyss. Nonetheless, dammit, the work must be done. How did I ever get into this? the old man muses. Who got me into this one?

His name is Rubén Procopio. I curse the lesson and bless the knowledge.

He is an excellent artist.

He is also a gracious and great-hearted man, and his friendship manifested itself one day last year in the manner of his arriving at my home bearing gifts. Sumptuous gifts. Sculptures by Rubén. The Phantom. The Green Hornet. (And Andy Panda, but he doesn't make any more than this cameo reference.) Rubén had come to tell me how much he admired *my* work, and we stood around like two seven-year-olds, praising each other's toys. And as I stared at the magnificent double-statue of the Green Hornet and Kato, back to back and radiating all the grandeur I'd known through their radio exploits as a little boy in the early 1940s, the beginning of the lesson Rubén was dragging me into learning, began.

I said, "Boy, wouldn't it be wonderful if there were a story in which The Green Hornet actually *met* The Phantom?!"

The old man pauses. He needs to explain a theory. Because the theory lies at the heart of the trouble, of the lesson, of the anguish.

Sometimes, what is...simply *is*. It is that way because the universe has decreed it so. No larger, no smaller, no more blue, not patterned with stripes. Just because we *can*, doesn't mean we *should*. What an arrogant, transitory little species we are. Change, always change; just for the sake of spewing NEW! on the carton. No better, no richer, no more profound... just *other*. The great French poet Mallarmé wisely pointed out, "To define is to kill. To suggest is to create." The old man smiles and concurs.

Besotted with technology, but no greater of heart or innovation, the world goes a-whirling, onward ever onward, but loses its shadow. The moment is suffused with a cobalt blue miasma, and a kind of cultural hypnosis takes us all. We stare at the unreal, creating nothing of our own, providing willing customers for the Company Store. And all that was, is lost, unremembered, ridiculed, and discarded.

Because we *can*, we do.

No better, no nobler, merely one more pony added to that dog-and-pony show that recycles the old ideas, but leaches from them their freshness.

For instance, the old man points out, we *had* one *King Kong*. A perfectly good one. We never needed five or six others, just because we had the ability to articulate the great beast a little better.

One still goes back to that stop-motion black and white artifact, and the wonder is not dimmed. One watches for a while all "re-imaginings"—theft is too harsh a word—and after a time there is a nasty buzzing between the ears. Just because they could, well, they needn't have. The universe created that first, miraculous *King Kong* and said "Never again." But we are a duplicitous little species. Give us a knife, and we can whittle a flute to charm a child, or to cut our meat to survive. But because they *can*, some use the knife to bury the blade in someone's skull, to build the bomb, to strap death onto an old woman and send her into the marketplace. The knife makes no flutes, quarters no loin of beef: it kills.

Because we are capable, if we can, we do. Even though the universe makes it clear: sometimes, what is, *is*; and sometimes what *ain't*, shouldn't be.

The old man looks back on the theory, and sighs. It seems diffuse. Does it parse at all? What all this of a universe of IEDs and fat people losing weight on television? If one were just encountering such maunderings, or if one were younger and had no idea who, say, Willis O'Brien was, or Christy Mathewson, or Ma Rainey, or Jim Tully, would this theory make any sense? Or would it merely resonate with a great and deep, heartfelt sense of loss?

The world is run by the geek-boys. Anything they can think of, is ooo *awesome!* Kewwwwwl!

And the geek-boy said to Rubén Procopio, "Woooo, wouldn't it be neato keeno kewwwwl if The Phantom met The Green Hornet?!" And Rubén Procopio said, "I am seven years old, too. And I'd *love* to illustrate that!" And the geek-boy, overcome with gratitude and respect for the great gifts the artist had given him, being only seven years old himself, let Rubén Procopio take it to his publisher. And the geek-boy did nothing to stop the publisher from making it all real, asking permission of two elegant gentlemen—David Grace of the firm of Loeb & Loeb, that represents the Trendle holding of The Green Hornet, Inc.—and Brendan Burford of King Features Syndication—and the seven-year-old geek-boy cozened them, and chatted with them, and told them of the sublime story that could be written. Not knowing that this was a lesson brutal in the learning, defying the universe and its message: what is...just *is*. Let it lie, old man.

And so, arrogant and naïve, even after all these years, after chasing down and capturing every one of those fleeing little creatures, and gaining power over them by uncasting the runes and learning their true names...

I could easily lie, and say it was the fault of Britt Reid and The Ghost Who Walks. I could lie and say I held sway over them, that they were just fictions and so many hundreds of others had done with them as they chose...why not I? I could lie, but I won't.

It was arrogance. A fool's pride and refusal to bend to the will of the universe. I had to learn that lesson, finally, after all the years I had pulled that plough.

Yes, it was Procopio who abetted my fecklessness. He had no way of knowing that's what he was doing, but if I lie and attempt to blame Rubén, I might get away with it, oh poor sad old man, he didn't know what he was doing, and I might get away with it. But always, inevitably, the fault is mine. More than sixty years at this typewriter, I should've known what the hell I was getting into.

But I was arrogant. No other word for it.

It is an explanation, but not an excuse.

I have to eat that rotting, redolent fish, head and bones and all.


So I began to write. That was April 5th 2009. It is now nearly ten months later. And here is the beginning of that story. It is all you'll ever get of "The Soul of Solomon."

```
My name is Kato.
    At one time or another, I have been asked thus:
"Ah, well and good. Kato. Yes, we know that name. But
what is the full of it? Kato Who?"
    The asking is simple. Unsullied and clear, without
twist or turn. The answering is much more difficult;
and never fully satisfying. Kato Kikigaki, the faith-
ful Japanese house-boy. Kato Aguinaldo, the staunch
Filipino aide; Kato Tung-hu, of what you might call
"royal" Manchurian lineage. Kato Yutang, who was
definitely Chinese; and Kato Nguyen, who might have
been Korean, Vietnamese, even Laotian, there is no
certainty.
    My name is Kato.
    Let that suffice for the duration of this
narration.
    I would tell you of two men I knew: Mr. Reid, for
whom I worked many many years, until he committed
suicide--and this telling will disclose the reason for
his final act of life--and Mr. Walker, who said to me,
"When the devil is your landlord, you had best begin
humming 'The End of the World Blues.'" Immediately
```

after the events of which I will treat here, Mr.
Walker shunned his other self, and turned what you
might call the "family business" over to his son. He
then became hermitic, as one with Aramites; and
sequestered, let the ashes of his final days disappear
on the winds of the years.

My name is Kato, and I worked for the man who was
known as The Green Hornet, and once, just once, I was
of avail to The Ghost Who Walks, he who called himself
both Mr. Walker and The Phantom. Beside them in the
most terrible moments of their lives, on the path that
forced them to cut trail with each other as I say,
once, just once.


The beginning, if you believe, was long before the
birth of Christ. If you believe, it was long before
the Neolithic peoples of Middle and Lower Egypt, more
than a thousand years before Mentuhotep II reigned in
the Middle Kingdom. Perhaps even before, as one has
said, "the oceans drank Atlantis," if you believe.
Again, the asking is simple, any fool can play in that
field. Not even belief, not even faith, suggests that
the beginning occurred at the same moment most life on
Earth succumbed to the flaming cudgel that snuffed out
the saurians. No...no one can believe that.

It has been said that the second beginning was
during the excavation for the Temple of Jerusalem. Not
the Haram al-Sharif, not Herod's Temple on the Mount,
not the temple of Zerubbabel, but the first Temple,
the one called Solomon's. It was erected based on
plans given to Solomon by his father, David; and
decades before Solomon completed his father's dream,
ground was first broken, the soil was first turned, in
959 Before the Common Era.

Beneath the blade of one such exploratory spade, an
Israelite laborer struck something that rang with the
sonority of a carillon. When it was unearthed, it was
carried to the overseer, who held it away from himself
as he rubbed it clean. And he took it to the Master
Builder Hiram, who had been sent to Solomon by the
ruler of the Phoenicians, and Hiram was dazzled by it,
and he took it to Solomon, and the King held it,
staring into its abyssal depths for a very long time.

It was neither stone nor gem, neither coral nor
petrified wood, neither scoria nor glass. It was
exquisite; and it rang sonorously; and it gave back
the sunlight and starlight in colors and shadows whose
hues could not be named.

They came to call it The Soul of Solomon, and it
was put in the inner sanctuary, the Holy of Holies,
the <u>debir</u>, nearby the Torah and the Ark of the
Covenant and the twin cherubim covered with gold that
were fifteen feet tall, each with a fifteen foot
wingspread and there, for three millennia, it lay
waiting, there atop Mount Moriah, on the threshing
floor of Araunah where (if you believe) not only had
Abraham sacrificed, but so had Adam, Cain, Abel, and
Noah.

There it remained, for almost four hundred years,
till the First Temple was burned and plundered by the
Babylonians of Nebuchadnezzer.

And so vanished from men's eyes, The Soul of
Solomon. If you believe.


Night had dropped its tonnage...

I wrote in a frenzy, all of that opening in one sitting. I was so drunk on it, I called Josh and read it to him. And he was knocked out by it. Then I read it to Susan and *she* was knocked out by it, but she loves me, so I can't trust that. Then I called Joe Gentile, and *he* said, "Britt Reid commits *suicide*?! You can't do that!" And I, arrogant and puffed up like a pouter pigeon, replied, "Trust me. I'm the fuckin' king of the universe; you'll only *love* it when you see where I'm going with this." And Joe trusted me, because he didn't know he was talking to a seven-year-old geek-boy.

Goshwow, wouldn't it be so kewwwl if Godzilla battled The Creature from the Black Lagoon while Flash Gordon and The Bowery Boys joined forces to bring down The Red Skull who travels around in the TARDIS! There is a balance in the universe, dear friends. Trifle with it at your peril. I sat and stared at Rubén Procopio's magnificent sculptures of The Phantom and The Green Hornet, and I wrote as well as I could write—Josh said so, Susan said so, even Rubén said so—but I didn't realize, till the white heat of my beginning cooled, and I had to contemplate how I was going to run down that fleeing creature called story, and gain the power of its name. Then I began to learn that lesson, and began to fear the knowledge.

What happened was this...

I knew *how* I was going to tell the story: from Kato's viewpoint.

But why had Britt Reid killed himself? Why had The Phantom passed over his active life to his son, the *next* Walker, after the affair of The Soul of Solomon. And what *was* the Soul? I knew! It is no less than the conscience of god; the ability to know, and to do, good or evil.

It would have a powerful, possibly deleterious effect on anyone who possessed it. For instance, on Mount Moriah, Abraham *would* have sacrificed his son; Solomon *would* have cut the baby in half. Cain *did* slay Abel, there on Mount Moriah, because the Soul lay just beneath.

What a great concept. Bigger than I'd planned, more complex and ethereal than I'd intended, but what a kewwwwl idea. In pursuing the Soul, for whatever reason, The Phantom comes to Chicago, where he and The Hornet cut trail, and this happens, and that happens, all of it written with all the skill and imagination of a lifetime of unraveling storylines and creating characters.

I even went so far as to seek out a pseudoscientific reason for that stellar object to possess the qualities I needed to move the plot. And I called my friend, the (also) stellar science fiction writer, Jack McDevitt, and shared my plot-problem with him. And Jack, good friend, went to a prestigious reference source with geek-boy's conundrum.

"Michael," Jack wrote, "Harlan Ellison is working on a story. He has a meteorite which puts out radiation that effectively bifurcates the nature of an observer, causing him to go to one extreme or the other. Think the Lone Ranger deciding he has had enough and shooting the bad guy. Or an individual who is normally extremely selfish sacrificing himself to save someone else. What he needs is an explanation—something that can be encapsulated in three lines or so; how might this happen?"

Already, the universe was trying to tell me...what is, simply *is*. If it were condign for The Phantom to meet The Green Hornet, it would not require this convoluted, cobbled-up *Lara Croft, Tomb Raider* jiggery-pokery. You are suddenly in the middle of doing what only the crappiest kind of Michael Bay filmmakers do...you are twisting and corrupting your own story to achieve an artificial end. I was doing exactly what I'd spent a lifetime avoiding—I was lying.

And the "Michael" whom Jack had asked to intercede on my behalf, Michael Fossel, MD, PhD, MA, FACEP, wrote back and said, "...the quantum nature of consciousness. It goes something like this: consciousness is absolutely dependant upon the quantum nature of reality and its inherent unpredictability (hence free will). The radiation (it immediately makes me think of 'Bizarro' from *Superman*) inverts the relationship between normal neuronal function and consciousness by producing a mirror image of the normal quantum connection (and here a great deal of hand waving occurs)..."

The Green Hornet possesses the Soul. He does something so tenebrous, so impossible to live with, that he kills himself, even though what he did was sunk to the roots in the greater good.

*What* "greater good?" What am I talking about here? What sort of nebulous Judeo-Christian morality am I trying to sell? Why didn't I just do a simple, silly story about gangsters and goons in the jungle and Chicago back'o'the'yards? What the hell have I gotten myself into here?

And that was in May. Then June. Then year-end. And now I come to the end of my tale.

The old man sits hunched as he has been for decades, tapping out line after line. He has learned a terrible lesson, and it may be the very last one of his life:

Rubén responded to the geek-boy. Wouldn't it be kewwwl if...

If what? If worms had wings? If monkeys bit the heads off every lubricating vampire-loving teen? If a thought got lost and found its way into Sarah Palin's arid Sahara of a skull? If this and if that; it is a terrible lesson finally to learn that just because we *can*, it doesn't mean we *should*.

I spent a year near the end of my life, trying to write what should never be written. The Phantom stands, The Green Hornet stands, they need never meet. They have nothing in common, ultimately, save the arrogance of an old man who has learned at the last doorway that sometimes what ain't, shouldn't be.

Wisdom come late, is wisdom nonetheless.

# I HAD A
# THOUGHT TODAY...

Editor's Note: This column started life as a series of lengthy posts made on the Art Deco Dining Pavilion, the HarlanEllison.com forum frequented by Ellison. After a few informal online installments, the column found a home at the *Funny Times*, where "Guys Are Pigs" was published in February 2012, "Batman" in March 2012, and the first page of what became the "Mondegreen" essay in April 2012.

After the fourth segment (presented herein as the latter portion of "Mondegreen") went unpublished by the *Funny Times* editorial staff, the column moved to *Jamais Vu: The Journal of Strange Among the Familiar*. A new "Whitey Bulger" essay from HarlanEllison.com debuted in the January 2014 issue, followed the "Guys Are Pigs" segment in the April 2014 issue, and a conflated version of the third *Funny Times* piece and the unpublsihed fourth installment in the September 2014 issue, which—unfortunately—marked the end of the periodical.

The *Jamais Vu* sequence is presented here, with the second *Funny Times* piece—described by Ellison as a "Substitute Thought"—at the end.

# 1: 15 November 2013

In a stately New England courthouse yesterday (Thursday, 14 November 2013) a man named James "Whitey" Bulger was sentenced by a judge and jury to two (2) lifetimes-plus in a maximum security prison after an 80-something-year-long lifetime as a hit man, extortionist, drug trafficker, multiple murderer, and kingpin behind the notorious "Winter Hill" *apparat* that ruled Boston and surrounding environs for decades. Mr. Bulger had been on the lam for 16 years, hiding out under an alias, with his longtime girlfriend, in no farther a venue from me than Santa Monica. In June 2011, they got him. He is in his 80s; he will die behind bars. Some might say: too little, too late.

Like many another Great Criminal—brought to mind are Idi Amin, Saddam Hussein, Adolf Hitler, Burke&Hare, Senator Bilbo—I suppose "Whitey" got what was coming to him for a long time. It was a bed he made for himself and, despite having spent considerable time in the slam earlier in his life, he was by his own hand His Own Man...and I guess he got what he had coming to him.

Yet—as one with all the Great Criminals except two (whose names I've legally agreed not to subject to calumny)—"Whitey" Bulger never did me a disservice, never was less than courteous to me. On the one occasion that we crossed paths.

Yes, my children, among the Great and the Near-Great with whom I've cut trail, I once spent an evening in the company of "Whitey" Bulger. And though it is neither THE ILIAD nor THE ODYSSEY, though in terms of Great Events it is mere an anecdote, I have promised the telling for some time, and so here I am to tell.

The names to remember here, as much as mine and Mr. Bulger's, are Malcolm Braly, Knox Burger, and Walter Fultz.

213

Permit me to lay in a short background:

Started reading Hal Ellson's novels about juvenile delinquency in 1950 in Cleveland. Got fascinated by the subject. Got beaten up in front of the Paramount Theater on Times Square, NYC by street thugs out of Brooklyn. Got booted out of college. Moved to Manhattan in the early '50s. Ran with the gangs in Brooklyn for six weeks incognito. Wrote WEB OF THE CITY (aka RUMBLE) and got drafted. Got out of the Army, went to Chicago to edit *Rogue* magazine, went back to New York, started lecturing about juvenile delinquency (a sideline), got busted by the NYPD for the Sullivan Act (possession of an unregistered firearm), went to jail in the legendary Tombs for 24 hours, finally got my day in court, 31 October 1960, Grand Jury dismissed all charges. Wrote about The Tombs for *The Village Voice*. Went back to Chicago to create and edit Regency Books. Regency published MEMOS FROM PURGATORY, about the gangs and jail, in 1961. Also, that year, Gold Medal paperbacks published my rock novel SPIDER KISS (aka ROCKABILLY). Wound up in Los Angeles in 1962. The anecdote that follows took place circa 1964–66, as best I can recall.

Gold Medal was one of the paperback imprints of Fawcett Publications, which had lost the use of Captain Marvel as an enormously successful comic book in an infamous lawsuit brought by DC Comics some years before. But Gold Medal was a top-rate hardboiled house, publishing John D. MacDonald, Peter Rabe, Gil Brewer, Richard Prather, Charles Williams, early Vonnegut and a host of others, mostly originals. In 1961, as they were publishing SPIDER KISS, I was living in New York, hanging out at Fawcett a lot, and had become good friends with the Senior Editor, the legendary curmudgeon Knox Burger, and his brilliant associate, *my* editor, Walter Fultz. I admired Walter unreservedly. (His suicide, some years later, has never ceased to dishearten me, and I shall never forget it.)

Knox literally saved my life once. I wrote a story about it. "Punky and the Yale Men."

He also started publishing the novels of an ex-con named Malcolm Braly. Pronounced BRAW-ly. They were (and remain) spectacularly well-written, gritty, knowledgeable books. You MUST read them: FELONY TANK (1961), SHAKE HIM TILL HE RATTLES (1963) and IT'S COLD OUT THERE (1966) are his first three, and his best. One night, Knox and Walter invited Mal and me to dinner at O. Henry's Steak House in the Village. Mal, who lived on the West Coast, and I took to each other immediately. I was wowed by his first book, and he was a fan of both WEB OF THE CITY and, later, MEMOS FROM PURGATORY. Malcolm had done heavy time in the joint. He arrived at that point in American Letters where Norman Mailer had gotten Jack Abbott out of the pen, and gotten him published to considerable attention; and it was around the time of Truman Capote's IN COLD BLOOD; so paying attention to a guy in stir who could write like a twopenny nail angel was a smart editorial move by Knox Burger, who had a flawless eye for new talent. Thus and so, Mal and I became buddies. He drank, I didn't, and having done big time in prison Mal always thought it hilarious that I, who may have been in and out of small clinks since I was pre-teen, had been arrogant enough to turn 24 hours in The Tombs into an entire memoir. I was Bucky to his Captain America. He was a wonderful guy, had served his time, and was at the outset of what looked to be an impressive, extended writing career.

Malcolm went back to L.A., I went back to Chicago for a year, MEMOS was published, I booked out of Chi with my second wife, came out to California, got divorced, settled down to writing more books and stories (occasionally paying my bills by writing honorable whoredom for *Confidential* magazine), soon tv, then movies. Lived in the treehouse in Beverly Glen from 1962–66, got married again, moved to The Lost Aztec Temple of Mars in '66, got divorced for the third time after 45 days, linked up with Malcolm Braly in L.A. sometime during that period.

We'd go out pub-crawling, or see movies, or go bowling. He was good company. As I said, he drank—not to excess—and I was—as have always been—dry. And once in a while we'd go to a "safe house" bar frequented by ex-cons. There were, in them days (as there no doubt still are), watering-holes where guys and ladies who shared the experience of having pulled long jolts felt among their own, a community of commonality of times past. There was one joint, in a tiny 90-degree-angle pod-mall just off Santa Monica Boulevard, midway between La Cienega and La Brea, the name and existence of which are decades flensed from both recollection and neighborhood, where Mal would take me, where he cut trail with past cellmates, newly-sprung cons, visitors from out-of-state, mob hoods, visiting villains, and total strangers with misty, suspicious backtrails. I wallowed in the venue. I was nothing better than a wannabe thug who'd been around riff-raff and petty culprits more than a little in my life, and like most "bling gang" hangers-on, I was slavering to get a toe in that underworld-celebrity swamp.

Mal tolerated, and I think was amused, by my sidekickiness. I had what're called "walkin' smarts," so I didn't embarrass him or speak out-of-turn the way those caricatures in sitcoms do. No one ever groaned, and I was treated squarely. If not an equal, at least an "okay kid." But, oddly, I was already in my thirties. We spent many times in each other's company. Lost track of him years and years ago; never found out what happened to him. He did a couple of adaptation-novels based on movies of the period, but nothing under his name for a long time.

But. Back to the anecdote. We're somewhere in the middle Sixties now.

One day, Mal calls me, says, "Y'wanna go to a Party?"

I says, "Where, who, when?"

He says, "Tonight. About eight. Drive down, I'll meet you at Dino's."

He won't tell me more, but I says, "Okay," and hang up.

At that time, Dean Martin owned a restaurant located at 8532 on the south side of the Sunset Strip; it was used when shooting exteriors of the *77 Sunset Strip* television series. Much frequented. If you were going to meet up with someone in New York City, you'd often say, "Meetcha under the Clock," meaning Grand Central Station; in L.A., meetcha at Dino's was commonplace.

So that evening, about eight, I pulled my (then) Austin-Healy or the Camaro (whichever) under the portico of Dino's Lodge, got my parking stub (no, not from "Kookie" Byrnes), and walked out to the curb on Sunset Boulevard, where Mal was waiting; smiling, if I remember. Malcolm Braly was a big guy, looked a lot like a sideman or a bouncer, without the scars or cauliflowers, pleasant countenance. He didn't *tower* over me, but I was 5'5" and he was shorter than Captain Marvel to my taller-than-Billy Batson. I paint you the pictures, I tell you the stories: it's my job.

"Where we off to?"

"C'mon, I'll show you. You'll get a kick out of this."

Malcolm and I started walking.

I cannot remember now, half a century later, whether we were walking left—west— or right—east—on Sunset Boulevard from Dino's Lodge. But we didn't walk far. Perhaps one or two longish blocks.

(In preparation for telling this anecdote, I drove down from my home, same route as that night, and remembered very well what the area was, and the large building across the street where Malcolm Braly and I went, that night. The building may well still be there, but L.A. eats its Past and Facelifts it every few years, much less fifty. I *think* the building I'm now about to describe, on the north side of Sunset, is still there, but I'll be damned if I can figure out WHAT IT NOW CONTAINS! I have tried, not once, but twice, to provide you the exact address, but without walking and re-walking a substantial distance, I am forced back onto your willing acceptance that I ain't shittin' you.)

Across the street was a four or five storey Gilded Age, Belle Epoch, old L.A.-style apartment house that had obviously been—at some stage of its existence—a hotel.

It was now apartments.

We crossed the street and Malcolm said to me, approximately this: "We're going to a party being thrown by a guy from outta town. I think every guy here is an ex-con, and I think you may've met a few of them. I don't know if I'll know everyone, but it's cool; everybody knows SOMEbody or they wouldn't've been invited."

I said I understood, and we went in and took the elevator to an upper floor. There was a discernible echo from behind one of a number of ornate wooden doors off the foyer. What may have been an entire floor-through in posher times, had obviously been divided into separate multi-roomed apartments. The place was in excellent shape, and knew constant attention because its age notwithstanding, it was still a Gilded Age, Belle Epoch, old-L.A. style mansion.

Malcolm went before me, knocked, and somewhichway in a moment or two we were in a gigantic living room or what may have been a ballroom, and it was well-filled. Men and women, all duded up, with glasses in their hands, and food everywhere, and smoke rising like the clouds in a NASA silo. I recognized no one.

Let me, at last, cut to the core of this story. You've been patient long enough.

An hour or more into our stay at this gathering of many clans—and we were there a *loooong* time—Mal and I had gotten separated, and he was off somewhere in the place, and I was sitting on a sofa with a glass of Perrier or suchlike. The noise level had grown, there may have been more than a hundred people in the room, Mal and I had clocked the space pretty thoroughly, I'd met a couple of guys who seemed familiar, and Malcolm amazed me by producing from his jacket pocket, early-on, a copy of MEMOS FROM PURGATORY, and reveled introducing me as the Author with a *précis* of my time with the gangs, and my brief stay in jail.

I was embarrassed, of course, because with each new introduction, and Mal's recounting of who I was, and why I was there, every time he would say something like, "Spike, I want you to meet the Author of this book, Harlan Ellison..." and he'd quickly recap my escapades, and then with his arm around my shoulders, say to me something like "...Harlan, this is Spike: he did 25–to–30 in Joliet for..." and it would always *ALWAYS* be some heavy lug about butchering an entire family, or robbing 132 banks, or running the mob in Conshohocken, Pennsylvania, or assassinating the Premier of Tasmania, or boosting *Oaxacan Gold* shipments from mules on dusty side-roads and beheading the couriers so the shit could be resold without any backtrail...and every single guy Mal knew, and introduced to me, and regaled with my by-comparison pitiable tale of Villainy, roared with laughter because...

Among that vast congeries of crooks, thugs, criminals, poltroons, street scamps and killers, the amassed time behind iron bars and stone walls had to exceed the entirety of the Years of the Crusades! What I'm saying here, is that these were "made men" and bums and full-time lawbreakers who laughed like a *sonofabitch*, every one of them, every time Mal ran it down, and clapped me on the shoulders, mussed my hair as if I were a cute handbag-puppy, and welcomed me into their roistering as if I were Conan the Barbarian, not some snot-nosed whelp out of Painesville, Ohio.

I cannot tell you how smaller than 5'5" I felt all that evening and into the night into the early hours, but how *congenial* it all felt at the time. Without for an instant losing the Reality of what was happening, and how filled with the bitter vetchroot of epiphany that consumed me: of my hubris and piddling belief that I was, and had always been, a Scourge, a Reaver, a Rapscallion, when I now had rubbed scarred shoulders with the *real* pirate horde.

Hours went by. I had a wonderful time. Mal and I got separated. I sat on the sofa near a giant cathedral window looking down on the Sunset Strip. I was tired, but not ready to leave.

*Then.*

Then a guy sat down next to me on the sofa.

And he started talking to me. Very pleasant. *Bahston* accent.

"They tell me you wrote a few books? That right?"

"Yeah," I said. "I'm Harlan Ellison." Hubris. Even under torture, with bamboo slivers flaming within my fingernails.

"Yeah," said the asshole, "I'm Harlan Ellison."

"You can call me Jimmy," he said.

And then he had me recount in detail everything you've read in WEB OF THE CITY, MEMOS FROM PURGATORY, my childhood, and most of what's preceded in this anecdote. In detail. Maybe half an hour, Jimmy and me schmoozing, sitting on a sofa in L.A.

Then, at the point in which I confessed to him that I was truly gobsmacked being in a roomful of guys who'd done long *long* jolts, truly impressive Hard Time in calabooses from Attica to Zimbabwe, Malcolm Braly, himself a long-stretch sufferer, my pal Mal, emerged from the savage swarm, walked up, smiled at Jimmy and said, "Oh, you've met my friend Harlan."

To which James "Whitey" Bulger, then-still-kingpin of South Boston's Winter Hill gang, and only a few years older than I was, sitting right next to him, replied, "He's a good kid. Only thing wrong with him is he suffers from PENAL ENVY."

That's my story, and I'm stickin' to it.

# 2: 18 March 2009

One of the irrefutable core truths of the Universe is that guys are pigs.

Uh, well, not ALL guys are pigs, but as women will attest—even those so stump-stupid they have eight babies out of wedlock, or bail their favorite scumbucket out of the clink—MOST men are pigs.

"Pigs," may be too harsh and unforgiving a word. I do seek to be *au courant* and P.C. in this case, so permit me a minim of back&fill: in place of "pig," let us conjure "unclean," "untidy," "careless," "unsanitary," "imprecise," "unnoticing," "unaware," "casual," "slovenly," "slatternly"!

Or just short-hand it, and call it piggish behavior.

All right, so perhaps not *all* men, since the first humped hominid began etching beauty on the Chauvet Cave, perhaps not *every* man has been, is, will be a pig: possible that Amenhotep III wasn't a pig; maybe the great English novelist Charles Reade, who famously created the Core Lesson for all wannabe writers when he said "Make 'em laugh; make 'em cry; make 'em wait!" wasn't a pig; possibly Steve Rogers, who became Captain America, waren't no pig, neither. Yet—hyperbolic drift-exceptions discounted—

One of the irrefutable core truths of the Universe is that guys are pigs.

Now, how I came to this profound realization occurred in one of the public men's toilets on the American Airlines concourse at O'Hare Airport, Chicago. Oh, perhaps eleven, fifteen years ago.

I stood next to a guy about, possibly, thirty-five, forty, thereabouts and, while I do not consider myself a snoopy neighbor, it was impossible for me to blindfold myself to the New Directions in Public Pissing this dude was initiating. It was no less than as a

219

daredevil, a veritable Evel Knievel of the *Pissoir*, that I was able to broken-field avoid the firehouse hose of power-driven *baño* urine emanating from the Citizen Traveler's tumescence. He hit the urinal cup, the urinal walls, the walls AROUND the urinal, the floor, his own shoes, the floor next to *MY* shoes, a passing lady bug minding her own business, and the near perimeter of the guy to the right of him. Echoes of Al Jolson doing "April Showers," please sing along with me.

Then he shook off his diddle, zipped his trowz, and proceeded to walk out of the bathroom, without so much as a look upon the wash basin. Now, again, I confess to aberrant behavior, in this instance, because I am a prodigious and showboating hand-washer in public terlets; on the demented theory that if I set a really sterling example of Civic Cleanliness, others will note and follow suit. "Look!" I penultimate, projecting to the last row in the theater (or last piss-pot in the abattoir, as the dice may fall), "I am laving myself here! Clean! Clean! My hands are so clean you could *eat* off them!" And on and on, making the usual toad's-*tuchis* of myself.

But THIS time, I was so blinded with nausea and naked hatred for La King of the Pig People, that I barely zipped my pants, barely shook off the last Dew of Summer, barely kept my head from exploding, and as he made for the door, I began shouting at this Typhoid Tommy, "Hey, fellah, wash yer hands! Yer hands! Hey guy, aintcha gonna wash yer hands, ya took a piss, hey ya got piss all over yer hands, aintcha gonna wash yer FUCKIN' POLLUTED MITTS, ya oozing testicular gobbet of piss-engorged douche-fluid!???!!!" And other encomia equally as well-phrased and cozening.

The guy spat panic from his eyeballs (you'll go with me on the metaphors) and ran for his life. Out the door. Into the jammed concourse. Knocking passersby into walls.

I chased him, screaming Disease Carrier and Plague Bearer and Leper and suchlike, till he ran down a flight of stairs to nowhere. One can only hope he missed his flight.

I, of course, now found myself standing monolithically, back somewhere near my Right Mind, with terrified men, women, children, and airline minions staring at me. Not a great moment, this part, so I'll skip over it and get back to my thesis.

Men are pigs.

I have seen hundreds of creatures of the male persuasion, at *least* hundreds, perhaps thousands by this time—I piss a lot more these days than I did prior to the upcoming 2015—honkin' their comet in the men's room, since I was a tot, and my Mother—the late Serita Ellison, a woman so clean you could eat off her—made it abundantly clear to me that anyone who neither wiped nor abluted absolutely, would burn in the NINTH and innermost CIRCLE OF HELL, with Shia LaBeouf, which was worse than all the other eight spackled together, because in the 9th, everything that could happen in the previous eight was your necrotic lot PLUS a "But wait! There's more!" of truly Machiavellian/ Satanic horribleness...you are submerged up to the cleft in your chin in a Great Endless Lake of boiling, maggoty, disease-ridden Moroccan Baboon vomit...and imps in motorboats circle you for all eternity, making waves.

So.

Nowadays, as I have for decades, I am required to sit and sign books at various public functions, and I do it—if not with a smile, then at least with a dyspeptic smile, however death's-head it may appear—like a good professional, as the Worldwide Viral Treasure I've become. Humbly, I can live with that. But everyone wishes to shake my hand.

You see where I'm going with this Thought for the Day?

I am not a bacteriaphobe such as, say, the big film producer, the late Arthur Freed, or the also-late Michael Jackson. I cannot seem to remember to take one of those travel-size bottles of Purell when I venture forth into the airways or byways. I do put toity-paper down on the seat, wherever; but when it comes to the pressing of flesh in public, well, I am reluctant to suggest by spraying myself *post hoc ergo proctor hoc* that the hand just extended to me is cold-welded to the body of a Pig-Man.

But I've seen them five dirty digits still bearing the pustulant redolence of the dreaded one-eyed worm touching door handles, phone receivers, slips of money, and finally, circling for a landing in my right mitt.

So.

My Thought for today is that from now on, when I appear for a public do of some sort, I will have beside me a glove. Not a plastic glove, nor one of those scab-like disposables, nor yet even a mitten. I will have a workman's glove, a good honest blue-collar, brakeman or thresher-pilot or ingot vatman's triple-strength glove; the kind you use when you're trimming out the roses or the Crown of Thorns bush. Heavy, but easy to slip on and off. A non-insulting Joe the Plumber kinda guy's phalanges-fit.

And I will say to whoever it is seeks my benison:

"Put on the glove."

And he or she will say, "Whuh...?"

And I will repeat, because I am a FINE man, "Put on the glove before I shake your hand, please."

And s/he will say, rolling like the 20th Century Limited, "Whuh...?"

And I will say it thrice because, as we all know, "What I tell you three times is true." Would you kindly put the glove on your paw, and I will shake it as you have requested.

This seems to me, this looms large in my legend, this bulks weightily and with a condign gravitas, this seems to me a peachykeen social condom when I go, in mufti, among you, my people.

I am only defending myself because, as women will confirm, men are pigs.

# 3: 2 May 2009/12 March 2012

Actually, and in truth, I had this thought two weeks ago last Thursday. Notwithstanding the dilatory presentation, due to my attention being otherwise directed till now, I think it is one of the few more-than-casual thoughts I've ever had. Quotable, I think. And it is that which brings one up short, flashing the possible that it is an idle thought with some gravitas in its core.

And *that* thought brings me—as it would others, I'm sure—up short.

I do not consider myself a Great Thinker, because I have imbibed the wine of the Great Thinkers since I was a kid, and I know the real from the *manqué*. No, I'm sure I do not even have a chit to enter the Great Thinker Race, but every once in a while I get a peek through a rent in the cosmos and I say something far wiser than I'm equipped to have said.

And it is then, at that scary moment, that I dare to think I may have had a Great Thought.

This is one of them.

And here it is, from Thursday the 23rd of April 2009:

People tell me I am witty or clever or smart or intelligent. I like that, and I'll happily batten on it. Many people tell me my biggest problem is that I expect everyone to be as "smart" as I am. In truth, I go to bed every night, and in my way, as a confirmed Atheist, I pray that I wake up tomorrow as smart as I am...and I'm the *dumbest* person on the planet.

There is entirely too much casual "road"-style rage in America today. Too gahdumm muddlefuggin caulksuggin sheetfaced who the fugg you lookin' at, geddaway from my car you dhiggwwhad peeza schat azzwhole bastidch crazy rage. I, for instance, have been getting a great many—may I proffer plethora—yes, I'll proffer plethora—a plethora of street confrontations, resulting in ass-chowdering fistfights. Over the dumbest, smallest, most inconsequential misunderstandings.

But I had a thought today.

And fortunately we have the DICTIONARY.

*Mondegreen* is the answer.

I'll get back to this, my central thought point, in a moment.

It was 1976, around the holidays. I was at a small party at the home of my friends Walter and Judy Koenig. (I am loath to drop names, but in this instance, it is condign.) I was sitting on the ledge of the fireplace talking at length with Walter's brilliant son, Josh, age 8. All around us in the living room people were hors d'oeuvreing, drinking, chatting. It's not that I don't like parties—I *don't*, but that has nothing much to do with this particular thought of the day—but I *do* like Walter and Judy, and I was nuts about Josh. He remains, to this day, one of the brightest, cleverest, most courageous kids I've ever known.

And we were sitting side-by-side, discussing the atlas of the ancient world, or bunny-hopping, or something equally arcane, while the conversations swirled behind us through the atmosphere. And out of the corner of my peripheral, I heard an actor I barely knew, Jack Danon, say—or I *thought* he said—something like "Jeff is fine. He's always fine."

But I didn't *hear* "Jeff is fine. He's always fine." What I *heard* was "Jeffty is five. He's *always* five." And my storyteller's brain made that leap of the abyss from eight-year-old wonderful Josh beside me, to a boy named "Jeffty" who was five. Who was forever and *always* at the age of five, as the world aged around him.

And I went home and wrote the story.

It is now quite a well-known piece of my *oeuvre*, filmed, done as a recording...well, just first rank in my proudest of productions. All from that moment with Josh when I heard what I didn't actually hear.

It is mondegreen.

We're back.

(I pause for a moment to make my living: this heartbreaking story is available both on spoken word and in a number of my books. Under award-winners. Shame is for those who live well enough not to feel it; you may quote me. Now back to our Major Thought of Cosmic Proportions, intended to protect you from all the frothing gibbons wearing clothes from The Gap. And who the fugg *you* lookin' at, terd-bucket?)

The OED and other reliable sources say of the philological origins of the literary term "mondegreen":

"The term was coined by Sylvia Wright in 1954 in an article in the *Atlantic*." Apparently, when Ms. Wright was a child she had been impressed by a folk song that included the lines "They had slain the Earl of Moray / And the lady Mondegreen." As one with hearing "Jeffty Is Five" (a tragic, yet brilliant story, he vociferated with humility), or *mis*hearing same, she didn't realize her mistake for years. "The song was not about the tragic fate of Lady Mondegreen, but rather, the continuing plight of the good earl: "They had slain the Earl of Moray / And laid him on the green." Got that through yer guhdamnt skull, idjit?

Mondegreen.

Purposely mishearing to save yourself a confrontation; one of the numberless stupid bump-shoulder road rage encounters that boil and blight our daily lives to no advantage whatever, and often result in a sad hospitalization or dinged side-panel.

Mondegreen as a useful daily tool of self-preservation in these parlous times, as valuable as a spanner, a hair pin, a belt, or a jack-knife, occurred to me today after a minor encounter that ordinarily would be as significant as a bubble in a betatron. But since I live to serve your every need, I let the thought expand. (For application, just let your mind recapture the last episode you watched of *Operation Repo* or *Hard Core Pawn* or *The Real Cheap Ho's of Jerseylicious Shore* for hundreds of frighteningly commonplace daily uses for this remarkable mondegreen lifesaver. You'll thank me later.)

You talkin' to *me*, ashwipe? You *mush* be talkin' to me...dooood, cuz I'm the only one standin' here with my finger up my nose an' a marmoset in my mouth!

Preceding paragraph, only slightly altered from the actuality, happened to me today, mentor of this Great Thought:

That was the unspoken attitude of a total stranger who had chosen to watch me— on a somewhat shabby street in North Hollywood—as I stooped, literally—to tie my shoelace. He was about thirty feet away, ass hugging a wall, and when I looked up casually, this is a stranger, remember, he got the look of a howler monkey in dire need of an enema, and he snarled at me, "Whut the fuckke you think you're starin' at, ersewhole?"

Now there is almost no answer you can provide that won't start a brouhaha, because this jamook is clearly outta his tree, pissed off at the cosmos, and spoilin' for a fight.

Which is the moment my thought blossomed. And I grinned like a three-year-old and went back on my haunches, and replied:

"Yeah, my lug nuts *feel* loose! How could you tell from over there? You got a lug-wrench I could borrow? I was gonna buy a fuck-me starin' at lug-wrench, but I was too broke. You are a helluva guy for pointing it out...you got an extra?"

He gave me a disgusted look, turned and walked away.

The small war that would have ensued, had I not gone mondegreen all over his ass, I cannot conjure. But he was looking for a squiff, and I just babbled on, down on the side-walk, kept talking till he was so confused he didn't remember that "what the fuckke you..." had been translated into a jeremiad about lug nuts.

Same thing happened to my friend Alan Brennert day before yesterday. He and another car were jockeying for position in a pair of parking spaces, and the other guy didn't think Alan had given him enough of the Known Universe to lumber his tug into the allotted environ. So he starts screaming and cursing and propounding the specious theory that Alan was being "rude," when Alan pointed out that there was plenty of room for both of them, and it was *he*, the gaboon, who was cursing, thus the true placement of "being rude."

Well, I shall not belabor this incident. Alan had to unship his Glock and kill the muthuhfugguh right there in the street, resulting in a $2 ticket for littering the street with spent shell casings and a stern reprimand from his mother.

Mondegreen would have saved the day.

*"You're rude!"*

"You're right! I shouldn't be driving around nude. But aliens from Ganymede stole all my clothes, and my presents for my nephew Darren, and I'm so sorry for being out here nekkid in the street..." and on and on till the guy realized he was dealing with a nut-job, and that he would wind up last in line at the Krispy Kreme if he didn't get away at once. Oh, I do love dat Mondegreen!

I feel just like the first mongoloid-jawed pithecanthropoid who figured out that lightning was made by Ryan Seacrest on a wild Malibu weekend. Great thoughts can blossom from the smallest snippet of slippery slime, you know. Try it sometime, feel how enriched you are!

*"Watch where the hell you're going?!?!"*

"No, it's not going well at all. Do you happen to know what time it is? I think my watch stopped. I have to pick up dog food."

*"Don't touch me!"*

"Oh, yeah, I used to use touchme, it worked very well for my arthritis. I could tell you a good drug store where they still carry it, if you'd like; but it's called *Swee*-Touch-Nee tea; that may be why you're having trouble finding it."

And on and on. You'll have to be on guard, for the lame rude remark; but there are only a limited number of rude and imbecile threats that can come to minds between the ears of which blow nothing but the arid *khamsins* of thought-starved winds, so you will mostly be having fun choosing which quick-wit ploy you wish to use to befuddle the road-rage ruffian. Be quick, be sharp, be off-the-wall. The word "fuque" can, with just a little bit of jackanappery, be mondegreen misheard as "folk," "fork," "foolk," or even "frog."

And once you've begun your completely askew answer, it is a matter of a minim for you to lay down "Oh, what a sweet guy you are, wanting to help me take off my fork, because I have an aunt with pleurisy and I have to get to the hospital for visiting hours."

And if this doesn't simply confuse the hell out of the mook, if it doesn't tend to make him think you're utterly insane, and he turns away in disgust, and leaves you untroubled, remember, if you keep running your mondegreen mouth long and crazy enough, it'll give you all the time you need to pull a crowbar out of the trunk and shove it up the moron's ass.

Thus preserving the peace. Just a thought.

Photo by Steven Barber

# Substitute: 29 March 2009

In truth, this is more or less a little casual thought, not the major Thought I had last Sunday, and was prepared to visit on the world...had circumstances of a trying nature not obtruded, obstructed, and otherwise obfuscated my outlook, overlook, and objectives. This is a substitute Thought. A small one, as set purposely apart from the Cosmic Thought lying just over the horizon. Which Thought you will only slightly love a lot.

Meanwhile and meantimes, this:

Every once in a while you'll see a panel in one of the Batman comics—usually set in the Batcave—where the careful observer can identify, in a large glass case or cabinet or clothes closet, supplementary Batman uniforms:

The white Bat-Suit, the gold Bat-Suit, the rainbow Bat-Suit, the zebra Bat-Suit, the spacegoing Bat-Suit, the knight-in-armor Bat-Suit, even a cowboy Bat-Suit. These are actual for-real Bat-Suits from decades of comicbook issues, and there are likely more neither I, nor Mark Evanier, nor Len Wein, can remember off the top.

Such as, I was thinking:

A tempered and case-hardened chrome steel Bat-Suit for battling OhShitI'mOn-Fire Guy; a plastic, Velcro fastened Bat-Suit for staving off magnetic tractor-beam technology developed at MIT for use at Gitmo; the Arctic Bat-Suit with mukluks and a tush-warmer, in the event of the mythical Global Warming; the 3-D Bat-Suit that always looks as if a No. 2 pencil is being hurled at you, and gives a blinding headache to evildoers who stare at it; a dirndl and pinafore Bat-Suit for obtaining clues at The Push-In Pub; the savanna grassy plain disguise Bat-Suit that comes fully equipped with pith cowl and underarm-deodorant dispensers; a gangsta butt-crack baggy pants Bat-Suit for

229

undercuhvuh wo'k in d'hood; the polar bear disguise Bat-Suit for use in Alaska, in case Sarah Palin manages to shuck out of the straitjacket and runs amuck; an Armani-designed double-seamed Bat-Suit, we're talking really dope, good lapels, double-vent jacket, scarlet jacquard lining, possibly shantung; an Aurora Model kit mud-encrusted Bat-Suit in case Batman has to battle the Predator again; the Great Books model Bat-Suit which comes equipped with a hi-tech scanner and readout cowl that can instantly flash anything from Aesop to Stefan Zweig, in case Batman has to face off with Alex Trebek, and so on.

Big closets, lots of walk-in space, down there in the Batcave.

Yet...I had this vagrant Thought...

Batman has an unending congeries of horrid threats coming at him, in (currently, at least) several dozen different eponymous comics, arcs, series, crossovers, graphic novels, amalgams, movies, animated series, and theme rides. None of which cost 10 cents a pop any more. (Apparently DC Comics doesn't yet "get it" that there's a crippling, cataclysmic economic "downturn"—dontcha just luuuuhhv that euphemism—in progress.) And there's very little dispensable frivolous expenditure cash floating around. So the more Batman books (at, minimally, four bucks a shot) with which DC floods us (along with the 10,000 dumb crossover *Crisis on Final Crisislike Crises World of Semiannual Crisiseses* crap they fling out monthly, like a hiatic-hernia hamster upchucking), the less any one publication (at a puny 36 pages, of which 10 are ads) can continue to attract its Loyal You'n'Me audience. Even the long-time beloved *Batman* or *Detective Comics*...if the choice is food on the table, gas in the tank, a roof over your mortgaged head. Comic books?!?! COMICthefuckBOOKS??? C'mon, wake up, get real, think clearly.

And I've been reading/saving both since 1940!

Where was I? Thoughts upon a Thought. (Your Doctor would call it thread-drift.)

Perils. Facing Batman. Lotsa perils. Yes, he is brave, he is muscular; he is experienced, he is field-tested, he is tempered against fear; he is a multimillionaire. Yeah, sure, he is wily, smart, forensically insightful; he is well-read, except for the later works of the Essenes and French Modernists, including Colette. Uh-huh, he got him some terrific sense of spatial relationships, he got a great sense of smell, he got even common sense. All of that!

Nonetheless, a hundred and sixteen times a month, Batman has to face down sudden, unexpected, unbelievably dangerous and demented perils, menaces, perplexities, and hazards that would give Spartacus the bump-nodes, that would make Achilles and Atlas and Ares himself whimper, that would make The Dirty Dozen go white with terror (and that includes Jim Brown). Malevolent manifestations loopier than Kiev's current mayor, Leonid Chernovetsky (who wants to erect a giant cow statue and a monument to street lights). What I'm talkin' here is giant ant stuff, boiling lava stuff, the kind of stuff would make God His/Herownself drop a cookie and run! Dr. Moreau would hand in his diploma. Prince Valiant would lay down his sword. James Bond would whimper like Shirley Temple. The Shadow would fade in fear. Muhammad Ali would take a dive. Wonder Woman would plead to be recast as Rebecca of Sunnybrook Farm. Paul Revere would pull up short and beat hooves in the other direction. Joyce Carol Oates would fumfuh. We're talking incredible, horrible, awful threats and terrors here, folks! Real sphincter-clutcher stuff, by your leave.

Batman gets his rib-cage squashed by giant robots; Batman is trussed-up and dropped into vats of molten metal; Batman is drowned, punctured, chomped-on, frozen solid, asphyxiated, and really disrespected big time. Batman is flung off skyscrapers; Batman has his spine broken; Batman gets buried alive beneath sixteen cubic yards of Portland Cement; Batman is masticated by giant carnivorous worms; Batman is stabbed in the eye-socket by spike-heeled Jimmy Choos; Batman is knocked loopy and dropped into trash compactors; Batman is run down by everything from a Go-Kart to a McCormick Thresher; Batman is eaten alive by cougars, catamounts, lions, cheetahs, jaguars, voles, Kleenex dispensers. Any-thing that draws breath has it in for mere flesh and blood Batman... and...on top of all that...Batman gets regularly pissed-off by, and winds up getting the bejeezus beaten out of him day in, day out, by foes *and* friends...Robin and Nightwing and Cat-woman and Superman and Scribbly and Green Arrow and Prez and Brother Power the Geek and, jeezus, even the FedEx delivery guy! Can you *imagine* what his blood-pressure is like? Batman has to deal with demented creeps like The Joker and The Penguin and Two-Face and Poison Ivy and Mr. Freeze and Bane and The Scarecrow and Red Hood and Clayface and the Ventriloquist & Scarface and Catman and Ra's Al Ghul, not to mention that asshole Kite-Man.

We're talking here about swinging around up there in nosebleed-heaven, seventy-two storeys above smashdeath concrete Gotham pavement; imbibing pure death in poisoned beef Stroganoff; hydraulically-powered arrows the thickness of Rush Limbaugh's waistline; clockwork-oranged with prongs holding open your ears, strapped into an electric chair and being forced to listen to endless hours of Ann Coulter as the merciless villain *refuses* to give you blessed electrocutionary release; shark attacks; ninja thugs; Mafia thugs; Crips thugs; Blood thugs; *thuggee* thugs; Scientologists.

You are Batman, and every second of every minute of decades and decades since

1938 or so...you have been chained to the railroad tracks of mind-paralyzing unending no-weekends-or-Federal Holidays-off terror...and here comes the 5:09!

So the unasked question is:

How many times has Batman pissed himself, how many times has Batman crapped his drawers, how many times has Batman soiled himself? How many dumps has he taken unwillingly? How many "Oh, Kriiiiste, it's the Killer Croc in that crane and here comes the fuckin' wrecking ball!!!!??" How many biscuits? How many yello-mellos? How often the ooo, whooops!?

I don't care how good you are, how much money you have, how many times your suave alter-ego has gotten laid by starlets, how much Pilates you do, how buff you are, how many chunks of metal you've got replacing your arms, legs, liver, or spleen...I don't give a damn how athletic you are, how lucky you are, how adept and sinewy and flexible you are...Jack, don't tell me that looking up from the bloody deck and seeing a twelve-foot-high, drooling, snakeskin, mass murderer with the moves of a Sonny Chiba and an intestine-festooned pickaxe lunging over you...

You do not piss yourself!

This guy leads a life that would make a sandworm whiz.

So.

What the hell does Batman do with his smelly tighty-whiteys?

Does he burn 'em on return to the Bat-Cave? Incinerate 'em so no enemy can glom his DNA? Does he vaporize 'em in the Bat-O-Craperator? (Westinghouse, pat. pending.) Does he just toss them in a closet or slide-chute from which poor Alfred has to shovel them up with a spade or, more appropriately, a Silent Butler? Do they begin to get maxi-redolent after a week of his battling the Slimy Grub Men from Arcturus, without he can manage even a minute to get the befouled items to the launderette? Does he get them to the Fluff'n'Fold? Is there even a laundry room in Wayne Manor? Yeah, sure, suits of armor everywhere you look, but how about a Maytag? And Alfred...how the hell much would you have to pay *me*, much less overworked Alfred (who apparently keeps that enormous mansion *and* the Bat-Cave dusted, sprayed, mopped, and clean all by himself), to shovel up a hundred crap-filled Jockeys a week? Does Bruce Wayne have an entire Underwear Annex, the deep south wing, to store drawer after drawer of, well, drawers? Poop heaven, we're talking here. I don't give a, well, a *shit* how heroically magnificent the Dark Knight Detective is, this man is still a simple human being, with natural bodily functions, and has *got* to have an odorocity problem that transcends mortal explication.

I had a thought today.

# The Captain of Fate

Mostly, it's a boxcar full of incomprehensible terminology. Mandelbrot sets. Linear versus non-linear systems. That trite and wearying "butterfly effect" everyone uses when they want to sound informed. Fractals. Simple attractors. Strange attractors. Iterated growth and erosion. Self-similarity. The Koch Curve (same as fractal). Random behavior, in seemingly normal patterns. The manner in which smoke disperses; the manner in which cream permeates a cup of coffee; a lone walker standing at a fork in the road. Chaos Theory.

None of that gibberish will help you. But:

Using the underlying concept of Chaos Theory and its universal application to flawed, fallible, mostly ridiculous human beings—that's you and me, kiddo—I can codify for you The Big Secret. I can tell you how to attain riches, fame, true love, avoid accidents, reap the benefits of being well-liked, assure your future, and in short, make Life a Sweet Song for you. Pay attention.

> "Chance favors the prepared mind."
> LOUIS PASTEUR

I'll start with an anecdote. It never fails, not even once; at every lecture I deliver, whether at the Yale Political Union, or MIT, or the London School of Economics, or Caltech, or Estrella Mountain Community College, hundreds and hundreds of lectures over more than fifty years, it never fails: someone will come up and ask me for The Secret. Like Willy Loman in *Death of a Salesman*, where he demands of the hallucination of his brother Ben, "What's the secret? What is it, Ben? Tell me how to achieve success! What is it, Ben?!" And the ghost says something useless like "be well-liked, Willy" or "I went into the jungle and hewed an empire out of the vast waste...it's *diamonds*, Willy!"

That's what they want to know. What is The Secret? As if we who have made something of our life ascend to the attic at dead midnight, bearing a chamois bag filled with the knucklebones of a Chacma baboon, and we cast the runes, and come down in the foggy morning light with The Secret.

All that is as useless as Chaos Theory terminology.

But Chaos Theory *isn't*. Because, as Pasteur said: "Chance favors the prepared mind." So when a student, or a businessman asks me—in one way or another—"What's The Secret," I tell him or her: "Read the Sherlock Holmes stories. The entire Conan Doyle canon." Because all the stories are built on the concept of using logic, of ratiocination as a weapon and tool to control your own existence. The more you know, the more clearly you look at all aspects of the problem, the more likely you are not to wind up in bad situations with lovers, not to enter into illogical and blue-sky business plans, never to get involved with time-wasting or demented leaners who will lead you into the morass. If you understand that *there is no such thing as chance*, but only patterns we do not understand, you will cease to believe in phony religions, astrology, flying saucers, heroes and demons, good and evil (most of what we call "evil" is usually only ineptitude), ghosts, the infallibility of politicians, and all the other coocoo distractions from clear thinking.

There is no chance. There is Chaos. And Chaos is Entropy Misunderstood. The world is not run by secret cabals, it is run by people who do not understand the systems within which they operate; and so they attempt to bend them to alternate purposes. But Chaos will have its way. Those rivers will find their true courses, no matter how many dams of bigotry, greed, hatred, and frenzy are erected.

Chance favors the prepared mind. Chaos works to your benefit. *Know* as much as you can. Understand and remember.

Life has only one great lesson. It says to you: PAY ATTENTION. Whether in Chaos or Entropy, the more you know, the cleverer and more well-informed you are...the easier it is to ride the tide of Chaos, to achieve The Secret.

You're welcome. And you didn't even have to sign up for a seminar. Chaos is a highwayman, wild and free.

Chaos is when a man walks ahead, but his soul lags behind.

---

Editor's Note: The preceding piece was commissioned by New Line Cinema to promote the 2004 theatrical release of *The Butterfly Effect*. It was featured on the movie's website, and makes its print debut here.

# Terrorists

> "Sir, if a man has experienced the inexpressible, he is under no obligation to attempt to express it."
>
> SAMUEL JOHNSON

It is wickedly difficult attempting to generate a sense of gravitas when you have convinced yourself that you have nothing to say that anyone should properly need to hear.

Let me try this:

Why can't I get that portion of the human race to which I have access to understand that it has been systematically gulled, hoodwinked if you will, had enough smoke blown up its kilt to refloat the *Lusitania*, by disingenuous egalitarian bunkum, into believing "Everyone is Entitled to His or Her Opinion" when, in truth, everyone is only entitled to his or her *informed* opinion; and all the witless upchuck devoid of fact or common ratiocination is merely the chittering of intellectually-arid hominids swathed in Old Navy *shmatahs*.

No, can't launch into it that way. Sounds too Elitist. Don't even *dare* to suggest that some folks are smarter than some other folks. That ain't The American Way. All opinions have the same weight: Herman Kahn, Debbie Reynolds, Miss Cleo, Colin Powell, Joyce Carol Oates, Adam Sandler.

Okay, let's go a different way. How about this:

In the dead of night, masked marauders should stalk and ensnare Jerry Falwell in his bed, his coiffed cap of majestic silver hair mussed as a haystack, drag him into the bayou, to an abandoned crayfisherman's shanty, hang him up with his arms handcuffed behind his back on a slaughterhouse hook screwed into the top half of a Dutch door, strip him to his gourmand gut, slick and pale as a planarian worm, and beat him across the belly with an aluminum ballbat till his piss runs red.

Oh, whoa! Can't do that, either. Sounds—at *best*—stone vicious, meanspirited, sadistic. This is Moral Jerry, the voice of Gawd Above. Can't write such stuff, not The American Way. Jerry talks to the Lord, and the Lord gets right back to him. Only a card-carrying member of the ACLU would doubt that. So, um, let me see...would this work:

The phone rang. It was October 19th 2001. Only thirty-eight days after the September 11th attacks on the World Trade Towers and the Pentagon. No one was talking about anything else, because nothing mattered as much; but the fabricators of *tchotchke* novelties were already casting the molds for the cute antimony ashtrays with the rubble stumps and American flags unfurled. And my phone rang.

It was Carole Chouinard, one of the "talent coordinators" for the ABC-TV talk show *Politically Incorrect with Bill Maher*.

They wanted me to come on the show as part of the usual disparate quartet of opinionated citizens, some of whom (like me) had a tenuous yet deathlike grip on the appellation "celebrity."

I'd done the show perhaps fifteen or twenty times over the years, all the way back to its original incarnation out of New York on Comedy Central cable. But I hadn't heard from them in more than a year, ever since the telecast in which I'd explained to Maher (with some difficulty of comprehension on his part) that I didn't fantasize about other women when my gorgeous and brilliant wife, Susan, and I were in bed, mostly because my dick had fallen off years ago in a particularly frigid high-wind-chill evening in Manhattan, outside the St. Moritz.

So I was glad to hear from them.

When you've been writing professionally for just abaft fifty years, it gets more and more strenuous trying to keep any sort of a commercially viable profile that permits you—if you're a freelancer—to continue earning a decent living without recourse to scripting a film that will star Pauly Shore, or doping racehorses, both of which will send you to the 9th and inner circle of Hell. (Only difference: with the former, you take the express.)

So doing *Politically Incorrect* didn't pay much; but in terms of keeping one's name and kisser in front of the fickle masses for an extra eyeblink or two, well, it was a halibut swimming in a benificent sea.

So I said, sure I'll come on the show. When? And Carole said we'll be taping as usual at CBS Television City after our hiatus, Tuesday, November 20th. I said that's peachykeen, and what will the topics be?

And Carole—quite correctly—reminded me that they don't finalize the discussion topics till the day of the telecast, in order to keep *courant* with the savory flavors of the breaking news; but that I'd get my *précis* probably on Monday the 19ᵗʰ.

Ah, I thought, no more beaks and feet; my fifteen minutes has done rolled 'round again!

*T*V *Guide* carried the listing, and I was the only name officially slotted in (I'm usually a last-minute replacement for Queen Latifah. Other than that I'm a short, white, Ohio Jew, age 68, we could've been separated at birth, y'know what I'm sayin'?) In fact, the fax I received from Assistant Talent Coordinator Stephanie Lynn on November 19ᵗʰ, the other three guest chairs were to be occupied by ex-*M.A.S.H.* star and political activist Mike Farrell, a very smart cookie; actress Charlotte Ross, now on *NYPD Blue*; and ultraconservative Representative Dana Rohrbacher. Now, I have no idea of how deep and wide runs Ms. Ross's intellect or awareness of current events, but those other two guys are sharp and knowledgeable.

Thus it was, one day before the telecast, that I received advisement of my on-camera companions, along with the three topics that had been chosen by Maher and his staff for discussion.

And here are the topics, exactly as presented to me:

1.  *America has taken great pains to assemble a coalition of nations in its fight against terrorism. Is a coalition important?*
2.  *President Bush says the noose is getting tighter around Osama bin Laden. When he is caught, what should we do to him? Should he be killed on sight? Should he be tried in court? Should Saddam Hussein be next?*
3.  *Undoubtedly, the fight for increased homeland security could benefit from increased tax dollars. Are Americans more willing to sacrifice—financially and otherwise—than politicians admit?*

I stared at that faxed page for a long time.

One spends a lifetime wondering if one's ethics are report card "A"—buttressed by courage sufficient to understand at every test-point not only that you gotta *do* The Right Thing, but to *know* when it's time to do The Right Thing. We are a weasely little species, capable of alibi and obfuscation at a level of instant adroitness that would put a turkey vulture to shame. If you doubt it for a second, pick a television court show like *Judge Judy*, and watch it for a week. Will make your gorge buoyant.

I stared at that faxed page for a long time.

*Everybody* wants to be on television. Everybody. At the scene of a fifty-car-smashup, bodies strewn everywhichway like bloody pick-up-sticks, there will invariably be some gobbet of human phlegm who, with slack jaw and extruded tongue, positions him- or herself behind the stringer with the mike, who waves to the world or to Mom while squishing an ejected large colon neath his/her Nikes. Pedestrians in malls, passersby in markets, patrons in moviehouses, all pant and drool as their progress is impeded by a total stranger with a hand-mike, seeking their oracular wisdom. The late British Prime Minister, Harold Macmillan, once wrote, "I have never found, in a long experience of politics, that criticism is ever inhibited by ignorance."

And, hell, we *pay* politicians to have opinions.

Everybody wants to be a dancing bear on television, and everybody *deserves* to shoot off a big mouth on the tube because, as *everybody* knows...We Are All Entitled To Our Opinion.

Doesn't matter if we're dumb as a box of Hamburger Helper, as uninformed as a hemorrhoid, as surfeited with jingoism and urban myth as a foot-soldier in the White Aryan Army, by gosh we're entitled to express that bone-stick-stone opinion, endlessly, at the top of our lungs, ungrammatically, like uh *totally* and, gawd willin' and the crick don't rise, on *tele*muthuhfuggin*vision*!

I stared at that faxed page for a long time.


Then I called *Politically Incorrect* and told Nora Burdenski or Carole or Marilyn Wilson or Stephanie or *some*one that I was going to have to do what I had never ever done before, in more than forty years of talk-show appearances. I was going to have to excuse myself from the panel. Tomorrow night.

When you tell someone who has booked a talk show slot cut and sewn to fit your shape only, that you are doing a bunk, there is—first—a moment of silence one encounters only in undefiled Pharaonic tombs. That moment, as they refer to it in Indonesia, is *djam karet*, the moment that stretches. A cæsura gorged with billions of Roentgens of incipient hysterics.

Then they take that esteemed cortical-thalamic pause, for they know if they explode it will only serve to solidify your dastardly intention. The voice grows soft, cashmere, Reddi-Wip, plangent; soothing and as confidential as words whispered in the death cell at Dannemora.

"Oh my."

I say nothing.

"Well, this really is terribly short notice, Harlan. We even have the limo laid on to bring you to the studio."

"Yes, I know, Nora [or Marilyn, Carole, Stephanie], and you've worked with me enough times to perceive that this is an unusual circumstance, because…have I *ever* pulled this sort of thing on youse guys?"

"No, you haven't. Are you sick?"

"Not in the accepted, non-psychiatric sense of the word; no, I'm just fine, dear heart. But I cannot sit on that show with the topics Bill is planning to throw at us."

"Why, what's wrong with them?"

"Nothing's 'wrong' with them; I just don't have any intelligent opinions on them. I truly have nothing to say."

"But you're so *funny*; you *always* have something to say on *any*thing! That's why we call on you so often."

"Yeah, you'd think I'd have something to shoot off my big bazoo about, wouldn't you? But, in truth, kiddo, I just *don't*."

"You have no opinions about 9/11?" Astonishment trembled in her voice. This was a concept she could not parse. A Flat Earth Theory for the 21st Century. In the word of the evil Sicilian, Vizzini, who kidnapped Buttercup, *Inconceivable!*

"I was three thousand miles away from ground zero when it happened," I said, beginning to get annoyed. "I saw it on teevee, fer chrissakes! I wasn't *there*, though I know there are people who delude themselves that they 'saw' the Manson murders or the Lindbergh baby kidnapping or the assassination of JFK because they glommed a docudrama on the tube. It was a horror show, and I was watching live as the second plane dissolved through the wall of the second Tower, and I spent days trying to reach friends of mine who lived in the area, or worked in the buildings, but…"

How the hell do you say what comes next?

"…but *I wasn't affected*. I didn't lose anyone close to me. I was a spectator. I'm enraged at the atrocity, just like everyone else, but what the hell does *my* opinion mean? It's just more hot air and posturing, expelled like all the hot air by the hundreds of wannabes who've been on the tube for the last month. I have nothing to say that anyone needs to hear!"

"But you'll be great on the show. You can say what you've just said to me."

"I can go drain valuable airtime on a coast-to-coast hookup, to say that I'm empty of opinion? That I know nothing more than what I read and see in the news, and there are actual people out there who've been through it, but I'm a bigmouth on the other end of the continent who should shut up and sit down? Is that my contribution to the advancement of Western Civilization on this particular topic?"

"But this is really inconvenient, it puts us in a hole."

"Don't you think I'm well aware of that? Don't you think I sat and stared long and hard at those topics *trying* to dredge up something meaningful that would validate my sticking my teeny opinions in the faces of three million viewers? And I don't delude myself that *Politically Incorrect* is news, kiddo: it's mere show biz, it's entertainment. Nonetheless, I am affronted when you put on guests who are as uninformed and as outright stupid as—" and I named half a dozen recent guests, "—so I'd rather not be a hypocrite and balm my own cheap need for exposure, at the expense of three million people's patience. I grant you the show, and even the lowliest opinion by the dopiest standup comic pseudo-pundit, is better than the entirety of those Grand Guignols presided over by Letterman and Leno and Conan the Borebarian, but it ain't *Nightline* or the editorial page of *The New York Times*.

"I understand that jerking you around like this will likely mean I'm persona non grata at *Politically Incorrect*, but I find myself inexplicably troubled by the ethical considerations of pretending to know something in front of so many people, when I just don't have the vaguest opinion on these weighty topics. So...well, maybe you can get Queen Latifah to stand in for me. We were separated at birth, you know."

Well, there were a couple of cajoling calls an hour or so later, but by that time I'd firmed my resolve, though I knew such behavior would redound to my detriment profilewise.

There was even a call from the new Producer who had taken over when Scott Carter left the show to produce Candice Bergen's short-lived chat-a-thon. He said he understood perfectly what my bizarre concern was, he assured me *he* felt sanguine about my coming to do *what I'd agreed to do*, and he further assured me that even if I screwed them over this summarily, it would IN NO WAY deter him from inviting me back, and soon. Very soon. Almost sooner than I could envision.

I thanked him for his understanding and compassion, and told him that as a lifelong blabbermouth of infinite hubris I found this spike of ethical constriction most unnerving. But I was, for better or worse, fixed in my decision.

He said he'd make sure I was invited back in December.

We parted amicably.

That was five months ago as I write this. Listen, *amigos*, do we hear the silence of

Pharaonic tombs? The silence of petrogeny? The silence of Coventry? I'll be placing a small personal ad in the *Green Sheet* seeking the whereabouts of my lost fifteen minutes. Maybe on milk cartons.

I have never expressed a public opinion on the nightmare of 9/11. I've been asked by others, but I just shrug and mumble something to the effect that it isn't my *place* to have a public opinion. Even though I hold with Voltaire: "My trade is to say what I think," there are some things in this sad and painful world that are too large, too significant, too troubling for the squirrel chatter of the mook in the street. My pal Tony Isabella notes: "Hell hath no fury like that of the uninvolved." But, boy, did I catch the shit. On one of the websites "dedicated" to my comings and goings, a guy went on at sibilant length as to how "unpatriotic" I am, not man enough to let others know how I felt about the sudden vaporized disappearance of a few thousand innocents. I chose not to reply.

Then, something straight out of the *Manual of Synchronicity* went down, and I found to my chagrin that I did, indeed, have an opinion—if not about 9/11 directly, well, at least it was a *strong* opinion about terrorists.

You won't like it, and you may echo that gnat's e-post that I'm not a Good Amurrican, but I'll pass it along, anyhow. Do with it what you will.

(A pause. I am an American. Says so on my passport. I served in the U.S. Army for two years, I have paid loads of taxes for half a century, I marched for civil rights with Martin Luther King, Jr., worked with Cesar Chavez on the grapefruit strike in the Coachella Valley, spoke for more than 1100 actual hours in dozens of venues on behalf of the Equal Rights Amendment, and I once sued a large corporation for screwing its customers, and won a rebate for them, not to mention a policy change. I am an American. My response to your cavil that I'm "unpatriotic" is a soft, sane, reasoned bleep you and the snake you slithered in on.)

On September 17th, less than a week after the suicide slaughters, when Bill Maher's show went back on the air for the first time after the 9/11 events, he made some comments about the turmoil, the roiling and chaos, the vast number of opinions by everyone from Jennifer Aniston to Geraldo Rivera, the intrepid war correspondent. Among his remarks was one that prompted White House Press Secretary Ari Fleischer to chide him, "This is not a time for remarks like that."

The remark. Maher suggested—and I concur with his proper use of terminology—that you could call those brutal skyjackers rabid, you could call them demented, or brainwashed, or merciless, amoral, devoid of kindness or compassion, the heartless dregs of a mad society…but you could not, rationally, call them "cowards." Cowards do not saddle up a flying coffin filled with something like 24,000 gallons of high-octane jet fuel and hurtle at full throttle into a World Trade Center spire, turning themselves into screaming flaming gelatine, their eyeballs melting, their rib cage exploding, their hair burning down through their brain. Assholes, maybe. Religious fanatics, damned skippy. But not cowards. Wrong word.

A bit of convenient jingoism used by the Ashcrofts and the Bushes, to demonize what is already demonic. But not cowards. To an enormous segment of the world's population they are the equivalent of Audie Murphy, Sergeant York, Captain America, the kid who throws himself on the grenade to save his buddies, the old lady who pushes the toddler out of the way of the Peterbilt and gets turned into roadkill for her trouble. We call those people heroes.

See, I told you that you wouldn't like it, where I was going. But don't expend all your outrage just yet; I plan to take this a lot further.

Maher's remark loosed the Apocalypse upon him. Now, I am not a friend of his, nor do I agree with him most of the time, nor has he ever expressed so much as a fartwhistle of interest in getting to know Susan and me. When I do the show, he is always sedulous in making a green room appearance to thank his guests, but apart from exchanging passing courtesies, I know *you* better than I know Bill Maher. But I became incensed at the mindless, lockstep behavior of empty patriotism that the great manipulable wad of American slopebrows unleashed on him. Samuel Johnson had it screwed down tight when he observed that "Patriotism is the last refuge of a scoundrel." I offer Timothy McVeigh and Richard Nixon as examples.

And while the *New York Times* was running a special section titled "A Nation Challenged"—a four-month long project that included more than 1800 "Portraits of Grief" remembering the victims of September 11th—and setting itself up to win seven Pulitzers, Maher was fighting to keep his sinecure. He became a pariah. For expressing a logical but not hysterical opinion.

Sure, here in our beloved republic you are "entitled to your opinion," just as long as you don't voice it when the lynch mob is raising the flag and the cross.

But, still, I didn't post my agreement publicly, because it wasn't necessary. Dozens of righteous (as opposed to *self*-righteous) commentators jumped to Maher's defense, including that blowhard bully Bill O'Reilly. "Censorship of anything, at any time, in any place, on whatever pretense, has always been and always will be the last resort of the boob and the bigot." Eugene O'Neill. Now dead, so no one can bust *his* chops.

But what happened next, almost simultaneously with Maher's oh-spare-me-the-imprudence-of-it-all, was the force that yanked the wooden stake out of me widdle vampire heart.

Jerry Falwell, the pimp of religious recidivism, went on Pat Robertson's tube and blamed the World Trade Center Towers bombings on those who run abortion clinics, homosexuals, feminists, and the liberal scum who refuse to allow Christian Fundamentalists to take over the schools more than they have already. (The fact that something like sixty-five per cent of all science teachers in high schools believe in the wacky creationist theory of the universe ought to scare the crap out of anyone but a bible-thumping true believer.) There he was, that smooth, slick planarian worm of a minister, telling everyone that it was the fags and the feminazis and the baby-killers who were to blame.

Now, just to remove the thorn from your paw, to deny you that disreputable forensic-debating rathole into which the Blind Faithful predictably scuttle—"Well, Dr. Jerry is bein' quoted outta contex'"—I will now offer for your predilection vast windy sections of Pat Robertson's interview with Falwell from the 13 September 2001 edition of *The 700 Club*, two days after the great death. Two days into the American heartache. (Please note, all pecksniffs: in the original manuscript of this essay, I reproduced the *totality*, every last word of this obstinately wearisome exchange. Just so no one could *possibly* suggest there had been any flummery. But the good barristers who vet this material pointed out that even though I'd taken this from *The 700 Club*'s own website, where it appears sans copyright; and even though it had been broadcast live over the public airwaves; and even though there was a surety that this was what is called "fair use," that the censorious carrion birds who serve the Messrs. Falwell & Robertson might, nonetheless, initiate a nuisance lawsuit if I was to republish the entirety of the tv duologue. So we cut it, this seriatum babble by Tweedledum and Tweedledumber. Here's the essence. If you think, in a last-straw grasp at paranoid justification for the monstrousness you are about to read, that I have misrepresented even by a scintilla, I urge you to go to the anointed website to fill in the blankety-blanks.) Clip and save: Falwell in full flight, followed by the comments of Robertson on the same episode of *The 700 Club* prior to Falwell's appearance.

The Interview with Jerry Falwell:

PAT ROBERTSON: Well after Tuesday's attacks, many Americans are struggling with grief, fear and unanswered questions. How should Christians respond to this crisis? Well joining us now with some answers is a dear friend of ours, the Pastor of the Thomas Road Baptist Church and Liberty University, the head and founder of that, Dr. Jerry Falwell. Jerry, it's a delight to have you with us today.

JERRY FALWELL: Thanks, Pat.

PAT ROBERTSON: Listen. What are you telling the church? You called your church together. What was your response at Thomas Road to this tragedy?

JERRY FALWELL: Well, as the world knows, the tragedy hit on Tuesday morning, and at 2:00 in the afternoon, we gathered 7,000 Liberty University students, faculty, local people together, and we used the verse that I heard you use a moment ago, Chronicles II, 7:14, that God wanted us to humble ourselves and seek his face. And there's not much we can do in the Church but what we're supposed to do, and that is pray. Pray for the President that God will give him wisdom, keep bad advisors from him, bring good ones to him, praying for the families of the victims, praying for America. And, you know this thing is not a great deal different than what I remember and you Pat. We're about the same age. December 7, 1941, when we entered the war against Japan, Germany, Italy. Hitler's goal was to destroy the Jews among other things, and conquer the world. And, these Islamic fundamentalists, these radical terrorists, these Middle Eastern monsters are committed to destroying the Jewish nation, driving her into the Mediterranean, conquering the world. And, we are the great Satan. We are the ultimate goal. I talked this morning with Tom Rose publisher of the *Jerusalem Post*, and orthodox Jew, and he said, "Now America knows in a horrible way what Israel's been facing for 53 years at the hand of Arafat and other terrorists and radicals and barbarians."

PAT ROBERTSON: Jerry, I know that you shared several 40 day fasts for revival in America. We here at CBN had a couple of 40 day fasts during the Lenten season, and Bill Bright, I don't know, eight or nine. Do you think that this is going to be the trigger of revival, a real revival in the Church where we truly turn back to God with all our heart?

JERRY FALWELL: It could be. I've never sensed a togetherness, a burden, a broken heart as I do in the Church today, and just 48 hours, I gave away a booklet I wrote 10 years ago. I gave it away last night on the Biblical position on fasting and prayer because I do believe that that is what we've got to do now—fast and pray. And I agree totally with you that the Lord has protected us so wonderfully these 225 years. And since 1812, this is the first time that we've been attacked on our soil, first time, and by far the worst results. And I fear, as Donald Rumsfeld, the Secretary of Defense said yesterday, that this is only the beginning. And with biological warfare available to these monsters; the Husseins, the Bin Ladens, the Arafats, what we saw on Tuesday, as terrible as it is, could be miniscule if, in fact, if in fact God continues to lift the curtain and allow the enemies of America to give us probably what we deserve.

PAT ROBERTSON: Jerry, that's my feeling. I think we've just seen the antechamber to terror. We haven't even begun to see what they can do to the major population.

JERRY FALWELL: The ACLU's got to take a lot of blame for this.

PAT ROBERTSON: Well, yes.

JERRY FALWELL: And, I know that I'll hear from them for this. But, throwing God out successfully with the help of the federal court system, throwing God out of the public square, out of the schools. The abortionists have got to bear some burden for this because God will not be mocked. And when we destroy 40 million little innocent babies, we make God mad. I really believe that the pagans, and the abortionists, and the feminists, and the gays and the lesbians who are actively trying to make that an alternative lifestyle, the ACLU, People For the American Way, all of them who have tried to secularize America. I point the finger in their face and say 'you helped this happen'.

PAT ROBERTSON: Well, I totally concur, and the problem is we have adopted that agenda at the highest levels of our government. And so we're responsible as a free society for what the top people do. And, the top people, of course, is the court system.

JERRY FALWELL: Amen. Pat, did you notice yesterday? The ACLU, and all the Christ-haters, the People For the American Way, NOW, etc. were totally disregarded by the Democrats and the Republicans in both houses of Congress as they went out on the steps and called out on to God in prayer and sang 'God Bless America' and said 'let the ACLU be hanged'. In other words, when the nation is on its knees, the only normal and natural and spiritual thing to do is what we ought to be doing all the time—calling upon God.

Not counting the occasional "Amen!" used in place of their natural grunts (human speech not being their native tongue), this extended badinage was in no way percipient for our little town meeting here. It was mostly hype and hustle, disingenuous back-slapping and mutual greasing about what a powerful force for paleolithic thinking Jerry is, and how we'uns is all gonna git t'gethuh in Bedford on Sunday for an exploitative prayer memorial and pocket picking. I have excised these sections because they put my typewriter to sleep. I had to bitch-slap it to get it to continue. I am sedulous in trying to present the full indictment here, but when the self-serving palaver is about as appropriate as argyles on a turtle, well, you'll just have to take my word for it—untrustworthy though I may be—that between what you've just read, and what is to follow, there was nothing, how shall I put it, exculpatory. Just boring. But now, let us surge forward.

Pat Robertson's Comments Preceding the Falwell Interview:

> PAT ROBERTSON: And we have thought that we're invulnerable. And we have been so concerned about money. We have been so concerned about material things. The interests of people are on their health and their finances, and on their pleasures and on their sexuality, and while this is going on while we're self-absorbed and the churches as well as in the population, we have allowed rampant pornography on the internet. We have allowed rampant secularism and occult, etc. to be broadcast on television. We have permitted somewhere in the neighborhood of 35 to 40 million unborn babies to be slaughtered in our society. We have a court that has essentially stuck its finger in God's eye and said we're going to legislate you out of the schools. We're going to take your commandments from off the courthouse steps in various states. We're not going to let little children read the commandments of God. We're not going to let the Bible be read, no prayer in our schools. We have insulted God at the highest levels of our government. And, then we say 'why does this happen?'
>
> Well, why it's happening is that God Almighty is lifting his protection from us. And once that protection is gone, we all are vulnerable because we're a free society, and we're vulnerable. We lay naked before these terrorists who have infiltrated our country. There's probably tens of thousands of them in America right now. They've been raising money. They've been preaching their hate and overseas they have been spewing out venom against the United States for years. All over the Arab world, there is venom being poured out into people's ears and minds against America. And, the only thing that's going to sustain us is the umbrella power of the Almighty God.

So get this straight: all you've been told by the left-wing liberal kneejerk commie-and-queer-dominated news media is *all wrong*. You now have the straight dope from the straightest dope in America. Jerry Falwell, who speaks to God, and God *speaks back to him*, has told you that it wasn't religious fanatics serving an all-powerful god who threw themselves into fiery hell, it was the ACLU, the American Civil Liberties Union, the ones who take up the cases of poor schnooks who've been fired for blowing the whistle on corporate polluters and subhuman sweatshop owners. The ACLU, that says the First Amendment is pretty much sacrosanct, even when it means defending scumbags like serial killers and members of the much-beloved American Nazi Party.

But the gargoyles of the ACLU couldn't have brought down the Towers alone. Hell no, they needed those godless self-involved sluts devoid of Family Values, those ferocious harridans who reject their rightful role as punching bags and soup makers for Manuel and Meyer Machismo. The heathen Feminists, damn their uplift bras! And, of course, the faggots and lesbos, those unmentionable corrupters of the young—unlike the good priests of the Catholic Church, princes all, who merely seek little princelets with whom they can share the *Divino Afflante Spiritu*—who so upset the Falwells and Robertsons of the world that mere mention of them causes Righteous Televangelists to lubricate embarrassingly.

See, isn't that all clear now. Not the dedicated children of Islam, but home-grown nasties right here. And not even the stand-up American patriots who shoot physicians and bomb medical centers, who tie niggers and butt-fuckers to trailer hitches behind SUVs and drag 'em till they plow a decent furrow, who blow up half of downtown Oklahoma City in the name of God and the American Way...but people who pay dues to the ACLU and want to decide what happens to their lives and bodies themselves instead of having self-appointed little autarchs like Falwell and Robertson calling the shots.

I didn't have an opinion worth voicing on 9/11, till I read what that termite Falwell had to say on 9/13. Now I have an opinion; but not one I much think would go over well with the studio audience at *Politically Incorrect*.

But here it is.

Osama bin Laden and his crew of degenerate thugs, and Jerry Falwell and *his* cadre of sicko-pervo-freakos, with Pat playing the Gabby Hayes sidekick, all worship the same god. Not the gentle succoring Jesus, and not the kindly warmhearted Allah, but some third entity, some horned and astigmatic sulfur-breathing deity who battens on hatred and loathing and the spreading of Elitist snake-oil promising 73 virgins or the Pearly Gates, if only you will waste your lives in pointless denigration of everyone Pat and Osama and Jerry point to as enemies of the all-powerful God. It is hard to slam religion when there are so many decent Christians, Jews, Buddhists, Muslims, even Atheists. But if nobody notices that the same religious insanity that drives little girls to wear bustiers of C-4 is the one that Falwell and Robertson slather across our daily bread, then we become as one with the hypocrites who manifest astonishment that priests bugger choir boys. As though it hasn't been going on for five thousand years!

How many lives has Falwell ruined? How many walking zombies inculcated with religious lunacy has he set on the path to murder and arson and rape and madness? There is no difference at all, *in my opinion*—which I'm entitled to—between a terrorist egomaniac like bin Laden and his *al-Qaeda*, and Falwell with his Moral Majority. No difference.

Neither of them serve a sane god; neither of them will go to heaven; neither of them belong in a world as sad and troubled as this one.

You want an opinion...try this:

Falwell and Robertson ought to be in chains, sharing a hut at Gitmo's Camp X-Ray, where the good terrorists are sent.

All over the globe, people are being slaughtered in the name of God, said Salim Muwakkil in the *Chicago Tribune* last April. It's been that way throughout history, but no one dares "take religion to task for the evil it has ushered into the world."

And don't give me any of that banana oil about all the wonderful things like the Renaissance and illuminated manuscripts that religion has proffered. That's what a man-made succoring faith is *supposed* to do! It's not, however, supposed to do all the *rotten* stuff it does. Like burning Giordano Bruno and turning Galileo into a craven wimp; like stoning witches to death and flinging people onto the *strappado* for the pleasure of the Inquisitions; like banning books and art and dance; like dynamiting gloriously beautiful ancient Buddhist statues; like telling the gullible and uneducated that they must empty their pockets of milk and medicine money even as they hate and hate and hate all those with lifestyles unlike the ones Jerry and Pat and Osama trumpet as Moral Values; lifestyles of honor they cannot live up to themselves.

I have no opinions on what happened September 11th, 2001. None that need be voiced, because they're even less informed than yours, and frankly, if you're like me, you don't know actual jack...

But you asked, and you persisted in asking, and you pressed me to shoot off my big bazoo, so I give you the opinion to which, as a dumb-as-ditchwater average American, I am entitled.

Do with it what you will.

While I go in search of some gravitas, and my lost fifteen minutes of fame.

HARLAN ELLISON® has been characterized by *The New York Times Book Review* as having "the spellbinding quality of a great nonstop talker, with a cultural warehouse for a mind." *The Los Angeles Times* suggested, "It's long past time for Harlan Ellison to be awarded the title: 20th century Lewis Carroll." And the *Washington Post Book World* said simply, "One of the great living American short story writers."

He has written or edited 76 books; more than 1700 stories, essays, articles, and newspaper columns; two dozen teleplays, for which he received the Writers Guild of America most outstanding teleplay award for solo work an unprecedented four times; and a dozen movies. *Publishers Weekly* called him "Highly Intellectual." (Ellison's response: "Who, Me?"). He won the Mystery Writers of America Edgar Allan Poe award twice, the Horror Writers Association Bram Stoker award six times (including The Lifetime Achievement Award in 1996), the Nebula award of the Science Fiction Writers of America four times, the Hugo (World Convention Achievement award) 8 ½ times, and received the Silver Pen for Journalism from P.E.N. Not to mention the World Fantasy Award; the British Fantasy Award; the American Mystery Award; plus two Audie Awards and two Grammy nominations for Spoken Word recordings.

He created great fantasies for the 1985 CBS revival of *The Twilight Zone* (including Danny Kaye's final performance) and *The Outer Limits*, traveled with The Rolling Stones; marched with Martin Luther King from Selma to Montgomery; created roles for Buster Keaton, Wally Cox, Gloria Swanson, and nearly 100 other stars on *Burke's Law*; ran with a kid gang in Brooklyn's Red Hook to get background for his first novel; covered race riots in Chicago's "back of the yards" with the late James Baldwin; sang with, and dined with, Maurice Chevalier; once stood off the son of the Detroit Mafia kingpin with a Remington XP-l00 pistol-rifle, while wearing nothing but a bath towel; and sued Paramount and ABC-TV for plagiarism and won $337,000. His most recent legal victory, in protection of copyright against global Internet piracy of writers' work, in May of 2004—a four-year-long litigation against AOL et al.—has resulted in revolutionizing protection of creative properties on the web. (As promised, he has repaid hundreds of contributions [totaling $50,000] from the KICK Internet Piracy support fund.) But the bottom line, as voiced by *Booklist*, is this: "One thing for sure: the man can write."

He lives with his wife, Susan, inside The Lost Aztec Temple of Mars, in Los Angeles.

# CHRONOLOGY OF BOOKS BY
## HARLAN ELLISON®
### 1958 – 2016

**NOVELS:**

WEB OF THE CITY [1958]

THE SOUND OF A SCYTHE [1960]

SPIDER KISS [1961]

**RETROSPECTIVES:**

ALONE AGAINST TOMORROW: *A 10-Year Survey* [1971]

THE ESSENTIAL ELLISON: *A 35-Year Retrospective* (edited by Terry Dowling, with Richard Delap & Gil Lamont) [1987]

THE ESSENTIAL ELLISON: *A 50-Year Retrospective* (edited by Terry Dowling) [2001]

UNREPENTANT: *A Celebration of the Writing of Harlan Ellison* (edited by Robert T. Garcia) [2010]

THE TOP OF THE VOLCANO: *The Award-Winning Stories of Harlan Ellison* [2014]

**OMNIBUS VOLUMES:**

THE FANTASIES OF HARLAN ELLISON [1979]

DREAMS WITH SHARP TEETH [1991]

THE GLASS TEAT & THE OTHER GLASS TEAT [2011]

**GRAPHIC NOVELS:**

DEMON WITH A GLASS HAND (adaptation with Marshall Rogers) [1986]

NIGHT AND THE ENEMY (adaptation with Ken Steacy) [1987]

VIC AND BLOOD: *The Chronicles of a Boy and His Dog* (adaptation by Richard Corben) [1989]

HARLAN ELLISON'S DREAM CORRIDOR, Volume One [1996]

VIC AND BLOOD: *The Continuing Adventures of a Boy and His Dog* (adaptation by Richard Corben) [2003]

HARLAN ELLISON'S DREAM CORRIDOR, Volume Two [2007]

PHOENIX WITHOUT ASHES (art by Alan Robinson and John K. Snyder III) [2010/2011]

HARLAN ELLISON'S 7 AGAINST CHAOS (art by Paul Chadwick and Ken Steacy) [2013]

THE CITY ON THE EDGE OF FOREVER: *The Original Teleplay* (adaptation by Scott Tipton & David Tipton, art by J.K. Woodward) [2014/2015]

BATMAN '66: *The Lost Episode* (adaptation by Len Wein, art by Joe Prado and José García-López) [2014]

**SHORT NOVELS:**

DOOMSMAN [1967]

ALL THE LIES THAT ARE MY LIFE [1980]

RUN FOR THE STARS [1991]

MEFISTO IN ONYX [1993]

**COLLABORATIONS:**

PARTNERS IN WONDER: *Collaborations with 14 Other Wild Talents* [1971]

THE STARLOST: *Phoenix Without Ashes* (with Edward Bryant) [1975]

MIND FIELDS: *33 Stories Inspired by the Art of Jacek Yerka* [1994]

I HAVE NO MOUTH, AND I MUST SCREAM: *The Interactive CD-Rom* (Co-Designed with David Mullich and David Sears) [1995]

"REPENT, HARLEQUIN!" SAID THE TICKTOCKMAN (rendered with paintings by Rick Berry) [1997]

2000$^X$ (Host and Creative Consultant of National Public Radio episodic series) [2000–2001]

HARLAN ELLISON'S MORTAL DREADS (dramatized by Robert Armin) [2012]

**AS EDITOR:**

DANGEROUS VISIONS [1967]

NIGHTSHADE & DAMNATIONS: *The Finest Stories of Gerald Kersh* [1968]

AGAIN, DANGEROUS VISIONS [1972]

MEDEA: *Harlan's World* [1985]

DANGEROUS VISIONS (The 35th Anniversary Edition) [2002]

JACQUES FUTRELLE'S "THE THINKING MACHINE" STORIES [2003]

**THE HARLAN ELLISON DISCOVERY SERIES:**

STORMTRACK by James Sutherland [1975]

AUTUMN ANGELS by Arthur Byron Cover [1975]

THE LIGHT AT THE END OF THE UNIVERSE by Terry Carr [1976]

ISLANDS by Marta Randall [1976]

INVOLUTION OCEAN by Bruce Sterling [1978]

# CHRONOLOGY OF BOOKS BY
## HARLAN ELLISON®
### 1958 – 2016

## SHORT STORY COLLECTIONS:

THE DEADLY STREETS [1958]

SEX GANG *(as "Paul Merchant")* [1959]

A TOUCH OF INFINITY [1960]

CHILDREN OF THE STREETS [1961]

GENTLEMAN JUNKIE
*and Other Stories of the Hung-Up Generation* [1961]

ELLISON WONDERLAND [1962]

PAINGOD *and Other Delusions* [1965]

I HAVE NO MOUTH & I MUST SCREAM [1967]

FROM THE LAND OF FEAR [1967]

LOVE AIN'T NOTHING BUT SEX MISSPELLED [1968]

THE BEAST THAT SHOUTED LOVE
AT THE HEART OF THE WORLD [1969]

OVER THE EDGE [1970]

ALL THE SOUNDS OF FEAR
(British publication only) [1973]

*DE HELDEN VAN DE HIGHWAY*
(Dutch publication only) [1973]

APPROACHING OBLIVION [1974]

THE TIME OF THE EYE (British publication only) [1974]

DEATHBIRD STORIES [1975]

NO DOORS, NO WINDOWS [1975]

*HOE KAN IK SCHREEUWEN ZONDER MOND*
(Dutch publication only) [1977]

STRANGE WINE [1978]

SHATTERDAY [1980]

STALKING THE NIGHTMARE [1982]

ANGRY CANDY [1988]

*ENSAMVÄRK* (Swedish publication only) [1992]

JOKES WITHOUT PUNCHLINES [1995]

ВСЕ ЗВУКН СТРАХА (ALL FEARFUL SOUNDS)
(Unauthorized Russian publication only) [1997]

THE WORLDS OF HARLAN ELLISON
(Authorized Russian publication only) [1997]

SLIPPAGE: *Precariously Poised,
Previously Uncollected Stories* [1997]

*KOLETIS, KES KUULUTAS ARMASTUST MAAILMA SLIDAMES*
(Estonian publication only) [1999]

*LA MACHINE AUX YEUX BLEUS*
(French publication only) [2001]

TROUBLEMAKERS [2001]

*PTAK ŚMIERCI* (THE BEST OF HARLAN ELLISON)
(Polish publication only) [2003]

DEATHBIRD STORIES (expanded edition) [2011]

PULLING A TRAIN [2012]

GETTING IN THE WIND [2012]

ELLISON WONDERLAND (expanded edition) [2015]

PEBBLES FROM THE MOUNTAIN [2015]

CAN AND CAN'TANKEROUS [2015]

COFFIN NAILS [forthcoming]

## NON-FICTION & ESSAYS:

MEMOS FROM PURGATORY [1961]

THE GLASS TEAT: *Essays of Opinion on Television* [1970]

THE OTHER GLASS TEAT:
*Further Essays of Opinion on Television* [1975]

THE BOOK OF ELLISON
(edited by Andrew Porter) [1978]

SLEEPLESS NIGHTS IN THE PROCRUSTEAN BED
(edited by Marty Clark) [1984]

AN EDGE IN MY VOICE [1985]

HARLAN ELLISON'S WATCHING [1989]

THE HARLAN ELLISON HORNBOOK [1990]

BUGF#CK! *The Useless Wit & Wisdom of Harlan Ellison*
(edited by Arnie Fenner) [2011]

# CHRONOLOGY OF BOOKS BY
## HARLAN ELLISON®
### 1958 – 2016

**SCREENPLAYS & SUCHLIKE:**

THE ILLUSTRATED HARLAN ELLISON
(edited by Byron Preiss) [1978]

HARLAN ELLISON'S MOVIE [1990]

I, ROBOT: The Illustrated Screenplay
(based on Isaac Asimov's story-cycle) [1994]

THE CITY ON THE EDGE OF FOREVER [1996]

**MOTION PICTURE (DOCUMENTARY):**

DREAMS WITH SHARP TEETH (A Film About Harlan Ellison
produced and directed by Erik Nelson) [2009]

**ON THE ROAD WITH HARLAN ELLISON:**

ON THE ROAD WITH HARLAN ELLISON
(Vol. One) [1983/2001]

ON THE ROAD WITH HARLAN ELLISON (Vol. Two) [2004]

ON THE ROAD WITH HARLAN ELLISON (Vol. Three) [2007]

ON THE ROAD WITH HARLAN ELLISON:
*His Last Big Con* (Vol. Five) [2011]

ON THE ROAD WITH HARLAN ELLISON:
*The Grand Master Edition* (Vol. Six) [2012]

**AUDIOBOOKS:**

THE VOICE FROM THE EDGE: I HAVE NO MOUTH,
AND I MUST SCREAM (Vol. One) [1999]

THE VOICE FROM THE EDGE: MIDNIGHT IN THE SUNKEN
CATHEDRAL (Vol. Two) [2001]

RUN FOR THE STARS [2005]

THE VOICE FROM THE EDGE: PRETTY MAGGIE MONEYEYES
(Vol. Three) [2009]

THE VOICE FROM THE EDGE: THE DEATHBIRD
& OTHER STORIES (Vol. Four) [2011]

THE VOICE FROM THE EDGE: SHATTERDAY
& OTHER STORIES (Vol. Five) [2011]

ELLISON WONDERLAND [2015]

WEB AND THE CITY [2015]

SPIDER KISS [2015]

THE CITY ON THE EDGE OF FOREVER
(full-cast dramatization) [forthcoming]

**THE WHITE WOLF SERIES:**

EDGEWORKS 1: OVER THE EDGE
& AN EDGE IN MY VOICE [1996]

EDGEWORKS 2: SPIDER KISS
& STALKING THE NIGHTMARE [1996]

EDGEWORKS 3: THE HARLAN ELLISON HORNBOOK
& HARLAN ELLISON'S MOVIE [1997]

EDGEWORKS 4: LOVE AIN'T NOTHING BUT SEX MISSPELLED
& THE BEAST THAT SHOUTED LOVE
AT THE HEART OF THE WORLD [1997]

**EDGEWORKS ABBEY OFFERINGS**
**(Edited by Jason Davis):**

BRAIN MOVIES: *The Original
Teleplays of Harlan Ellison* (Vol. One) [2011]

BRAIN MOVIES: *The Original
Teleplays of Harlan Ellison* (Vol. Two) [2011]

HARLAN 101: *Encountering Ellison* [2011]

THE SOUND OF A SCYTHE *and 3 Brilliant Novellas* [2011]

ROUGH BEASTS: *Seventeen Stories
Written Before I Got Up To Speed* [2012]

NONE OF THE ABOVE [2012]

BRAIN MOVIES: *The Original
Teleplays of Harlan Ellison* (Vol. Three) [2013]

BRAIN MOVIES: *The Original
Teleplays of Harlan Ellison* (Vol. Four) [2013]

BRAIN MOVIES: *The Original
Teleplays of Harlan Ellison* (Vol. Five) [2013]

HONORABLE WHOREDOM AT A PENNY A WORD [2013]

AGAIN, HONORABLE WHOREDOM
AT A PENNY A WORD [2014]

BRAIN MOVIES: *The Original
Teleplays of Harlan Ellison* (Vol. Six) [2014]

HARLAN ELLISON'S ENDLESSLY WATCHING [2014]

8 IN 80 BY ELLISON (guest edited by Susan Ellison) [2014]

THE LAST PERSON TO MARRY A DUCK
LIVED 300 YEARS AGO [2016]

BRAIN MOVIES: *The Original
Teleplays of Harlan Ellison* (Vol. Seven) [2016]

# ON THE ROAD WITH ELLISON
## VOLUMES 1 - 6

The *On The Road With Ellison* series of CDs collect some of the best moments of Harlan Ellison live on stage from the past 30 years. Each volume comes with an exclusive essay written by Mr. Ellison and rare photos from his archives. Hear him talk about mailing a dead gopher, exposing himself during a lecture, getting fired from Disney on his first day, and so much more. This is not Harlan reading his work; it's a collection of observations and stories from a life lived on the road. You get inside the head of America's most outspoken wordsmith. This is Ellison live on stage, and anything goes.

available now from

DEEPSHAG
R E C O R D S

# www.deepshag.com

## VOLUME

## SEVEN

## COMING

## 2016

Made in the USA
San Bernardino, CA
16 June 2016